BROWNING

PLEASANTVILLE

Disclaimer

I have tried to the best of my ability to recreate events, locales and conversations from my memories of them. In order to maintain their anonymity in many instances. I have also changed the names of individuals and places, I may have changed some identifying characteristics and details such as physical properties, occupations and places of residence. Although the author and editor have made every effort to ensure that the information in this book was correct at press time, the author and editor do not assume and hereby disclaim any liability to any party for any loss, damage, or disruption caused by errors or omissions, whether such errors or omissions result from negligence, accident, or any other cause.

Cover Design by Marshall Shorts
Edited by Patricia Bolton

ISBN-13: 978-1975990695
ISBN-10: 1975990692

First Edition: September 2017
10 9 8 7 6 5 4 3 2 1

Printed in the United States of America

Dedication

Bear (Charlie) and Hollis (London)
You are my "A Lots". I love you…

Acknowledgements

Mommy, thank you for being my impetus for social justice, my counselor, my listening ear, my motivator, my storyteller, and even my book editor!

Daddy, I did not make it easy for you to parent me and you loved me through it. You softened my hardened heart and I appreciate you for teaching me patience, stability and forgiveness.

Volk and *Erika*, KiMISTRY wouldn't exist without your partnership and friendship. Thank you for believing in my talent, abilities and my heart.

Posthumous thanks are given to two of my ancestors in particular: *Jennie Garland*, my great, great, great, great grandmother and a Virginian slave who raised her grandchildren in the undocumented absence of her own child(ren). And to German-born Chief Bugler *Charles Schorn*, my great, great grandfather who was awarded a medal of honor for capturing a Confederate flag while serving in the Union army during the Civil War; Grandma Garland and Ururgroßvater Schorn, we are still fighting your fights. I promise to keep this house and rally the troops until we all sustainably win and are all sustainably free. With reverence and humility in recognizing that I stand on African, Slave, Appalachian and German shoulders, I begin my story...

CONTENTS

Introduction

"Remember who you are."

-The Lion King

I was born in 1976 and that makes me a bona fide, quintessential Generation X kid. Casio keyboard music, Three's Company TV show, break-dancing to new musical noise called rap, Aqua Netted and/or Jheri curled hair, neon everything and WHAM! The Royal 'They' referred to us as "Latchkey Kids". And in fact, my brother, sister and I were raised in a single parent household and returned home from school every afternoon to an parent-free house because our mother was at work. My older brother wore a house key on a string (or a latch) around his neck. That's how we all poured into the door ...with the exception of those afternoons when my brother forgot or lost his key. On those days when the key was forgotten, he hoisted me up and into the tiny window of our first-floor bathroom to enter and unlock the door from the inside.

I remember how important television was to me as the community outside my home grew to be more and more dangerous. TV granted me a different way than my zip code to make my world bigger. I remember the beginning of MTV when the only thing the network played was music videos – novel idea for a channel named Music Television. I remember, "Video Killed the Radio Star", the Talking Heads and eventually Yo! MTV Raps. My family and I watched the Richard Simmons Show as we ate dinner together. The Young and the Restless and Guiding Light soap operas were how the intergenerational women in the family made peace with each other when puberty, menopause and geriatrics all hit at once.

It was my generation, the GenXers, who arguably felt the most impact when TV didn't end with the Star Spangled Banner and a snowstorm of static nothing. The only box reality I know is not unlike a lowercase god. Infinite. No beginning. No end. All-knowing. Omnipresent at the time of the greatest joys and the most wicked of sorrows. TV would become the greatest accessible tool I had to reinvent myself. I was searching for intimate social acceptance. It provided me with a menu of options of who I should be and how I should portray the role. I was "before" and somewhere in the box and its wormhole called "cable television", I could access endless perspectives on the human experience and narrow down what my "after" should be.

When I watched TV shows as a young girl, the episodes I always gravitated toward were those involving some kind of makeover or re-creation of self. Ever since I can remember, I have had an obsessive interest in any and every kind of makeover. More than that, I needed to blindly believe that past and present states do not dictate future states. I needed to believe that we have second chances; that we can be made over into better versions of ourselves. In both dream state and real life, I find myself drawn to the lure of makeover stories. Any kind will do. Even now in adulthood, my attraction to stories is still grounded in the fantasy of the makeover.

To me, this transformation means present tense is not a permanent state. If I am in pain, before and after means a cure for my suffering is on the way and the pain will not endure. If I am displeased with my life circumstances, before and after means it won't last. If I am invisible in any way, before and after means there exists a path I can take to intentionally become more visible – and audible. Perhaps before and after didn't and doesn't matter much to others; I, however, needed to know change was possible. I envisioned a secret door through which I could walk and be transformed into a new and improved version of me; a metamorphosis of sorts. My external circumstances didn't match where I was trying to go or who I was trying to be. As a child, I feared I would suffocate in the perceived mediocrity of brown poverty culture.

I don't know if it was because of specific, impressionable childhood experiences or other factors, but I love the idea that one can overcome certain challenges with a little willpower and elbow grease. Note: "elbow grease" is entirely different from the idiotic idiom of "pulling oneself up by one's own bootstraps". Ain't no boots or bootstraps. I know that there is something bigger than individual bad luck working against me as well as people who look like me. That "something" is more complex than leather upper shoes. As the adage says, "The cavalry isn't coming; we have to save ourselves."

I am acutely aware that I need to have myself polished and ready when an opportunity presents itself (or when I kick the door down and loot an opportunity). My poise and talent must be undeniable. In that case, I have to put in my work so I can be ready to accept the invitation (or be ready for the coup d'etat, whichever presents itself first). There's something beautiful about knowing broken or unfinished people and situations can be made whole. There's something relieving about believing we are all in draft form. We are all susceptible to being edited. We can always do a little better. We all possess the power to make ourselves better in the after than we were before.

As I mature, I have greatly distanced myself from regular TV-watching, but I still get my "before and after" fix through the big screen. One of my favorite movies that demonstrate a beautiful and artistic expression of the concept of before and after is the film *Pleasantville* starring Reese Witherspoon and Tobey Maguire.

In *Pleasantville*, a brother and sister from the 1990s portray typically unpleasant stereotypes of the decade. The older sister is rebellious and sexually promiscuous. She rejects the notion of academia and intelligence in lieu of attracting boys. Her younger brother is fascinated by TV life in the golden era. They live in a single-parent household where mom is never around because she works hard to be a good provider. And in this household, the younger brother has essentially created an alternative reality for himself. He is a dreamer, unfocused and undiscovered to both the world and to himself. He is nursed by the alternative universe through which he finds peace in a fictitious household from the simpler times of the 1950s.

One evening, the brother and sister are fighting for control of a TV remote control. In an instant, the magic of Hollywood happens and they are transported into TV land circa 1958. Transported into a world when life was uncomplicated.

Pleasantville, the town where the brother and sister are transported, exists only in black and white. Everything in Pleasantville is practically perfect. The weather is always sunny. Dads go to work and the moms stay home, take care of the house, and have a hot dinner ready. All days in Pleasantville are awesome and when they're not, don't worry. Any problem can be solved in 23 minutes. Kids have balanced lives in addition to a guaranteed circle of friends which fit their particular interests and hobbies. Everything is beautiful, squeaky clean, and free from conflict or tension. Oh, and one more thing. There is absolutely no race, class, sexual orientation or gender expression diversity in Pleasantville. Is it a coincidence that this place would be a straight, white, middle class, gender binary utopia? I think not.

To imply or even directly state that 1958 wasn't the most "pleasant" year for people of color in the United States would be an exceedingly gross understatement. Everyone in Pleasantville looked the same – white. There was no racial difference which means there were no racial challenges. There was no "Negro problem" as 20th century brown sociologist and historian W.E.B. DuBois might say. (The "Negro problem" referenced the white opinion that brown people were a burden or a nuisance to white culture.)

Yet, while there was no one in Pleasantville who was brown like me, I found myself wanting to be there, too. I wanted a simpler life. I wanted sunny weather all the time. I wanted a stable, two-parent home where dinner was hot and ready to be served when I got home from school. Everybody seems to want Pleasantville, or at least what Pleasantville means and implies, which is to have some distance between *it* and anything that *isn't* Pleasantville. This complicates matters when I am everything that isn't Pleasantville, but it is impossible for me to escape from who I am.

What we discover as the film progresses, is that the Pleasantville people are just like everyone else. When they are challenged to think, feel, process emotion, and deal with tension, the colorless town transforms into Technicolor. Things are no longer as simple as black and white. The complexity of life even transcends the gray areas. At the peaks of discovery, the peaks of emotion, at the precipice of creation or disaster, we find diversity. And, in Pleasantville, once diversity manifests itself, folks live life in color.

The older sister changes from a sexually promiscuous and rebellious teenage girl to someone who has discovered her softer, quieter, and more intelligent side. The younger brother transforms before our eyes from a boy who has no clue about who he is or what strengths he possesses to a young man with focus, incredible passion, character, and conviction. Inside of Pleasantville, the brother and sister discover who they really are. They become their authentic selves there.

Before long, the entire cast of the film, thanks to anti-establishment thinking and frankly, white liberalism and counter culture epiphanies, begins living in color. The entire Pleasantville community is able to live in color. What a beautiful way of showing diversity in thought! It really is a gorgeous film.

I have probably seen the movie *Pleasantville* 10 or 15 times. But it wasn't until recently that it dawned on me how devoid Pleasantville was of black and brown people. This movie, which I have loved for nearly 20 years, is cinematography of a re-imagined throwback suburban society. It is a freeze frame of my grandparents' golden years. It is a sneak peek back to the good ol' days Archie Bunker reminiscently serenaded in the theme song to *All in the Family*.

Pleasantville is a community which was likely a perfectly formed souvenir of the days of "redlining" when the government used red markers to map residential areas where brown people could and could not live. Pleasantville was a Promised Land of milk, honey and white skin. I now see the film Pleasantville decoded as a Mecca of everything that didn't include me or many people who love and look like me. Pleasantville was not unlike Mayberry from the Andy Griffith Show which was not unlike many current-day suburbs across the United States. In fact, in my adulthood, I have discovered many a person in suburban communities who have referred to Mayberry as the land of "Milk and Honey". …The land of Starbucks and liberal, post-racial society conversations about racism without racists.

My cynicism struggles to reject the likelihood and subconscious notion that part of the reason why Mayberry and Pleasantville are so ideal is because brown folk in both towns (if they exist there, that is) are barely seen and absolutely not heard. Maybe Mayberry and Pleasantville brown folks are invisible. Maybe their brown folks know their place.

Diversity, equity and inclusion are noble concepts in which to believe as long as you don't have to practice them on a regular basis. Inclusion efforts require an intentional engagement of discomfort. Discomfort for an hour is one thing. Perpetual discomfort is an entirely different thing. And unexpected or unrequested discomfort in and of itself is a "thing" white people and male people and straight people and financially secure people have more power and privilege to avoid than their fellows who live further down the continuums of race, gender, sexual orientation and class. Few people will blatantly and consciously state with conviction that they do not believe in or support diversity. Principled thought is actually pretty easy. Not just easy, but en vogue. Diversity is the "new black" …as long as its daughter or son isn't dating the old black. Otherwise, we could not live life under the belief that we are decent human beings.

Our brains need our value systems and behaviors to be congruent. If I present to have a value that I care about people, then one would expect my behavior to demonstrate a care for people. The challenge comes in when I say that I value all lives, yet my behavior demonstrates bias in the way I actually respond to situations and lives depending on the circumstances and colors of the bodies involved. I can say whatever I want with my mouth, but my behavior will likely show patterns of the way I authentically feel about people based on race, class, gender identity, sexual orientation, age, and the list goes on and on.

As a grown woman, I moved into my first home in the suburbs by age 30. My residential community, West Village, is the *after* to the projects of my childhood before the blessing of upward mobility. The West Village house, we were told by the builder, was the least expensive house she'd built in our middle class new development neighborhood at the time. Our family's funds were modest then. Therefore, our house was modest, but we were there. We made it to the suburbs and we were the first to "brown" our street.

Our community was a blizzard of bland. The trees are so young; it took ten years to see a squirrel in the backyard. We had no need to own a rake. Behind the front doors of each home in our neighborhood, there were one million variations of off-white paint on the new-build walls.

We paid monthly fees to a Home Owners Association that had the power to dictate where our trash cans and recycling receptacles were permitted to sit before and after trash day. Heaven forbid trash lie on the ground in plain sight! Private school bus drivers for "little kiddos" built "mom-chatting" at bus stops into their drive time. Every mailbox was black with white-stenciled lettering. Every yard was meticulously maintained. Every home looked like a subtle variation of the one next door - indistinguishable color. Pale green. Pale yellow. Pale blue. Pale tan. Pale pale. The number one rule was conformity; look the same and be the same. The snuff of residential diversity serves to maintain and increase property values. Sure, there were some residents brave enough to shake the underpinnings of the system. One of our neighbors, the Brady Bunch, built a pirate ship in their backyard. Rumor has it, they were working on the inside of the Home Owners Association when the project application was approved.

I'd spent my first 18 years in places others referred to as "hoods" and relative "ghettos", but upward mobility had plans for my family and me. I put my "hood pass" in a lock box. My brown corporate American husband at the time and I merged our "so to speak" superpowers and became "buppies" – black yuppies or black urban professionals. We had "made it". Many likely use our family as an example of pulling oneself up by the bootstraps; a statement I, again, reject and abhor. To many, my family was a classic case of black achievement. We were

13

living the American dream. Our dream, however, was not quite a vibrant red, white and blue, but rather a smidge less monochromatic than faded glory.

Jordan and I had the following stats: two children, one dog and a white picket fence. We lived in close enough proximity that our children could walk to and from school in a matter of minutes. The corners of my neighborhood were marked by a church, a fire station, a senior condominium community and one of the most awesome playgrounds I have ever seen. My suburb was bordered by an impressively expansive bike path that was heavily used by riders ranging from paraprofessional tri-athletes to families on a Sunday evening fitness adventure together. Down the street from our home was an equestrian center where horses pranced with their handlers and riders in tow. 20 years ago, I didn't know what the word "equestrian" meant. That was before; this is after.

A suburban afterlife sounds like dogs barking and yapping happily at roller bladers on the other side of invisible fences. It feels like summer breeze blowing through the jasmine of lifeguards' minds at the freakishly elaborate West Village aquatic center. It smells like happy, entitled teenagers driving Audis and commanding Stepford moms to grant wishes to them as if parents were obliged-to-serve. It looks like happy gardeners watering chemically enhanced vegetation, stretching its green necks up to the sun, growing for suburban farmers who have no intention of tasting the harvest.

All of this perfection was around me, but somehow, I knew it did not belong to me. Classic suburbia is perceived utopia and factually not very "brown". Its utopia is defined by white perfection. This is not better or worse than brown perfection, but it does feel incongruent to my brown utopia. I felt incongruent to West Village, my Pleasantville. The longer I lived there, the more I longed for a utopia made for people who looked like me. I wonder, though, if Mayberry is as "good" as it gets. My fear is the only way there will be peace is if Mayberry and Pleasantville force brown folks to behave whiter or Mayberry and Pleasantville themselves become quantitatively and qualitatively browner.

If Mayberry and Pleasantville weren't intended to have me as one of its residents, then is there a Pleasantville for brown people? Are white and brown utopias still governed by Plessy v. Ferguson rulings? Is my utopia somewhere separate but equal to Pleasantville and Mayberry? If diversity in thought alone transformed Pleasantville from black and white to color, imagine its transformation with the addition of people of color! What happens to Pleasantville's vibrant Technicolor if a critical mass of brown folks moves in? What happens when you *brown* Pleasantville?

Chapter 1

So What; Now What?

There are plenty of kids living my poverty story. I am not special and this narrative isn't terribly unusual. There are even more adults who survived much worse than I. I'm not complaining about what I did or didn't have. I'm not seeking pity, as I believe those socioeconomic stories were meant to be mine. I'm not using my experiences as an excuse or a crutch; we all did the best we could with the coping skills we had at the time. I'm merely illustrating that I know what pain feels like in the corners of marginalized identities. I earned my scars and my hope is that I can spend my adult life doing work that helps people begin or continue their healing processes as I am working to continue mine. This mission, of which I was unaware in college, resonated with me in everything I did. Every committee I joined. Every event I was drawn to attend. Every poem I wrote. I was born and bred to be a social justice activist and advocate.

As a brown person, I am both excited about and exhausted by increasing statistics of how the world – and especially the United States – is "browning". Statistics can prove in less than thirty-five years, there will be more black, Latino/a and Asian people on the planet than white people. Both media and the average Joe/Anna is obsessed with this coming trend of browning. We are obsessed in both positive and negative ways. Coexisting are both overpowering feelings of safety and threat about this browning of the planet. This browning could result in a sunset on the era of a white majority.

My borderline offensive and oversimplified report-out is this: brown folks think the revolution is around the corner. White folks fear the end of the monarchy. Biracial folks incorrectly assume neutrality either way. My opinion is that not much will change for the decision makers – unless they *want* it to change. It is true that decision-makers will soon lead masses who demographically outnumber them and have nothing in common with them. Brown masses could wake up and realize we've been well-trained in how to either evolve into a white mainstream or die. And if we brown masses can work through our trauma of marginalization, we stand a fighting chance at ensuring our voices are heard and our needs are met.

But…

I am compelled to be honest with you. If we are going to be in conversation with each other for the entirety of a book, I don't want to start this relationship by deceiving you. My truth places me in a particularly contentious position as a Diversity Practitioner. My occupational shop-talk precludes me from being negative about a more diverse planet earth. My soul's belief, though, is life will not change much for me when brown folks take 51 percent ownership of the planet. I doubt life will change because brown folks will not own 51 percent of the boardrooms and "c-suites". Unless the browning of the United States and the world also leads to the browning of executive level leadership, we've got the same problem with different census demographics to look forward to.

We're doing better now than before, some may say. We live in an era following two terms of the first black president of the United States, others may chime. True. What is also true is that fused to Obama's second presidency term was four years (and counting) of what felt like another, nay, a new race war. Nearly eight years of a black man in the highest position of power in the world being drawn somewhere in someone's racist publication as a monkey or a terrorist. The most powerful person in the world being publicly branded a liar by a subordinate while at work. I watched the most powerful person in the world be insulted, have his wife and children insulted and I watched him swallow insults like oversized vitamins that scratch your throat on the way down. The first black president, Barack Obama, swallowed public ridicule with clenched jaws, white teeth, nicotine patches and class.

The hair of the first black president grayed from the stress of having the weight of the world on his shoulders. He led amidst microaggressions and slept with a belly full of racism husks intestinal bile can't break down. He dialed back indigestion and the nausea of hate lest the president of the United States be labeled a vomiting thug for choking and unleashing angry black fists of rage on his oppressors. That's too brown and he was not allowed to be that brown after election day. That kind of behavior would've set all of us brown folks back to the Civil Rights Movement version 2.0.

Here's a quick timeline to put things into perspective. In 1865, Lincoln was assassinated, the Ku Klux Klan was founded and brown people were emancipated from slavery. Colorado and Oregon territories were stolen from Natives and thousands had already died on the Trail of Tears. Puerto Rican slaves would not be free for another decade.

One hundred years later in 1965, Malcolm X was assassinated. Over fifty marchers were injured during the "Bloody Sunday" massacre on the Edmund Pettis Bridge in Alabama. The Civil Rights and Voting Rights act had passed. Nearly 40 people died during a week of race riots in Watts, California and Caesar Chavez was fighting for the rights of LatinX and Chicano/a migrant workers. Tens of thousands of Natives were fighting in the Vietnam War.

50 years later in 2015, over 1200 brown people had been killed since 2011 from interactions with police. By 2017, we the people elected a presidential candidate who stated that Mexicans illegally cross the border and import their problems to the U.S., including drugs, crime and rape. We elected a presidential candidate who referenced a "Muslim problem" and suggested the government create

a database of Muslims and take care of "the problem" by sending all Muslims out of the U.S.

We are chin-deep in nearly four years of the Civil Rights Movement version 3.0. Our legs are tired from treading middle passage waters and we are still hydrophobic. The death of Trayvon Martin and the years following his death have been particularly anxiety-ridden. Institutions communicate their work and investment in a safer future; meanwhile brown male bodies can only guarantee their survival from day to day.

Since 2012, I have become hypervigilant to news stories of law and brown death. I cannot help but wonder if the victims were white, would these same interactions have resulted in warnings and arrests as opposed to protests and caskets? Since 2012, my daughters have become desensitized to brown men dying young and unexpectedly (and sometimes on camera) over the mismanagement of their brown bodies in public. Since 2012, mothers of young brown boys have sought advice and partaken in public discourse about how to rear brown children so the likelihood of their sons coming home alive is higher. I once heard a young brown woman complain about her boyfriend's apprehension to marriage. He figures, she explained, "Brown men don't live that long. If I'm not going to live a long life, what purpose is there in getting married?"

Fret not, though. We are in the era following a Barack Obama presidency; remember? Be comforted, knowing I have been assured that racism is over. Yes, it was rough for several hundred years, but "those" white people are gone and, well, all versions of the civil rights movements have been successful. [Note: that was sarcasm.] I must confess; however, I don't feel better, safer or more comfortable. Needless to say, even though I was proud of having a person in the oval office that looked like one of my family members, it was unexpectedly defeating to accept that his power did not eclipse his race. Race – when race is not white – is still an adjective while white is understood to be "normal". Clinton was president. Bush Sr. and W. Bush were presidents. Obama was "the first black president". He was an adjective president. What power is within my reach if even the president of the United States is still someone's n****? Will a nation comprised of 51 percent brown folks change that?

We've had a majority brown society before. Native or Indigenous communities are mostly brown. Africans are mostly brown. The challenge lies in temptation of power. Why look when you can touch? Why diet when you can be a glutton? Why lick when you can bite? Why be middle class when you can be wealthy? Why share power when there is such a thing as absolute power? The urge of a few to take over the many is so incredibly tempting.

Someone is going to read this book and think it's a bunch of malarkey. Someone is going to read this book and think, "What's so special about *her* story?" Someone is going to read this book and think, "This is not book-worthy. I

17

experienced the exact same thing." And *that's* my point. The disgusting part of my story is that it's not extraordinary at all. This is the story of *lots* of brown folks working and learning in predominantly white institutions. How is it possible for these experiences to represent thousands of brown folks who rank high enough in their organizations to be isolated, token brown leaders? How is it possible for the thousands who live these stories to have white colleagues and supervisors who don't know how heavy their baggage is?

None of this injustice changes until white decision-makers begin to acknowledge and feel the pain (as opposed to logically processing the injustice and pain) that comes with the lived experiences of "brownness". Once white folks can see brown folks as real human beings with real pain, they can aid in dismantling the very systems that create pain.

Chapter 2

The Hero/Villain Origin Story

"You don't have to be the hero and save everyone." I've heard that a time or two in my lifetime. Human beings are designed to be social and want to "fit in". We have a biological desire to want to be connected and to feel like we are a part of something bigger than ourselves. There is a *whole* and we want to be part of it. That desire is why we cling to our families and seek friendships. Once we know whose we are, we can begin to search for purpose and calling. That warmth we chase is our ambiguous recollection or requiem for the concept of "home". This is what is behind our quest for a higher power, love and *meaning*. Belonging and meaning are arguably the most important components of hero mentality.

I belong to parents whose marriage was sun-kissed (for a few years, at least) and so was I. My father is Caucasian; my mother is African American. Unrelated to race, my parents divorced when I was two and shared joint custody of me. I am their golden, biracial child. Yes, I also belonged to the color gold. My skin was golden and for years, my cottony hair was golden. My golden color didn't make sense or mean anything to me for a long time. Small children don't start life with an ability to process the concept of race or the power differential behind skin color, particularly children who are multiracial. In full disclosure, I didn't even know I was golden until some neighborhood kids called me, "yellow".

The neighborhood where I grew up with my maternal siblings was low income and highly ethnically diverse. My brother played with Filipino brothers down the street. Ghanaian sisters lived across the street and braided my hair on mild summer days. We listened to Puerto Rican Spanish spoken through the walls of our roach-infested townhome. I lived in a spectrum of color with all kinds of races, languages and nationalities at my disposal – except white. My neighborhood community, which was my entire world, was predominantly brown. Through visitation with my white father, I observed a white suburban world, but only in small doses.

In the height of the 1980s, there was a mere sprinkle of white folks at my predominantly brown parochial school. Outside of my white family members, the only white folks I saw were my teachers and the white parishioners at my predominantly white Catholic church. Ironically, my school and parish were approximately five minutes northwest of Pleasantville, one of the city's finest suburbs. Several neighborhood kids joined brown children from all over the city to attend St. Therese Catholic School. We were bused to a school where 99 percent of the students were African American and arguably only five percent of the students were practicing Catholics. I was one of a small Midwestern minority of brown Catholics. Singling me out of the brown crowd was simple with my gold skin, gold

"Jheri curl" and my keen awareness of proper genuflecting before the sign of the cross.

Isolated in a community of supposed peers, I was a different bird. Peers might describe me then as creative, intelligent and odd. My home life was different than my classmates. My mother was raised in an upper middle class African American household. Yet life, circumstance and the complexity of mental illness and mood disorders directed us to a low-income life and my mother's toolkit was not compatible. My "brought-upsy" came from second-generation college graduate thinking in an impoverished neighborhood. We had drug dealing and alcoholic neighbors, yet cassette tape loops of Pachalbel's Canon in D minor soundtracked our poverty perspective. Children can be cruel, but aspiration can be resilient. I aspired.

I was blessed early in life by being exposed to extraordinary brown people. They lifted my spirits. Unlike my neighborhood peers, I saw, tasted and touched brown exceptionalism – if only for moments at a time. A brown family with whom my mother befriended in college took me to my first Kwanzaa celebration. I was featured in my brown mother's class video during her pursuit of a master's degree in instructional design and technology. Every year, my family and I ate Christmas dinner in my brown grandmother's home. Grandma Lynn's home was spectacularly decorated; her living room was even featured in a JC Penney catalogue. A beautiful brown friend of the family, for years, tried to convince my mother to enroll me in an all-girls preparatory school. This woman, a school counselor, always said I had "the stuff" and silly me, I believed her. By my senior year of high school, I chose to follow in my mentor's footsteps, a successful brown attorney in the city, and attend his alma mater for my undergraduate degree. I was brown. My heroes were brown. The people I wanted to be were brown. I knew what was possible and people – both brown and white – had invested in me.

In 1994, I graduated from high school. Between 1990 and 1993, I attended six high schools and moved nine times – in two separate states. I survived inner-city schools while on welfare. I survived integrating a suburban school during the Rodney King era. I survived navigating school through the trauma of emotional abuse. I survived the bussing movement and being classmates with drug dealers and gang members, some of whom died before being fitted for a cap and gown. All of these changes were volatile, but I managed to maintain good grades and graduated sixth in my high school class. At the time, I completed high school, I lived in one of the rougher neighborhoods in my city. My street was two blocks from the Crip and Blood gang border. I had already lost two friends to shootings and served as a major support system for my family while my mother fought through a long and severe depression with suicide ideation. If there was anything at all I knew about myself, it was that I was strong and resilient.

I prayed for guidance. I prayed for a hero's rescue. By high school graduation, I wasn't sure what to believe anymore. Deep inside, though, I had a sneaking suspicion some power greater than me was preparing me for something big.

Who was I becoming? Were these the series of events that would change the course of my life? Which of these experiences would be the impetus for my desire to serve others? I didn't realize it at the time, but so many of my childhood memories were shaping into parables that had prepared me for the next phase of my life. More than ever before, events leading up to this moment in time were going to make sense to me. In times of desperation as a child and a young adult, I begged to be rescued. The girl in the mirror was weaker than I desired to be. She was more damsel than diva. She was more distressed than sharply dressed. Her "vibe" was more "in a bad way" than a total "badass". We, the girl in the mirror and I, had been saved so many times by teachers, relatives, friends of the family, government assistance and the kindness of strangers. Once I grew stronger, I believed I had a moral imperative to return the favor.

Chapter 3

Selling My Soul to Pleasantville

I once heard a brown sports commentator on ESPN involved in a discussion about the importance of racial integration in sports previously known for being historically white such as golf, skiing, swimming, etc. She made a valid comment I had never before considered. She explained that while the first person of color to integrate an environment is critical, in her opinion, what speaks more is the second person to integrate the same environment. Per her logic, if the door only opens for one person of color, one could argue that the environment has not yet been truly integrated. However, if the first person of color leads to a second, third and so on, the segregated culture of an environment has been successfully interrupted.

My early attempts to interrupt the working world of whiteness began when I was 21 years old. I sold my soul to the corporate world for a job as a "headhunter" or corporate recruiter. I am convinced my job was to use my personality to convince people to make bad occupational decisions for company's economic profit. Within three years of what felt like *slimy* work at different organizations, one of which I was certain was a cult, I "hightailed" from the cutthroat industry and thoroughly washed my soul and my hands of the bad karma.

I walked away from steady income because of my "moral compass". Though I was no longer a practicing Catholic, Catholic guilt won again. With one year of marriage under my belt and Charlotte, my newborn in my arms, I enrolled in graduate school for a master's degree in educational policy and leadership. My program required a practicum and I lucked up by stumbling upon Beaverpine College, a small, private, predominantly white liberal arts institution. I acquired a practicum in its admission office and aided the college's living legend, Ms. Totty, in minority student recruitment. To some degree, it felt like "icky sales" all over again. Imagine my discomfort in convincing brown students to pay nearly $40,000 for one year of college tuition in total cultural isolation. It was a "hard sell" for me, but I accepted the challenge and made great connections during the practicum with the *right* people.

After graduating a year early from my program, I interviewed for and was offered a permanent position with Beaverpine. There, I gained valuable student affairs experience in both admissions and career development, but I wanted to branch out into other areas of higher education. I had my eyes set on diversity programming, which is a virtual impenetrable career path. In the industry, we joke that one must wait for someone to die or relocate for a job to emerge. So, when an opportunity became available at another college, I ran to it with reckless abandon.

The heavens were smiling on me; and, I got the job. What followed was an adrenaline rush of purposed work.

In 2007, I "found my groove" at our city's large, urban institution, Downtown Community College as a diversity practitioner. In retrospect, diversity work was a natural "fit" for me. I was hired to plan diversity programs for the institution and I took my work very seriously. A large majority of the students had scars I recognized. I felt their stories, recognized their grit and it was easy for us to connect. They allowed me to be the *real* me without "putting on airs". Their pain was palpable and I was driven to provide opportunities for them to change their lives. ...To affirm them and their survivor stories. That kind of work is so much harder than hosting a movie or assembling a Black History Month panel discussion, but I knew our students needed some sustenance.

As a professional middle child and a talker from birth, it would have been too easy to plan events without controversy or conversation. I developed a habit of pushing the envelope through touchy topics and accompanying dialogue. What can I get away with? How can I make this more challenging? What do the people really need to talk about? How can we show people we're listening, we understand and we care?

I pushed and pushed at that job. Over time, I was incredibly fortunate to gain copacetic wealth of social capital and a large body of work that was respected by my colleagues and the community. Credibility from people who mattered gave me a little pleasure to accompany my pain. Sometimes the pushing landed me in the office of my supervisor or other institutional administrators to talk through the bold advocacy in choices I made, but ultimately, I was supported. Soon, I realized that programs weren't enough. What's the point of doing a festival of LatinX culture if their lives aren't improving on a daily basis? Why march in the lesbian, gay, bisexual and transgender pride parade if we still had transgender students who felt threatened in the community?

I wanted the work to be more meaningful, so I began looking into real action-oriented change. Naively, I attempted to implement big ideas and transformational change – all from my middle management role. While my curiosity was appreciated, bureaucracy's response is often, "Stay in your lane." My vantage point was deep and broad, but I was reminded that I was neither "at the table" nor "on the menu". Partial members don't have a decision-making seat at the proverbial table. My position gave me too much power to be on the front line of the struggle and too little power to affect change. I was too much of one thing and not enough of another.

The book, *The Souls of Black Folks* by W.E.B. DuBois, references a term called "double-consciousness". This concept links to a term we refer to as cultural code switching in modern times. Double-consciousness refers to identity and existence being split into compartments. To culturally code switch is to adapt behavior to the surroundings of the folks in the present environment. I understood both double-consciousness and cultural code switching in my work identity, my brown identity *and* in my biracial identity. For example, as a biracial person, I live a brown life but am reminded of my white identity by brown "monoracial" or single race friends and family members.

For a span of six years, I stretched my diversity programming role at Downtown Community College (DCC) beyond capacity. My portfolio was stuffed with advocacy work including poetry events, video projects, hip hop inspired activism, mentoring programs, cultural festivals – anything to edify our internal and external community. The plate became full. The cup "ranneth" over. The plates spun until they smashed into bits and pieces on the floor. I worked that job and my team and my boss to death. Clearly, it was time to move on.

By 2013, my face was smashed against the glass ceiling of middle management. No one was dying and no one was relocating anytime soon, so there was no job to which I could be promoted. I knew I had done all I could at DCC. As I matured in life and in my profession, I grew increasingly fatigued with managing multiple versions of myself. All I wanted was to be myself and do good work serving people who, themselves, wanted to be good.

Some call it the universe. Some call it fate. Some call it karma. I call it God. No matter its name, balance will always prevail. For me, God did not see fit for me to leave Downtown Community College until the perfect opportunity found me. Trust me; I tried and nothing clicked. In fact, God was cute about it. Every job I applied and was considered for resulted in me being the "runner up" candidate. One job opportunity even afforded me the opportunity to be considered for a diversity position at ESPN in Bristol, Connecticut. Alas, I came in second place. Always a bride's maid; never a bride.

Once desperation to find something new passed, I hit a place of peace with my job search. Panic hadn't made an opportunity come to me quicker; so, I *made* myself relax. My job search list had become too confining, so I started over without location barriers or industry barriers. I needed to leave myself completely open and let the job find *me*. That's when I saw it.

"Pleasantville Schools, Director of Student Services." My curiosity was piqued. I remember reading the job description and thinking, "This is my hippie dream job!" How crazy would it be if Pleasantville was the place where I could be myself and stop the double-consciousness insanity? I wasn't certain I was qualified or even a decent fit for the position; but, I believed I had absolutely nothing to lose. Second and third guesses started and stopped my process in submitting a letter of interest. I needed to know more.

I'd learned during my research that a colleague of mine was currently employed as an administrator in athletics at Pleasantville. She made one – *one* brown person on the administrative team. I was ahead of myself in my own daydreams, but I assumed there couldn't be more brown people in Pleasantville than her. If I were to be offered the position at Pleasantville, I would make *two* as the second brown person on the administrative team. She and I were both biracial with black and white parents. Therefore, I often joked that, technically, we still would only make one brown person. Yes, brown people joke about biracial identity, too.

Yes, this is right, I believed. This was my job; I just had to go through the process of fighting other people off to get it. It made no sense. I was urban; Pleasantville was quintessentially suburban. I was brown; Pleasantville was white. I was risky; Pleasantville was safe. I was rough; Pleasantville was polished. I knew poverty; Pleasantville only knew wealth. I fought for the powerless – folks with food insecurity, housing insecurity, limited money and demographic diversity. Pleasantville was made of power – doctors, judges, professors, entrepreneurs and attorneys you can call when you want to make your bad decisions "go away". Pleasantville and I had nothing in common. Still, I believed we were supposed to build something together.

I was Pleasantville's aggressor. I stalked her. In full disclosure, I had stalked Pleasantville for the better part of 30 years. Her landscaped streets were such a gorgeous and welcome contrast to the brick row townhomes of my "cooperative community". Pleasantville had trees. The cooperative had trees, but not like Pleasantville. Pleasantville was actually declared an *arboretum*!

Thinking too confidently about my abilities and the circumstances that sat before me, I fancied myself a potential hero. I thought, "I can make this a before and after story!" I imagined myself a meteor of humanity, crashing into the middle of nowhere. Maybe I would be Pleasantville's crested vigilante from an unknown planet far, far away. Heroes save the day. They unify the city. They make everyone feel like they belong and there is *nothing* like the feeling of belonging. It was grandiose, I know, but I daydreamt of being Pleasantville's unlikely hero. Before rescuing takes place, every hero needs to have a back story and indeed, mine had already been written.

It's not like I was individually and explicitly recruited to Pleasantville. I pursued the feat of disrupting Pleasantville's white culture with a little "brownness". I wanted it. I prayed for Pleasantville. I believed God's plan was to place me in Pleasantville intentionally. Pleasantville was, in my eyes, an opportunity to better understand systemic racism and implicit bias from the inside. So yes, I asked for it but in all fairness, I had no clue what I was getting myself into.

I read and re-read Pleasantville's position description many times before applying. I studied its people. Everything I could find about them, which was not much. Residents of Pleasantville built and maintained a very insular community. Private dirt and "house business" about Pleasantville was not readily available for public consumption. I read their city website, looked for online articles, asked

26

around and discovered nothing I had not already "googled". My hound dogs sniffed and picked up faint scents. We found ghost clues but no trails.

"Getting in" to Pleasantville was like pledging an elusive, secret society. One had to first be invited in. Did I need a special White House-like security clearance? Could I slip in behind a vampire, should he be given permission to enter Pleasantville's doors? The community was securely gated and I did not know the password to have the drawbridge lowered so I could travel without incident across the moat. All I knew was its city and schools' mission statements. Pleasantville was a beautiful mystery and I wanted in.

Pleasantville's Director of Student Services position description read like the manifesto from Jerry Maguire and I wanted to help build their dream of social emotional wellness for students from the ground up. My mother once said that Pleasantville was "the country club of country clubs". Even other suburbs of the city (though not all) were structured with less access limitations than Pleasantville. How, then, does one compose a written request to be invited into an exclusive and elite club where few brown people have been permitted to enter (except through back doors as "the entertainment" or "the help")– whether voluntarily or involuntarily? Here was a portion of my attempt:

Dear Dr. Springsteen:

Please accept this letter as evidence of my sincere interest in the Director of Student Services position currently available with the Pleasantville School District. In reviewing district information, it is apparent that Pleasantville believes in utilizing the strength of community to meet the unique needs of its students, which is incredibly commendable. As a leader within the diversity and inclusion profession, I believe my most meaningful work is community building. I do this by creating opportunities for individuals to be their authentic selves individually and in partnership with others. I am passionate about my vocation and I, too, have a commitment engage communities in order to remove barriers to student success. In doing so, we allow access for everyone to realize quality of life at its highest potential. Because of our linked visions, I believe I am a unique fit for this position...

That's right; I discovered that Pleasantville's district mission and my personal mission were aligned. Somehow, Pleasantville wanted what I wanted. They sought out excellence as did I. They subscribed to collective intelligence and I, too, believed it was the smartest way to solve community problems. I knew I was a wild card for the role as it seemed more 'social worker' than educational administrator, but I had to give it a try. I went on in my introductory letter to Pleasantville itemizing my work at Downtown Community College and my advocacy work over the last decade. I needed to convince them that my oddball skill set was exactly the addition they needed on their team to move the needle forward. What words I had left, I slipped into the end of my letter to them.

I believe in collective intelligence as a way to maximize productivity, inspire incredible innovation and to create supported and sustainable pathways to success. Please feel free to contact me to discuss how my addition to the Pleasantville school community may compliment the great work already happening and aid in the success of its students and educators.

Yours Truly,

Kimberly Brazwell

Pleasantville wanted a drug and alcohol abuse prevention counselor, a social worker and a diversity practitioner all rolled into one person, which was impossible. I knew from my time as a recruiter, though, that job descriptions are written for the "ideal" candidate. No one can meet every bullet item of the wish list particularly with brand new positions such as this. Decision makers can only hire based on best guesses and good intentions.

Well, it happened. I was the "best guess". My intentions were good. I was screened, interviewed and ultimately extended an offer for a position that over 100 people from across the nation wanted. Me; they chose me. I was the wild card; the diamond in the rough. The invitation came in the mail. The drawbridge was lowered. They picked me and I was ready to go to work.

To the amazement of friends, family and colleagues, I left my position at Downtown Community College with students whom I intimately understood and I accepted a leadership role at a small, high-performing suburban school district. In retrospect, I'm certain there was a collective jaw drop. I seemingly had nothing in common with its students, teachers or community members. So much of my work and my professional identity were embedded in community engagement and underprivileged advocacy. I was all about fighting for the "little man" and here I was, marching over to one of our city's most privileged suburbs. If I was a betting woman, I'd be pretty confident that the word "sellout" traipsed the lips of more than a few who knew me. Who cared? I dream big and I had a plan.

I wanted to understand and change the system. I wanted to penetrate suburbia and get a different, closer look at power and whiteness from the inside. I wanted to be the hero that saved Pleasantville from unconscious bias. It wasn't merely that I earned this job; I believed it to be mine through and through. The clouds parted. The sun shone on me. My heart warmed. I knew that the next position I stepped into would be the one that would change my life; and I was right.

Chapter 4

Walking on Water

I became obsessed with perfection at Saint Therese Catholic School. Miss Lane was my fourth-grade teacher, a tall, thin white woman who had never married. She wore 70's era clothing and her chestnut curls bounced when walked across the classroom. Even now, I can remember Miss Lane's full arm sways and the way she planted her legs into the carpet. Miss Lane was intentional in how she used her body and her mind. She wasn't afraid of the little brown bodies in her classroom. She had made several commitments long ago and had dedicated her life to fulfilling said commitments. Miss Lane was committed to Catholicism, the profession of teaching and the little brown faces who didn't quite realize how important education would be for them.

Mine was a multi-generation family who had attended Saint Therese Catholic School. My uncle was a student in its hallways in the same decade when Miss Lane's clothing was nouveau. My big brother attended Saint Therese Catholic school and, in fact, completing his primary schooling in its hallways through the eighth grade. He was a former student of Miss Lane's. She taught a couple of us and was under the impression that we were serious students. Then she met me. I was a legacy student and according to the unwritten rules of legacy students, my path would be easier in the space of student-teacher relationships. The hard work had already been done. My older brother made a great first impression for the family and my younger sister's great impression would follow mine.

Thank God for teachers – the good ones. While the jury was out on whether I was a regular student or a studious outcast, the word about me in teacher talk spaces was that I was a polite, bright and exceptional student. I was put on a pupil pedestal. I was revered and offered as the example other students should follow. Be quiet and obedient like Kim. Be a good listener like Kim. Be a quick learner like Kim. Be on honor roll like Kim. Perhaps the teachers hadn't noticed what was happening between them and me in classroom after classroom after classroom, but my fate was being sealed. My neighborhood peers knighted me as golden. My two shoes were deemed to be "Goody". My white, monogrammed cardigan was "crisp" and my knee-high socks did not slouch. On my head, teachers placed a golden crown to reign over all other students in my classes as a disliked but undisputed teacher's pet and golden child.

Saint Therese Catholic School was a small school, so peers in my class followed each other year after year together. There was only one section of each grade, so it worked to the benefit of every student to get along with our peers and to know our respective roles. I was labeled early on as the class nerd. Though I tried to shake it, I was too interested in grades and appropriate conduct while my peers were too interested in pointing out how odd I was. Perfection makes for lonely days on playgrounds and quiet indoor recesses. Early into my elementary schooling, I had accepted my role in the culture of my classroom. By first grade, I was sniffed out as a smart kid. By second grade, I had alienated myself from the cool kids by raising my hand to answer too many questions. Toward the end of third grade, the only thing that impressed my peers was my ability to draw. Heading into fourth grade, the divide was cemented in place. I had better and more frequent conversations with adults than I had with other students.

By far, my favorite conversation partner on the teaching staff at St. Therese was Miss Lane. Without her omniscient eye, I would have turned completely invisible and faded into non-existence. She noticed me. She called on me. She didn't call on me when I needed less attention. She gave me extra credit work to keep me busy. She complimented me when I needed it. She told me to walk with my head up so I'd look more confident. And maybe she knew what she was talking about. Miss Lane wasn't the prettiest teacher at Saint Therese, but she most certainly knew who she was and what she was about. She was confident in her story, her abilities and never attempted to take on others' identities to fit in.

Fourth grade was different; polarizing. After grappling with what it means to be one of the smartest brown girls in a brown school, I finally reached the end of the academic year. Even the class nerd feels a little relief on the last day of school. Emotions flooded as we prepared for bus rides home. We peaked at final grades on report cards. We had acquaintances, friends and maybe even a few foes sign our yearbooks. As I lined up to slip out of fourth grade for the traditional walk to the fifth-grade class, Miss Lane pulled me to the side. She slyly snuck a wrapped box into my hands and sternly asked me to put it in my book bag and not open it until I got home.

After a quiet bus ride on a loud bus of commotion and end-of year laughter, I rushed home to open the gift. Miss Lane, wishing not to openly dote on her favorite student, passed on a secret gift to me. I meticulously unwrapped the package to find a pristine calligraphy set. She knew I was "unique". I was her special student and she wanted me to know she knew it. That summer, I read every word of the manual. I studied all three styles demonstrated in the instruction pamphlet – Italic, Roman and Uncial. I practiced the styles in multiple color inks with my special pen every chance I got. To this day, I still practice my calligraphic handwriting and fondly remember the one year it paid off for me to be teacher's pet. Favoritism played in my favor.

That was then and this is now. What is a teacher's pet called when it's not a classroom anymore, but the world of work? What do you call the employee who is expected to know all of the answers? Is it a blessing or a curse to come into a new job bright eyed, bushy tailed, and with great expectations?

That's how I entered Pleasantville. They had a problem and I was brought in to solve it. They needed help supporting their brown kids and I just so happened to be golden, which was as good as brown. They needed to build and I had a shovel. They needed to tear down and put things back together. I came equipped with a sledgehammer. While leadership knew what they were getting themselves into with me and my new role, I wondered if everyone at Pleasantville would be as eager to get this social-emotional work done as the folks who had interviewed and hired me.

I have never been famous, but I did get a minimal taste of popularity in college. Downtown Community College kept me quite visible and then I was hired by Pleasantville. The hiring of K-12 administrators requires "vetting". It took at least a month for Pleasantville to dot the I's and cross the T's. Not only did the superintendent of Pleasantville Schools check my list of references, but he called a couple unlisted references, too. They needed to be certain I was, indeed, the right person for the job. This delay gave me an extraordinarily long amount of time to pack up, say goodbye and have closure as I transitioned from DCC and my DCC "family" there.

Imagine my surprise, then, to be visible to Pleasantville while still working at Downtown Community College. I remember packing up my office and noticing the blinking light indicating I had a voicemail message. After entering my secret access code, a small, feminine voice nearly squeaked on the line. It was a school counselor from one of Pleasantville School District's elementary schools. She congratulated me on my hire into the school district and extended contact information to field any questions I had. How had she found me? How did I feel about the call? How should I be receiving this early and intense of a welcome? In no other job I ever had had I been called a month prior to my start date to be told of how highly anticipated my arrival was.

When the hire was confirmed and I arrived in my new office, there was a welcome card and small gift waiting for me. A couple folks here and there stopped by to offer their greetings. Once my email was confirmed, a few messages were already waiting for me in my inbox. I was in disbelief! The welcomes were cheerful and the salutations were warm. ...Incredibly warm. ...Almost too warm. I was suspicious where I should have been thankful for the greeting. Folks popped their heads into my office as if looking for proof that the Easter Bunny was real. It was like being attacked by a blizzard of cotton balls or crowd-surfing on puppy dogs. I had never received so much verbal affection in an employment welcome in all my life.

There was media, too. Oh yes; the press wanted time with me. Legend has it that the realization of this position was two years and lots of long committee meetings in the making. The local newspaper had followed the history of this position's journey from its inception. My arrival was a big deal in Pleasantville. The district public relations rep rushed to get my headshot on the website and to the local reporter. I was connected to the community paper reporter for an initial interview. Once sound bites were harvested from my new boss, the superintendent, Dr. Springsteen, the article went to print.

Gossip commenced from all levels of power. Strangers shared that they had also applied for the position. Community members shared bits and pieces of meeting discourse, interoffice mailings, private meetings and staff break room conversation about the meaning of this role. Even a few school board members shared that other suburban districts were "watching us" to see what would come of Pleasantville's bold move to hire an administrator to lead social-emotional efforts on behalf of students fulltime. The watching eyes and listening ears felt like a lead vest on my chest as I prepared for them to examine my every move under x-rays. Invasive and yet there was nothing I could do about it. Again, I invited this. I wanted more responsibility, more room to have more vision. I wanted more trust to make some miracle happen in Pleasantville, which in turn led to more scrutiny.

The folks in Pleasantville were most certainly watching including my supporters, haters, critics and new colleagues. I even met candidates who interviewed for my position but were not chosen for the opportunity. The seat was hot but I was prepared to be more scented wax than flammable paper. When cooked, I made plans to be coffee beans, not eggs. One afternoon when meeting an assistant principal by the name of James Peep, he asked me a question I have never forgotten. "Do you walk on water yet?" I took that inquiry home to my partner, Jordan, for reflection. His five-word response startled me - no, it scared me. "This job is Mission: Impossible". "This job cannot be done," Jordan explained under a grumble. "They're setting someone up for failure". Mr. Peep likened my needed skill set to that of a "messiah" (lower-case). I needed to somehow form a "savior plan" for Pleasantville and myself in the process (that's lower-case savior).

"Can you walk on water yet?" Still now, I close my eyes and see his smile, hear his sarcasm when he questioned me. He was kidding, of course, but in his tone, it was as if he sensed something I didn't. I had not yet earned his trust enough for him to reveal his hunch to me. "Hmmm, tread lightly, girl," I cautioned myself. "Remember, you're hydrophobic and you can't swim. Jesus walked on water and they crucified Him." I'm hydrophobic and can't swim. If I can't walk on water, what might Pleasantville do to me?

Chapter 5

Making New Friends

"Have you met Luke yet?" This question had been asked of me over and over as I began the dog and pony show of meeting new friends and colleagues in the town of Pleasantville. The reputation of Pleasantville High School's principal preceded him. Before I was comfortable in my office, several people had given me unsolicited personal opinions of him as if revealing secrets. The common narrative was that Luke planted seeds of promise and watered them fast and furiously with a fire hose. His ability to create great relationships with students was always referenced as was his curiosity and willingness to learn more about diversity issues, especially as they impacted students' lives and students' abilities to be successful. His peers also cautioned, though, that Luke often worked so quickly in trying new things that sometimes he neglected to pay enough attention to the details. He started things too fast, went in too broadly and sometimes pulled the plug on ideas if the data didn't point to quick success. And yet, throughout all the private criticism given, there was still a presence of respect, admiration that orbited his aura.

These descriptions didn't intimidate me. To be completely honest, Luke didn't sound much different from some of the critical feedback I'd heard about myself from former colleagues. Besides, I was a professional "new girl". I knew better than to invest in other folks' advice about whom to or not to like – and why. My high school experiences taught me so much about people, namely not to believe everything you hear about how folks' images are formed or perceived before you get to meet them and develop your own relationships. Luke sounded like he might be a great ally for me. He seemed to be well liked; and, I'd always heard that his heart was in the right place. That's all I needed to know. In fact, I looked forward to meeting him and forming my own opinion.

Days before the school year began, my wish was granted. There was a knock at my office door, which was odd because I was brand spanking new and no one knew who I was, let alone where to find me. My visitor was Luke, the legendary high school principal in the flesh. To what did I owe this honor? This wasn't how I expected we'd first talk, but I ran with it. Luke stopped by my office, quickly introduced himself and asked if he could borrow me to meet a committee that was aiding him in the design and tweaking of a new high school program. Though Luke and I had casually and briefly met during my screening interview, the in-the-moment walk and talk was my first real introduction into the "method of his madness". He was charming, instantly charismatic and a fast thinker – a popular partner, no doubt. Luke was an undeniable leader and because of his magnetic personality, folks were drawn to follow him.

Luke seemed to be the kind of guy that filled the room when he wanted to. There's a very distinct difference between taking up space with your presence and sucking all of the oxygen out of the room with your energy. My instantaneous observation was that Luke had had years of practice to perfect the tipping point between space and suffocation. Brown men are in a constant state of managing their bodies so as to not appear frightening or intimidating. White men have the privilege of a different kind of body management. Theirs is always the management of power in their physique. And the taller they are, the more power they have. Research has proven that folks want to be led by males and by tall people. Luke was both. His appearance was almost intimidating. There was no doubt in my mind that he was – and had been for some time now – a member of the Good Ol' Boys Network. As I walked with him and listened to him talk, I had a fleeting thought that I'd never worked this closely with someone deeply entrenched in the Good Ol' Boys Network. Was it even possible for this connection to benefit my social justice cause? I was, naturally, a bit guarded. He could either be a great friend or an unfortunate foe.

Luke was from a small, Midwestern farm town. His present-day persona, however, emulated that of a person who had known and lived with the epitome of privilege. He was younger than those who'd earned the respect of senior level Good Ol' Boys. Luke was uniquely positioned, however, because his respect had already been earned. He was a military man, an athlete and a career-teacher. Luke was young enough to be spritely among his older peers, but old enough to be viewed as a respected elder in comparison to the club's younger members.

Yes, Luke was a card-carrying member of the best VIP club on the planet. Membership had its privileges. In fact, it – and he – had all the privileges. White. Male. Straight. Upper class. Christian. Tall and solid. He had all the desired "weapons" and he looked like he knew how to use them, too. Nice dresser; neat with everything in its proper place. His demeanor was more casual than his attire. The sleeves were rolled up on his expensive, perfectly-pressed button-up shirt. He wore a short haircut and clean-shaven face. I imagine he had worked in an administrative capacity for so long; he had begun to look the part – even if by accident.

Though his physical presence had all the qualifications to result in him being an intimidating figure, Luke had a hearty laugh and a friendly smile. In fact, there was something about him that reminded me of my favorite uncle, a gentle giant with an engaging sense of humor. Folks described him as likeable and friendly. Luke oozed "social capital". It seemed as though Luke knew everyone and could, if he desired, use the power he possessed through his affiliation with social networks to get things done for the greater good. Luke was someone you wanted to be around. Someone you wanted in your corner – a Good Ol' Boy and a good guy.

Luke was engaging from the very first handshake. And, he immediately wanted to connect me to faculty, staff and friends of the district. Already, he was asking for my help and "expertise" as he called it. There was a sense of vulnerability in his voice that I admired. He didn't have all the answers regarding cultural inclusion and he sought out folks who were "in the know". Luke wanted to take advantage of my network of colleagues and he wanted the students – who he cared about deeply – to benefit from my social justice subject matter expertise. I'd been warned that Luke moved fast and that insight turned out to be right. The truth was I had always been given professional feedback that I moved fast, too. Often, too fast or at least faster than organizations and their leadership were usually able to move. To me, Luke and I were going to make a fantastic team.

Luke walked me into a room bursting with papers, bodies, ideas, energy and challenging conversation. When the door opened, I felt the energy of their brainpower from the hallway. The space smelled of anticipation, collective intelligence and fatigue. As a waft of fresh air cycled through the room, Luke walked me in and began introductions. He gave me the names and titles of the folks sitting around the table and then energetically turned to me as he gave them my name. He stumbled through my title (as did most) and apologized as he excitedly shared with his colleagues what work I would be doing for the district.

To my pleasant surprise, when Luke introduced me, most faces smiled with familiarity, as if we'd made each others' acquaintances before. They'd heard about me and had anxiously anticipated my arrival. Though the meeting introduction was brief, they were relieved I was with Pleasantville Schools and all seemed interested in individually connecting with me to learn more about how we could work together. I was beaming. Not only did I already feel part of a team, but from the point of entry, I was being touted as a leader. I was shouldering responsibility and felt relief knowing I had a team of people who were ready to rally around me for the incredibly important work of supporting the social-emotional needs of Pleasantville's students. These were some of the folks I needed to link with throughout the year. They would be my allies and Luke, well, he would be a friend.

Chapter 6

Buffed Floors and Black Hallways

Though I had attended a few architecturally beautiful high schools, the Pleasantville School District main complex was like nothing I'd ever seen before. My new supervisor, Dr. Springsteen, gave my daughters and me a tour of the facilities during my first week of employment in the early summer. Charlotte, Paris (my youngest) and I walked slowly, rotating our necks in all directions down the hallways. The building was all but empty except for the sound of custodial workers buffing the floors into a near unnatural shine to be envied by Hollywood veneer smiles. In my head, Jordan's voice echoed, "Act like you've been 'there' before". Like many, my easiest lens to use was the one from my childhood. I understood poverty much better than I understood wealth and privilege. By telling me to act like I've "been there", Jordan advised me to pretend I see nice things like Pleasantville all the time. Likely, though, I failed miserably at maintaining my "poker face" after seeing all of Pleasantville "from the inside" for the first time.

The Pleasantville Schools main complex was palatial in my eyes. "If I'd had the opportunity to learn in a facility like this, how would my life have changed?" I wondered. There was an Art WING! Be still my beating heart. A Music WING. TWO theatres. TWO gyms. The students felt so secure, they didn't even use locks on their lockers. There was a traditional open lunch. That's right; open lunch. An open lunch meant for an hour, middle school and high school students had permission to leave the premises for a "break" from tedious study for a bite to eat. I realized rather quickly that this experience would be beyond my realm of reality. In fact, I was going to learn as much from them as they would learn from me. As an adult who had grown up in relative poverty, Pleasantville would test my character and my empathetic strengths as it related to socioeconomic status.

I tickled myself at the fleeting thought of Knuckles, one of my rough high school friends, and me attending Pleasantville for high school. Might we have turned out different? Would better futures have been actualized for us? Would I have learned how to study before my junior year of college? Would Knuckles have avoided prison? Would I have been a more disciplined art major when I first set out for higher education? Would Knuckles' art have been different than a beautiful paisley of tattoos that now drip down his body from his chin? Would extra-curricular inspiration have saved us from ourselves?

These were fair questions to ask. In fact, my sneaking suspicion is that Pleasantville already had parents and students in its district whom it attracted because Pleasantville – quite literally – might be the difference between someone's child living or dying. Parents living in low income and poverty-stricken conditions must make *different* tough choices than those who have expendable income. Tough love might look like-uprooting your family from everything they know and placing them in an environment where their very presence is likely spectacle. And what if they're not gifted in the art of being new? What if they feed their pain and frustrations with fist-a-cuffs? I kept wondering, "Is Pleasantville ready for real brown people?"

The bulk of my early childhood took place less than 20 minutes from Pleasantville's borders. St. Therese's Catholic School was minutes away from where I worked. Urban fringe, I believe it's called. Its north end border was literally a set of the railroad tracks. How do you like that? The town's reputation preceded itself. Since its inception, Pleasantville was rich, privileged, white and Jewish. Well-known for its deeply-imbedded cultural history – but not mine.

Pleasantville was not for people like me, so I was brought up to understand. If you were brown, you didn't drive through Pleasantville; you went around. And if passing through its city limits was unavoidable, you drove 5 miles under the speed limit. Whenever my mother and I would park and ride the bus downtown to get our government assistance benefits, we ironically always passed through Pleasantville.

As we crept through its streets, I imagined myself attending its private schools or living in one of its huge homes, a stone exterior sub/urban castle with lots of space. Free from alcoholic and drug-addicted neighbors. A place where I could have a pet dog kept in an actual yard with trees and a flower bed. Though I knew it wasn't mine, Pleasantville was an image for the foundation of what "making it" looked like to me.

One of the first secrets I learned at Pleasantville's high school is that the urban fringe had found its way into the building. There was a "Black Hallway"; and, apparently, everyone knew about it. Even more interesting, it was located in the hallway by the gym. So the story goes, this section of real estate in the high school was called "the black hallway" because most of the brown students frequented its space during open lunch. Stereotype threat and self-fulfilling prophecies abounded.

I even heard that some kids, when avoiding contact with the Black hallway, found a separate passage. The extended walk was called the "Journey to Africa". My goal was to somehow interrupt this culture. I had a great deal of work to do to earn trust and become the convener of a moral imperative for social emotional wellbeing.

Now, here I was in Pleasantville and it seemed like a mistake. A mistake I was grateful that had been made. An old neighbor of its borders. A new protector of its youth. I was hired to systematically address all social-emotional issues for brown students in the Pleasantville School District. My charge was to link the school district and community resources in efforts to create a supportive and nurturing environment for district constituents. The irony: a brown person was hired to be the bleeding heart for a community of people my brown family worked so hard to not bother. A job like this meant that Pleasantville was a different place than the suburb I grew up learning to avoid. This one sounded more diverse and liberal. This one was ready to be perceived differently and that excited me immensely. It seemed that Pleasantville had changed.

My new question became: If Pleasantville is different than before, how did my grandmother and mother's Pleasantville become the community it is today?

Chapter 7

Rose "Colored" Glasses

Perhaps I was a bit naïve when I first began the job. I was like a young bird locked in a cage; and, I was ready to be "let loose" and test my new wings. On day one, I showed up in the office with a notebook filled with ideas I wanted to act on right away. My pink notebook was filled with my rose-colored optimism and on the cover was a cartoon illustration of my "spirit animal". The beautiful sketch of an owl was a link to the "wild soul" that I hoped would guide my natural instincts. Owls reminded me to defer to wisdom and wisdom urged me to slow my pace and listen to what the environment was telling me. In one hundred pages, I had tons of doodles, flowcharts, book and article references and website links for the initial action plan. In my defense, I had plenty of time to obsess over my new job – and that's exactly what I did.

In my early days of work at Pleasantville, I read and researched everything that I could on the history of the town. I wanted and needed to hit the ground running. I wanted to let the job, the naysayers and, the Pleasantville School District see that I was a no-nonsense, "bad mother-shut-your-mouth!" as admirers said about the 1970s vigilante, Shaft. They needed to know that they might have more money, status and clout than I did, but they were not going to be able to outwork me. I was affirmed, confident and as my church friends might say, blessed and highly favored.

Was I suffering from delusions of grandeur? Perhaps. I felt special and so what if I did? Pleasantville chose me "unanimously" to lead this important endeavor and I felt I was up for the challenge. The notion that I am a grandiose thinker is fine by me, especially if it could one day help to end some of the world's greatest problems - "isms" like racism, classism, sexism and other power and control ideologies. Go hard or go home, right?

Within my first thirty days on the job, constituents from the district and the community met with me every day. At times, it was breath-taking and incredibly over-stimulating. If you can imagine, for six weeks, I was told a secretly dysfunctional story about Pleasantville nearly every day. The community's ideological drama was labyrinthine. Most of the problems were like a tangled ball of yarn. Some of the chaos was "hidden" with power and money. A select few of the major players were arguably untouchable. I didn't know where to start or what to do with the information. Weeks later, I met with a colleague whose subject matter expertise was in the prevention, intervention and recovery industry. What she told me, I'll never forget. After discussing larger-than-life issues that I might have to address on my new job with the Pleasantville School District, she offered that ending systemic oppression and mental illness was not possible. Those problems are too large and perpetual, she explained. "But what you can hope for is a ripple in the water. ...An interruption."

As Pleasantville's new Director of Student Services, I zoned in on the word "community" as a theme to my beginning ideation. I envisioned quilt-working the cultural history of Pleasantville into a beautiful district-wide student project. "How awesome would it be, I thought, "for the kids to research the progressive integration of their town?" Is it too much to say, that I could already hear all the Pleasantville children holding hands and singing, "We Are the World?" Probably not. As an 80s kid, the song changed my life; I believed its ideology still "had legs". How does a community of very little race diversity suddenly become ten to 15 percent race-diverse? Where did all these brown people come from? And how did a town with so little turnover feel about the fact that it was "browning"? Was the growth perceived as integration or infiltration? Was the "browning" a blessing or a curse? I decided to start there.

One of the first calls I made was to the Pleasantville Historical Society. An old, withered voice answered the phone and after introducing myself, I asked her, "What is the cultural history of Pleasantville?" I heard my father's mother in her voice, soft-spoken and sweet. She sounded old but still pensive and perhaps of German immigrant descent, just as I am. My mind drew her face in the image of Grandma Anna and I pictured her sitting in a tiny little... "What do you mean by culture?" she quizzically interrupted my thoughts. Thrown off by her question, I explained that I was interested in learning about how the different racial groups grew in numbers in Pleasantville.

I inquired about the "firsts"... I inquired if she knew who the first African American graduate of the high school was. The first Asian graduate? The first LatinX graduate? Silence fell on the other end of the phone. My intuition suggested that I was the only one on the line who knew what I was talking about. She was perplexed and notified me that they didn't keep track of any information like that. After the brief pause, the kind old woman responded, "Well, at the original high school, there were some colored students, but they likely lived with white families as 'the help'."

Colored. Like the woman to whom she was speaking on the phone? This was clearly not my grandmother's voice. My face tingled and Grandma Anna's wrinkled apparition and dimpled smile fizzled into the stale air of my office. This woman obviously had no idea I was also of African American descent. Otherwise, we both would have shared the awkward moment instead of me feeling flustered alone. But, my shoulders were broad enough to carry the embarrassment for both of us. She was clueless that she had offended me, so she didn't apologize. Still, I forgave her and excused "it". I told myself that she was older and "colored" might have been a socially acceptable term for brown folks in her era. I told myself, it was a generational lexicon issue. Alas, the School of Hard Knocks had begun.

Chapter 8

A Papyrus Sacrifice

Admittedly, for much of my life, I felt closer to my mother than I felt to my father. II matched my mother's side of the family on the outside as well as on the inside. My mother and maternal siblings understood me more uniquely than my I felt father could. We all "browned" in the sun. We liked Richard Pryor's standup comedy a little more than we should have. We shared the same struggles and triumphs on our coiled hair texture journey. Our music tastes were linked. We all were drawn to break-dancing and rap music like it was a genial language we all spoke. I felt enigmatically at home with the maternal side of my family through no fault of my father's; and, the strain was tactile.

I knew my white relatives were "family" and that they truly loved me. Still, the connection was labored and foreign with them. They loved me immensely; but, their only option for connection was via "Cliff's Notes" my father gave them to stay abreast of my life. Talking points on what was new in my neck-of-the-woods. My white grandparents – particularly my grandmother – didn't understand my hair. They could see it, smell it, and touch it; but, they didn't know what it was like to walk around with that head of hair day in and day out. My white aunts and uncles didn't appreciate my ability to dance as much as the "browner" members of my family.

My mother coached me on how to manage my body in the company of the white side of my family. No wiggling. Say please and thank you. Act like I have some sense. My white family heard the same music I heard, but I don't know if they "felt" it in exactly the same way as my brown family members. Maybe they did. To be fair, I never asked them. Were we all listening to Roberta Flack or Chaka Khan in some "spiritual" way? Or, was it just noise to them? They loved me, but more times than I care to recall, I wondered, does my white family really *know* me?

This is what it's like to be biracial. I am some of everything and all of nothing. I am half of a lot and whole of very little. I am the only "me" in my family on both sides. I did not have the words to articulate my race reality. With one foot in brown identity and the other in white identity, I was looking for somebody in the family who "looked" like me. Instead, I found fragments of this person's eyes and that person's chin. My brown family members explained that I was a *perfect blend* of those folks' faces. My color was a prototype. Understanding my biracial identity meant asking questions my family members were not able to answer.

It is amazing to me that I reached age fourteen and neither my mother nor father ever brought up a significant race conversation. We behaved as if none of us

45

noticed we were all different colors. With the exception of my father's obsession with Donna Summer and my mom's eternal crush on David Bowie, there was no explicit racial dialogue, let alone, how I came into being. My father didn't dare touch the subject. Perhaps, he didn't know how. My mother was still scarred from her own racial experiences. I was café au lait colored with brown eyes, a blonde afro, freckles and I was left to make sense of my mismatched family on my own. It took years for me to come to terms with what being biracial meant to me.

In recent years, Pleasantville was trying to make sense of its new mismatched family. Here, a whole community had spent its entire life predominantly white and by the 2000s, "brown" student enrollment was growing. There were, however, few if any communitywide conversations about race to prepare for the "browning". Maybe Pleasantville wasn't expecting the number of brown students to continue to increase; but, it did.

Alumni of Pleasantville High School in the 1990s recall there still being just "a handful" of brown students in their graduating classes. I can only speculate that the neighborhoods, businesses, schools, public servants and small town politicians did not coordinate orientation sessions and welcome baskets for the new brown residents of Pleasantville over the years. What I imagine is that both the existing white residents and the new brown residents utilized the practice of "color-blindness" to maneuver the changing demographics. They (told themselves that they) erased color and established relationships on a color-neutral case-by-case basis.

Maybe "Pleasantvillian" life was, well, "nice"; but, for some of the newer brown families, the definition of nice in Pleasantville culture versus brown culture meant two different things. New Pleasantville residents, regardless of culture, quickly learned to assimilate. There was, you see, a certain thing called "Pleasantville nice". Becoming a "Pleasantvillian" meant opting in to morning jogs, entertaining friends at dinner parties, wine and play dates, and Pleasantville School District yard signs proudly displayed in flower beds. From my initial conversations with a few of Pleasantville's brown residents, being brown and "Pleasantville nice" granted you some community member privileges, but not *all* of them. It admitted you into half of your culture and theirs but no whole cultural affiliation. It was a bit like being biracial. Being brown in Pleasantville, as a few of its brown residents described, required a fair degree of proficiency in cultural code-switching and double-consciousness.

Interestingly enough, Dr. Springsteen and I believed my biracial identity would be of benefit to me and to the community members who were consciously or subconsciously code-switching. My "United Nations" childhood neighborhood and biracial identity were perfect preparation to culturally serve a school district like Pleasantville. Most of my in-laws, nieces and nephews are veritable code-switchers. I knew that language; maybe I could be a cultural translator. Dr. Springsteen explained to me that several years ago, the district enrolled more biracial students

46

than monoracial brown students. According to the data, the biracial students were an entirely different set of kids than the monoracial brown students; I understood that. I fit that demographic as well.

I wondered if the multiracial students were aware of their surroundings and of who they were. I had what I now see as an advantage of coming up in a highly diverse nonetheless predominantly poverty—stricken neighborhood. Pleasantville kids, however, likely came up middle class. Sure, some had the experience of that "sweet life". Others had the unique "inconvenience" of living poor and socializing in a community that was overwhelmingly upper middle class. That's a tough tight rope to balance. From where did their race and class guidance come? Or, had it not existed at all?

As the school year grew near, only days away, I organized and finalized some of my academic year planning. One of the initiatives I'd be taking on was a quarterly community dialogue session. The plan was for the topics to be dictated by the attendees as an incentive to come back as an invested audience. Since the effort was new, I selected the very first topic to get us started. It seemed apropos in an environment like
Pleasantville to select the topic of cultural code-switching.

To be clear, cultural code-switching is imperative for success and everyone does it. Code-switching is the act of changing the way you speak depending on your audience or company. Youth do not speak to elders the way they might speak to peers. Workers do not interact with colleagues the way they interact with the boss. One would not interact with a romantic partner in the same manner as a distant family member. Each version of ourselves is assigned a specific way by which we communicate per each social group in our lives.

The degree to which we code-switch is dependent upon the variety in our lives from one environment to the other. Some of us do a tremendous amount of code-switching in our speech. Sometimes the switch is necessary in our body language, too. Other times, our dress and cultural artifacts change, depending on the environment. Those of us who are brown make a conscious decision – nearly every moment – on how soft or loud the volume of our cultural authenticity will be. If monoracial folks are doing a significant amount of cultural code-switching on any given day, can your mind even fathom the amount of cultural code switching that takes place for a multiracial person or a transracial adoptee?

I wanted to let folks in the Pleasantville School District know that there was a new administrator in town who was dedicated to creating a space where we could have conversations about our social and cultural experiences. Through community dialogue, I wanted to help us to build a relationship where we could honor the good and collectively heal from the bad. I figured we'd start that journey with the most important human relationship element – communication.

The theme of the first conversation was, "Talking Black, Acting White, Selling Out and Keeping It Real". We were going to grapple with the experience of cultural code-switching. My vision was to bring folks together for the first time in Pleasantville to openly discuss the unspoken undercurrent of race. Instead of pretending to be colorblind, my aspiration was to finally direct our attention to the elephant in the room so we could begin working on the challenge. That way, if we could "name the problem", we could then figure out what we wanted to do with it.

After I drafted the letter, I actually sat back and admired my work. It was so empowering for me to finally have a position high enough and important enough that I could essentially mail a "hug" right to my constituency groups. Once the letters were mailed, I waited with baited breath. As a highly-extroverted person, I tarried to receive the warm feedback from my letter recipients. I'd waited all summer to "make friends" and had readied myself for the coming relationships.

My arms were outstretched waiting for the brown people in Pleasantville to realize they no longer had to be silent. I wanted them to know I was ready, willing and able to be noisy on their behalf. Beyond the horizon, my new colleague Paula who headed up the fundraising organization for Pleasantville Schools, called me with surprising news. In her voice, I sensed the first wave of community energy coming my way.

Paula: [Whispering] Kim, I just got off the phone with a
                parent who's upset about the letter.

Me: [Chuckling] How is that possible? That's one of the
                nicest letters I've ever written.

                [Paula spoke almost cryptically. She'd lurked on Facebook and
                discovered my name had been referenced in a private group.]

Paula: I told her to talk to you; to give you a chance. She
                should be calling you so she can speak with you
                directly.

I sat, flabbergasted in my office chair, racking my brain to figure out what could have been offensive in a welcome letter. My brainstorming was interrupted when my phone rang. It was the parent who had been urged to contact me. For an hour, we calmly and politely debated on the LAN line. All the while, her "angle" perplexed me.

Jackie: My friends and I were so offended; we stood in my
                kitchen and threw your letters away together. It was
                like being mailed a race conversation that we weren't
                ready to have with our kids.

48

I was aghast that a mother of biracial children was this alarmed at the insinuation of her children being "lumped in" the category of students of color. Perhaps I interrupted her distain incorrectly. Perhaps she assumed her children were so "special", they weren't "colored" anymore.

Jackie: Both of my children are biracial and we have raised
            them to not believe that race is a barrier for them.
            We raise them to not notice race.

Me: Well, I am also biracial. My father is white and my
            mother is black. I know from personal experience that
            no matter what my parents told me inside our home
            outside of my family, the world will receive me as a
            black female.

I softened and chewed back my passion like a wad of curd.

            Everyone performs cultural code-switching. This
            dialogue session will simply allow attendees to start
            having conversations about it. It's not meant to
            "take sides" in any way. [She seemed to be relieved
            by my words.]

Jackie: I'm glad I called you. I don't completely understand
            where you're going with this; but, I'm going to give
            you a chance. I believe you have good intentions.

I inferred her concluding statements that to mean she and I agreed to disagree; but she was open. Before ending the call, I invited her to come to the community conversation, if only to listen to other perspectives. I also asked her to share her perspective on why she and her biracial children didn't talk about race. "I'll try," she hesitated. Good enough for me. "Try" is better than "no".

That Friday evening, I went to my one and only Pleasantville football game and brought my daughters with me. We bunched together like newbies in a sea of white folks who, thankfully, didn't seem to pay us any mind. Midgame, an athletic white woman sat beside me. The woman was the mother with whom I had spoken on the phone. That's how small Pleasantville was. A woman who hated my guts last week and gave me a piece of her mind only hours ago was now sharing a stadium bench with me. What were the odds?

I sat with a snarky smile on my face for several minutes, deciding whether the schadenfreude was worth it to make her acquaintance in person. Yes, it was. I tapped her and introduced myself. "*I'm* Kim Brazwell..." Her face lit up with surprise as she scanned her brain for transcripts of our phone conversation. Upon meeting me, my biracial identity suddenly mattered now. She insisted her biracial children meet me before my daughters and I left the game. They respectfully introduced themselves to me and I shook their young hands and offered myself as a contact after the game, should they ever want to talk.

They never came to my office. They never came to my community dialogues. The malleable process of neuroplasticity around race came to a screeching halt. She and I never spoke again.

Chapter 9

Black Faces

It was warm outside and in my soul. Early fall in a new school year means that you can still feel the excitement of things to come. Even on a late day in the office of the new job, the sun seemed to wait for me and accompany me on my drive home. The air was filled with hope and anticipation. We were anxiously looking forward to old familiarity and new discoveries. Lifelong friends were relieved to be reunited. New faces nervously learned the hallways and cafeteria food while masking desperation for welcoming smiles. Though the environment was ripe with opportunity, the climate of the district was porous. Maybe too porous. Unguarded; however, not yet in fear that it could be harmed by unfamiliar things.

One of the interesting things I've learned about predominantly white environments is that one has to wear his or her brownness a bit differently. Brownness or even more generally, "otherness" is this constantly evolving thing. Whatever one's "other" is, it has more than likely existed in some place on the planet since the beginning of time. Pigmentation. Gender. Sexual orientation. These are all natural occurrences in nature – including the animal kingdom. Meanwhile, it is the human, specifically the majority group, who acts as if this natural "otherness" is "abnormal or unnatural". An alternative. An oddity. Counter culture. And if survival in most any environment requires not existing in isolation, then the fate of the "others" is ominous.

One of my favorite quotes is, "Culture eats strategy for breakfast". A group's shared values, beliefs and experiences are incredibly powerful. That's why culture-shaping is so difficult. By itself culture isn't a bad thing. The issue is what folks in power positions do with things and people who are *counter* culture. Being part of the culture is exciting. It feels good to belong. It's exhilarating to *match* your family. It's powerful to know who you are and whose you are. One could argue that belonging is the beginning of pride, at least in the form of groups.

Take the notion of school pride as an example. It's football Friday night in the Midwest and every high school has the stadium lights on for the big game. Students and parents have filled the stands donning their mascot images and team colors. Cheerleaders root for friends, jersey numbers and call out school colors. For those few hours, everyone from that school community gets to belong to something. To one unifying thing. And win or lose, the momentum that carries everyone through the four quarters of the game is school pride.

In small communities, not unlike suburbs, that pride bleeds beyond the school district and flows into the entire community. And perhaps the pride gets so deep, authentic and passionate because the school community and the neighboring community become one blended unit. Houses and classrooms fuse. Faculty and families melt together. Now imagine a neighborhood community with very little turnover. Imagine that folks move in and out so infrequently, that you know the names and back stories of homes when a new neighbor finally does settle in the house down the street. In this case, pride far exceeds the current graduating class of the high school and its parents. This type of school pride gets passed on in the DNA of a community. Not unlike how certain diseases can be coded and transferred on DNA strands. Even sickness can be hereditary, but for now, let's continue to pretend we're all well.

The cool thing about a school district that was founded on class privilege is that the alumni have an immense sense of pride in their school – and resources to back that school pride up with money that "folds". After "snooping around" and asking more questions of folks in-the-know on the district staff, I was told that many alumni dedicated their yearbooks to the high school library. They were so *in love* with their alma mater that they bequeathed the hardcopy artifacts of their teenage memories back to the place where their pride began – school. In fact, the collection of yearbooks dated back as early as the 1920's. It was advised that I might page through these dusty artifacts to see if my questions about Pleasantville's cultural history could be answered.

I waited for a Friday afternoon when I could sit undisturbed. Still new to Pleasantville and its schools, I thought it might be nice to study the history in silence. All day, I answered emails, attended meetings, prepped agendas and researched ideas while waiting for the school to empty so I could concentrate on my task. I wanted to dive into the yearbooks; transport myself to 1920 Pleasantville. At around 5:00pm that evening, I made my way to the high school library. As well preserved as I had anticipated, the yearbooks were in chronological order right by the main doors of the library. The high school librarian graciously welcomed me in and stayed long enough to unlock the glass encased time capsule. He told me to take as much time as I needed and to just turn out the lights and close the door behind me when I was done.

The school was perfectly still. It was "Football Friday Night" and a stadium full of friends bundled together adorned with school-colored face paint. I, however, was the daughter of a teaching librarian. There was no better place to spend time alone than in a pile of books. The school and I could finally get to know each other a little better. Just the building walls, fluorescent light hums, weeklong dust from days of classes and a quaint study room in the library. I grabbed a stack of yearbooks and began my journey into Pleasantville High School's history.

I cracked open the first yearbook to a sepia daydream. My hand traced over fragile paper and I ran my thumb across the torn page corners. A waft of attic dust and basement mildew tickled my nose as I slowly turned the pages, careful to not crease or tear the fragile paper. Calligraphic-styled handwriting was grafted across the inside covers. Perhaps D'Nealian. It was as if I was dusting fossils from a rare archaeological find. I felt sheepish, paging through the yearbook like I was reading my grandmother's diary. Their whole lives were in my hands.

Smiling and mumbling to myself, I examined every detail of the students' faces. I looked at the etchings of their clothes and how they clasped their hands while standing in team pictures. I squinted to gauge hair texture in an effort to guess which curly-haired students were actually Jewish or Italian. Then, on the bottom, right page, I saw him. ...A brown face! "What?!" I gasped. "What are *you* doing here?" I interrogated, as if expecting him to answer me. Maybe someone had asked him the same question when he enrolled in Pleasantville High School in the 1920s.

This brown face was an athlete and a scholar. He looked handsome and distinguished; earnest and strong. The melody of fluorescent lights in the study room called my attention to the stillness of his eyes. His eyes... They were numb and distant. I averted my eyes from his, but I kept turning pages and searching for him. Every time I found him, he seemed all alone. For a moment, I trembled, feeling a chill in the room. Advancing deeper into the yearbook and then into subsequent chronicles, I serendipitously spotted a few other brown faces peering from nearly one hundred years ago. For effect, I'd release my eyes from focus to better catch the contrast. Dark spots in a sea of whiteness on a tennis or a football team photo. My elbows dug into my lap and I rested my chin in the fold of my hands. Reflecting on my conversation with the elderly woman from the Pleasantville Historical Society, I asked the photos, "Were you the help? Did you work for your classmates?"

A plastic grocery bag of snacks warmed in the room. I couldn't eat nor was I hungry anymore. Hunger pangs gave way to a burn in my diaphragm. In one yearbook, I discovered a family of three brown siblings. They were the lone brown folks in the school that year. Their onyx faces were sober and heavy. Holding the place with my left hand, I flipped to the back of the book and read superlatives and last will and testaments of the graduating seniors. Most students scribed jovial statements. Brown students' quotes were "short and sweet". "This place hurt you, didn't it? You probably left here and never came back." I sighed and sat back in my seat.

After several yearbooks, I took a break and let silence be a voice in the room. Questions raced and my heart fluttered a bit. What the times felt like for them ...in that skin ...during that period in the nation's history. I wondered how they found themselves in this entirely white community. How their brown peers treated them outside of Pleasantville. How their white peers treated them inside of Pleasantville. Did they study geometry with peers and then go home to servants' quarters and help clean house for "friends" from math class? Did they cook food for the fancy dinner parties of their community neighbors? Were there rare, wealthy brown-skinned blue-bloods that passed brown-paper-bag tests? What did cultural code-switching look like in 1924? Were they safe? Were they happy? Were they resilient and successful? Or were they swallowing a daily dose of pain as their sharp cheekbones and stiff jaws seemed to suggest?

Then I saw it.

Reading through one of the white classmate's profiles, I saw a phrase that made me do a double-take. *Minstrel Shows.* "That can't be right," I uttered. My face warmed and the insides of my cheeks salivated. I was growing nervous and angry, so I tried lying to myself. Maybe the yearbook was referencing a different kind of minstrel show. Surely, the students didn't participate in blackface and minstrel shows as a school activity. I tried scrubbing the words "minstrel show" from my brain shaking it away like Etch-a-sketch sand, but my skin began to crawl like it intuited the next page. In the advertisement section toward the back of the yearbook I was reading, I saw a caricature of a "sambo". Illustrated, likely by a student, he was shucking and jiving with eyeballs as big and white as cup saucers. His top hat was tilted and his lips were like water balloons dripping from his face. Out loud, I shouted, "Oh my God!" I shoved the book from the stack sitting in front of me and retrieved the book where I saw the first young brown man's graduating picture. I skimmed the student profiles again so briskly I nearly made myself dizzy. I had to confirm my fear and I did. That handsome, stalwart brown man was a current student at the same time his classmates performed in minstrel shows.

I was in pain. If it hurt me one hundred years later, how could he have *not* been in pain? Today, we would have affirmed he was living – and learning – with chronic post-traumatic stress disorder, returning every day to more hurt. Maybe he didn't even know he was hurting or, maybe he grew accustomed to it.

I sat alone and reticent in Pleasantville High School's beautiful library and imagined the conversations brown students in the 1920s and 1930s had over dinner each night with their family members. How did brown mothers and fathers build their children (back) up every night and coach them through being some of Pleasantville's only brown faces? Did the school offer students the opportunity to purchase the class picture? Could brown servant-students afford it with the money they and their families got from being "the help"? Did the brown students want to keep memorabilia of class picture where they were only recognizable as black dots in the corners among a sea of white faces? What about the classmates who mocked their brown faces at the annual minstrel show? Were they friends and teammates? Did they go to school functions together? Did they adorn school-colored face paint? Were *all* of the Pleasantville High School football players cheered for by proud patrons? Did they expect brown students to be the fastest feet on the track team? Did the brown students go to the minstrel show to share a belly laugh and cheer on their white friends? And if so, during those times, were the brown students proud to be Pleasantville Panthers? Was their pride darker than that of their peers? Did their cheers echo out as loudly or were they choked back with a little pain?

I was still disturbed as I tried to explain Pleasantville's minstrel shows away. Historians would likely tell me not to take it personally, but my coarse hair, full lips and relationships with brown family members made the pill a bit too jagged to swallow and the truth a bit too torrential to write off as just an overcast moment in American history. But, you have to believe I tried. "It was the 1920s," I told myself. Minstrel shows were quite popular around the nation at the time. It was a mainstream form of entertainment. Perhaps it would not have been uncommon for brown folks to see whites doing minstrel shows. "Maybe", I told myself, "it didn't hurt the brown students at all". But I knew that couldn't be true.

I spent a couple more hours paging through two additional decades of yearbooks and I watched the brown folk dry up like insecticide-treated weeds by the 1940s. "Where'd they go?" I wondered. And if the school reverted to being all white, how did we get here now with a ten to 15 percent race-diverse student body?

I neatly stacked the yearbooks in chronological order and placed them back in the glass display case carefully. It dawned on me that some of the benefactors of these yearbooks never imagined my brown hands leaving fingerprints on these post-depression era pages. Similarly, I never once thought that I or someone who looked like me would be seething or writhing over my ancestry, humanity and community through these books.

As I shut and locked the curio doors, I caught a glimpse of the handsome brown man's face in the glass. Of my maize complexion in the glass. My long, dark dreadlocks were pulled away from my brown eyes. My freckles looked like constellations across my round nose. My biracial hands resembled both my white and black grandmothers. It was surreal. I was Pleasantville's second administrator of color and I felt the weight of what it meant to lead the undertaking that had been entrusted to me.

I wondered how we'd moved forward enough for me to be standing in this place and yet we were still far enough behind that our present-day brown students were clueless about the work equity that was paid in full by the brown faces who suffered before them. How had we not documented and honored the cultural history of this community? Did they even notice that brown people were part of the school or had color-blindness become a real thing? How do students walk past this translucent and forgotten time capsule, sealing in white faces masked by black paint? Sealing in brown faces masking broken hearts? Did they have a clue about the racial history of their school and community? Did they even desire to know more than what was learned at home?

This is dangerous, I thought. Those who don't know history…

Chapter 10

Save the Drama

I don't make a big deal of it in my professional life; but, I was once a pretty fiercely competitive spoken word poet. My husband and I competed in poetry slams (competitive poetry readings) for many years. One year, I was even nationally ranked. With roots in the performing arts, I am always interested in approaching my social justice work from an artistic point of view whenever I can make it work.

During my time at Downtown Community College, one of my major successes was a collaborative effort between my diversity office and the theatre department. We joined forces and brought a readers' theatre version of *The Vagina Monologues* in connection with Take Back the Night – a national movement to raise awareness about sexual violence against women. The event was a huge success and prompted me to think of more ways to tie theatre into diversity work.

After joining Pleasantville's leadership team, one of the first living legends on staff who I learned about was the drama teacher, Bethany Mellow. Even better, Bethany's office was located right beside mine. "Perfect," I thought. I sent an introductory email with "new girl" hopes that a great friendship was on the cusp of beginning. In the quiet of the new school year, I waited to hear from Bethany and began planning in my head all kinds of cool collaborative efforts we could do together. So lost in my planning I was, that it took me a minute to realize the communication wasn't reciprocated in any form. No visit. No phone call. No email, text, Morse Code, smoke signals or dove with an olive branch. Nothing. I bopped next door and introduced myself. The meeting was cordial with lots of lovely voice inflection and toothy smiles, but nothing followed. I sent another email referencing the first introductory email. Goose eggs. I figured that Bethany was busy. "We're both artists, so this will be a natural bond," I maintained.

Later that fall, sometime after the discovery of black faces in old year books as well as brown faces of students in "the black hallway", I unexpectedly had what we would much later understand to be a panic attack. My heart felt as though it was pounding out of my chest. My vision dulled and the top of my lip sweated. I grew even more anxious, remembering my first-ever panic attack just months before. I could feel tension in my arms squeezing like a blood pressure cuff and feared I would lose consciousness. My instinct, as usual, was to try and not make mountains out of molehills. I needed someone to tell me that I was fine and that the feeling would pass, so I got the bright idea to call dial-a-nurse. Perhaps that would become my pattern; calling people whilst having panic attacks. While on the line, my symptoms worsened and my office tilted. Or maybe it was me who'd lost balance and sight of which way was true north. Fearing I was experiencing a potentially serious health emergency, the nurse on the line urged me to find someone nearby who could take me to the closest emergency room. Lucky for me, my theater neighbor was in the office and was able to come to my rescue.

Bethany and I hopped in her getaway car and I tried to have a normal conversation while my heart jumped double-dutch in my chest.

Me: [Narrowing wild eyes] Thanks for taking me to the hospital. I
                know you're all kinds of busy with things to do.

Bethany: [With nervous excitement] Oh, sure; it's no problem at
                all! [Pause.] So… what happened?

Me: [Hiding trembling hands] I just, all of a sudden, felt
                sweaty, lightheaded and my heart was racing. I'm sure
                I'm fine and it's nothing, but the nurse asked me to
                get checked out at the hospital.

Because Bethany and I had absolutely no relationship at all, it seemed she and I both felt overwhelmingly awkward in such close proximity in the front seats of her tiny car.

Me: You know, my oldest daughter, Charlotte, is interested in being
                an actress. She's scared of trying out for the school play.

Bethany: Where does she go to school?

Me: We live in West Village. She's at Legacy Middle
                School.

Bethany: [Fidgety] Oh, they've got some really great theatre programs in
                West Village Schools. I've worked with some of the teachers.
                There are some really great middle school plays out there.
                Grease, The Wizard of Oz. I think there might even be an
                adaptation of high school musical.

Me: [Dazed but anxious] Wow, I'll have to look into that.

Bethany: Yeah, you can do some really cool things with those
                productions. A few years ago, we… [Voice trails off]

I lost focus of Bethany's banter as I used every ounce of concentration to try and stop my limbs from buzzing. Main Street, where the nearest hospital was located, felt like it was on the other side of the country. My gut churned each time Bethany's car trounced construction potholes. Coin change, tchotchke and a couple small stage props sloshed around the car as we stopped and started through rush hour traffic lights. My body felt rubbery, but I knew I looked "normal". All I could do was pray that I would not lose consciousness in Bethany's car. I didn't want her to stigmatize me as a "hypochondriac freak" for the rest of my tenure in Pleasantville Schools.

Down the street, we traveled as I tried distracting her with my best attempt to get her to talk about herself. And, thanks to her equal desire to ignore the weird elephant in the car, she gabbed back with me. It was like we were on a 'ladies only' road trip, except instead of spring break in Miami, we were headed to the emergency room just east of the Pleasantville border.

Bethany obeyed traffic laws with white knuckled hands on "ten and two" of the steering wheel as she discussed set design of a past production with me. Needing to be believably lucid, I put on my best sane face and held it. It was like saying "Cheese!" for the longest photo prep ever. Moments before we depleted all forms of conversation, the tiny, cluttered car pulled up to the emergency room sliding doors.

Bethany: [With angst in her eyes] Are you sure you don't need any   help? Do you want me to wait with you?

Me: [All aquiver but with a calm voice] Oh that's sweet of you, but no. My sister and husband are on their way to meet me here. She just sent me a text and she's on her way. Thanks again for the ride. You can go.

Bethany: [Waving a hand toward the passenger window] No problem at all. I hope everything turns out alright!

Before the sliding doors had a chance to close behind me, I glanced back and she had already begun to pull away from the curb. Had I the strength, I would have chuckled. I'll bet she was looking for permission to bust out of that parking lot like a bat out of hell. I would have wanted the same thing if it were me.

That was a chilly and arduous evening. Hours of sitting in an emergency room lobby so long that most of my symptoms subsided by the time I was checked in and put in a bed. Doctors chased diagnosis possibilities about my cardiovascular health. X-rayed my chest. Monitored my pulse to see if I'd had a heart attack. Of course, they found nothing. No one had any clue what had happened. Again.

After being discharged, Jordan's car trudged behind mine as he followed me back to the school building. The night air was cold as was the trail on which the doctors traveled to determine my medical issue. The dark suburban street was lit by tall, dim lampposts. My car was the only vehicle parked outside of the building. The scene looked as if it was staged right out of a horror movie. The only thing missing was a maniacal criminal jumping out of the high school bushes. Twisted.

The night had been weird, and dramatic and dark and twisted. I'm sure my talented new thespian friend would agree.

The next day, I returned to work exhausted. I stopped by to thank my work neighbor for her hospitality the day before, but I wasn't able to reach her. Again. My office stationary set came in handy, though, and I wrote her a note of thanks for helping me. I sat the red card and matching envelope on a shipment of equipment outside her door.

No response. Ever. She *never* returned my emails. She *never* stopped by to check and see if I was okay. She just never… Our relationship never grew. Like a diseased plant that you watch die with each leaf that falls off the stem. In spite of water. In spite of fertilizer. In spite of sunlight. Sometimes a plant just won't grow for you.

Chapter 11

The Siren Song

When I was a little girl, I looked forward to Friday night TV shows with my family. We popped popcorn in the hot air machine and bunched together in the living room to watch now classics like "The Muppet Show", the Canadian Nickelodeon show "You Can't Do That on Television" and one of my favorites, "The Dukes of Hazzard". I always pretended that Bo was my boyfriend. The show had a special connection to us and maybe that was because at the time, my mom drove a blue Chevy Comet. Minus the awesome features and paint job, we had a car that looked a lot like the hot wheels of Bo and Luke Duke. Just some good ol' boys. Maybe I could've been a good ol' boy, too. Except for the "brownness", the "womanness" and the "yankeeness".

Every week I looked forward to watching the "Dukes of Hazzard". Uncle Jesse was like the white grandfather I already had, but with a scruffier face and a warmer heart. My brother and I reenacted show scenes and impersonated the different characters. Considering the climate of brown folks and police in 2015, it now seems comical how much I loved the Dukes of Hazzard. In an era where "Smokey and the Bandit" was king, I hissed at the corrupt law enforcement characters and cheered each time the orange Dodge Charger adorned with "General Lee" (as in Robert E.) and a confederate flag rooftop escaped from the grasp of the law. Never meanin' no harm. Fightin' the system like a true modern day Robin Hood. Childhood ignorance truly is bliss.

Television gave me a tiny glimpse at how the rest of the world might have been living. How it felt when your neighbors weren't drug dealers and addicts. Since our brains are file cabinets, whatever I watched went into the files. Unfortunately, my first image, definition and story for "the law" was "The Dukes of Hazzard", with characters Boss Hog and Roscoe P. Coletrane as the bumbling sheriff. Because I was raised in one of the rougher neighborhoods with grittier and grimier stories after those initial childhood days, the new files for my law enforcement folder weren't much better.

Until I reached adulthood, every place I called home was in a neighborhood where folks felt uncomfortable leaving their cars unlocked. By the time I realized my dream of being a bona fide suburbanite, I was married and had children. Though my house was located in a predominantly white neighborhood, it wasn't until suburban communities became my livelihood that I truly understood their nuances.

Pleasantville was my "School-of-Hard-Knocks", but much prettier and much more covert. This kind of school was less about formal education and more about the wisdom and experience gained by learning the hard way. I learned something fairly quickly about suburban towns within the first few months of my job there. Suburbs can be just as dysfunctional as inner-city neighborhoods and I mean any suburb – not just Pleasantville. Their definition of dysfunction, however, is different.

Poor people have "barriers". Wealthier people have "challenges". Everyone has problems; but, suburban household income can *dramatically* change the intensity of problems and the ease of the solutions sought. The most important factor, nevertheless, is whether to "fix" the problem or its symptoms. In a town like Pleasantville, image is everything. Infatuation with image requires one to analyze the extent to which the challenge becomes public-knowledge. Many of the town's greatest images were all-powerful, manmade and highly fragile. What I unearthed was that all drama isn't bad; just the kind that smudges reputations and leaves dirt trails. I suppose, when you climb your way to the top, the thought of being yanked down into the barrel of mediocre mortal life is unacceptable.

I have come to believe that there is an invisible rampart that borders suburban communities. It seems that everyone inside the community – particularly when the community is small – knows all of its dirty little secrets. Those secrets seldom see the light of day. There's too much at risk. The schools, the housing values, the property taxes, everything prized about a suburb is tied to its ability to be better than where the poor, brown people live. If your zip code doesn't communicate your status, how will people know who the most important people are? That essentially means, the whole community must be in sync about concealing dysfunction. They rise, they fall, they bury the bodies and maintain the secrets together.

Early in my tenure on the job, I'd attracted many people who wanted to give me individualized input on my charge. There were lots of players in the game. Some had been championing the rationale for diversity work for decades. Others, such as school nurses in the district, were fighting for more targeted social-emotional and behavioral health support for students. A core group of parents, particularly those who supported district co-curricular and extracurricular activities, wanted all efforts directed toward drug and alcohol abuse prevention. Still, another group believed bullying intervention should be the top priority. Those early days were filled with so many lunch and coffee talks; I almost considered myself a regular in a few of the restaurants, shops and bistros.

I had thirty different stories about Pleasantville's dysfunction that were all told to me voluntarily by its community members. One per day for *six* weeks. Excessive drug and alcohol misuse. Suicide attempts. There were a couple discovered incidents of youth sexual activity during the sacred space of the open lunch. Domestic violence and sexual assault, in a handful of complex circumstances, that resulted in non-arrests, to no fault of the police department in most cases. Parents hosted drinking parties for youth. The stories went on and on and the more I was told, the greater my concern grew, not only for the students, but

62

also for the adults in the community. Moreover, I began thinking, "What have I gotten myself into? If the adults are still partying, how will I get the students to change?"

In order to put my new job into perspective as it related to behavioral health and substance abuse, I began writing down the stories. I wanted to be cognizant of what I was brought to Pleasantville to do. As an ideator, it's naturally easier for me to lose focus; and, this job – my charge – was way too important to consign to oblivion. The more I learned about the secrets of Pleasantville's families, the more dedicated I became to my mission. The stakes were even higher than I had anticipated. A harvest (word and image collage) of the stories was created so that I could call to mind why I showed up to work every day. The social-emotional wellness of students was my laser focus, my single objective for the job.

One of my tasks in this new position was to host a monthly community meeting. For a couple years, a committee of select district personnel and community members met to develop the official charge and suggested direction for the work ahead. They created my job description. These were the individuals with the greatest amount of buy-in for social-emotional wellness. Excited to meet them and get started, I sent a welcome letter to introduce myself and my initial plans. I also used my harvest of the stories shared with me as the meeting agenda. I had a plethora of ideas on what I wanted to do and I was ready to go.

September 11th happened to be the date of the meeting. My first meeting with returning social justice advocates from years past – the Pleasantville "choir" of social change – was on September 11th, a day we remember tragedy and loss in the country. On this day with some still hurting from the absence of family, I was meeting my Pleasantville advocacy family for the first time. One might have assumed that I'd be nervous; but, I was actually excited beyond measure. All summer long, I'd been cooped up in my home office thinking about first steps. Finally, the first step toward action had come; and, I could not wait to be unleashed.

Minutes before the start of the meeting, a heavily-badged man in uniform walked over to me. The gentleman's hands were on his hips, thumbs tucked into a utility belt. I surmised from his careful placement of steps that he was military or law enforcement. Perfectly pleated pants hung from his waist and his shirt tails were precisely tucked. He was the police chief of Pleasantville; and, I was thrilled he'd come to the meeting. I smiled a little brighter in hopes to make my presence softer and more "palatable". Before getting a chance to greet the approaching man, he walked up to me and out of his snarky grin, he almost accusatorily declared, "So *you're* Kimberly Brazwell,"

The chief mouthed my name as if he was eager to flick it off his tongue. He leered as he planted in front of me. By his side was the chair of the advisory board for the police department. In light of the backup that had accompanied the chief, I had a feeling that they hadn't shown up to my meeting because they were excited to dive into social-emotional conversation. I had aired Pleasantville's problems, but I'm not certain the meeting attendees were convinced I had any solutions.

The room was buzzing with excitement to get started on improving the wellness of Pleasantville students. I, however, was stung by the chief's tight-jawed presence at the table. He kept bobbing into my peripheral vision like an eye floater. He was at my meeting and somehow, I felt unwelcome. There were no apple pies or muffin baskets in their arms. His presence was about confrontation.

We began the meeting and minutes into the introduction, the police chief was in a debate with me about an illustration. I'd drawn my "harvest" to creatively document, remember and honor the dysfunctional stories of Pleasantville as they had been told to me. The chief, however, didn't like my "illustration" one bit.

Have you ever been blind-sided by a challenge for combat? It's not that I was afraid or needed to flee once the tension began to build. I did note, though, that Pleasantville was not yet my "soil". I was a *visitor* on my opponent's home turf. It was not yet safe for me to fight back. Sure, I could defend myself; but, I couldn't strike with the power of a battle that would end future wars. Chief took issue with illustrated references of stories told to me that the police force had not made formal arrests for some past "criminal activities". I was taken a bit off guard. I hadn't worn my armor that day and was not prepared for battle.

My poster papers were taped to the ends of bookshelves in Pleasantville High School's library. The tables were pushed together in a semblance of a circle so we could all see each other's faces. I'd stacked handouts and writing utensils on the ends of the tables in an attempt to be a perfect meeting host. Tapping into my higher education student affairs training, I had incorporated an ice breaker to relieve some of the tension that might be in the room. I was nervous but excited about what could be accomplished with a team who had already bought-in to my objectives. This was our time to come together and my opportunity to establish myself as the "fearless leader".

Everything in the room was planned and intentional, down to my outfit. I wore a jean dress and riding boots. My hair, long, brown and neat cords of thin dreadlocks, swished behind my back as I briskly walked around the room. Only a few of the faces around the table were familiar and I could immediately intuit my leadership style was foreign to them. Hopefully, I could pleasantly surprise them by demonstrating I didn't have to dominate to lead. My desired approach was benevolent leadership; yet, across the table, my warm smiles were met with two thick mustaches resting on tight lips. When I moved, he watched me. The chief's body never relaxed. He remained seated in the rich, brown wooden chair with his elbows rested on the table top and his fingers interwoven in front of his chest.

64

It was rare for me to not eventually "win" people over, but the chief did not come to play games with me. Each time I looked in his direction, his eyes were locked on me as if he was waiting for the cue to sink my battleship. I was a stranger who had crashed a Pleasantville family meeting. I prompted attendees with questions and each time it was the chief's turn to share feedback, his comments pointed back to the "fine police force serving and protecting the community in Pleasantville". I inquired about folks' thoughts of the stories I shared with them. The chief responded that he'd "never worked with as fine a group of officers as the department in Pleasantville". He didn't come to develop solutions with the team on how we could improve the engagement of all of Pleasantville's students. Chief came, it seemed, to explicitly communicate to me that I was wrong about my perception of the Pleasantville Police Department. Further, I received his intimidating message loud and clear that I should be careful about how I portray officers' oath to serve and protect.

All my life, libraries had been a refuge for me. I felt protected in nooks and crannies of old papers, books, rocking chairs, literacy posters, pencil stubs, scrap paper clips and hard wooden table sets. Today, though, the safety of the library had been compromised.

At precisely the end of the meeting, he left the premises without speaking another word to me. I can't recall if he spoke to anyone on his way out of the library, but perhaps casual conversation would have been considered superfluous dialogue he didn't need. The chief wouldn't be back; he'd done what he came to do. It was one hell of an introduction. I felt a lot of things that night; but, welcomed wasn't one of them. It seemed I'd stepped on the toes of some of the "Good Ol' Boys". I didn't mean any harm. …Fighting the system like a true modern day Robin Hood. I was just like Bo and Luke Duke, except not.

Chapter 12

Peek-a-Boo

By mid-fall in my first year on the new job, I was already growing weary from being "one of the only" and, many times, the "lone brown face" in the room. I was constantly teetering between being both "too brown" for meetings and "not brown enough" for student hallways. At the new teacher orientation session, I was the only brown face in the room. It was just me. At the meeting on curriculum and special academic programs, I was the lone brown one. At an introductory conversation with parent leaders about my position and our students' special social-emotional needs, I was still uniquely colored relative to the meeting attendees. Perhaps I should have felt more comfortable with white folks, seeing as I am half white. In spite of being biracial, I have always had a comfortable and clear understanding that society will treat me like a brown female. Societal systems will not distinguish that I am technically biracial, nor would the white folks in all of my meetings, I suspected. I was beginning to ache for some semblance of my brown "home" culture at work.

I may get in trouble for divulging this secret; but, here goes nothing. In many brown communities, we have an unspoken avowal. Whenever we are in a predominantly white (or not brown) environment, if we see another person of color, we acknowledge them by speaking, smiling or giving the traditional backward tossing head-nod.

Imagine you are brown (and if you are brown, skip that instruction). Picture yourself on a busy sidewalk in Portland, Oregon, statistically one of the whitest cities in the United States. As you walk down the sidewalk, you glance over your shoulder and catch a glimpse of your reflection in the glass paneling of the stores. You are able to be instantly spotted as you seemingly crowd surf the white mass of bodies that surround you. You feel the awareness grow in your body, rendering you more conscious of your surroundings and less comfortable with your hands untucked from your pockets. Just as you begin to conjure up race-based "worst case scenarios" for yourself, your subconscious detects a break in the pattern. You look up and see a brown face. You cannot readily identify the specificity of the brownness, but you recognize immediately that the individual is not white. In a split second, you and the other brown individual, traveling in opposite directions, make eye contact. Without uttering a word, he looks at you, you look at him and you both bobble your heads back and your chins up at each other. Then, as quickly as you spotted each other, you both disappear into the sidewalk waves of whiteness.

What happened in the blink of an eye was no coincidence or happenstance. Though not directly instructed to do so, many brown folks "just know" when they are required to speak to another brown person whom they have never met in their lives. Whether it's a spoken utterance or a mere glance, it is understood that we are to do something to let the other person know, "I see you." In the African Zulu tradition, this concept is known as umbuntu, meaning humanity to others. The word "Sawubona" means, "I see you." Its response is, "Ngikhona" which means, "I am here." The literal translation of this exchange means, "Until you see me, I do not exist."

There were days in Pleasantville when I felt my link to brown culture was imperceptible – and that made me feel hollow. Navigating Pleasantville without a brown reference community was like keeping a secret about who I really was. The reality was not lost on me that I might be one of the only people of color on Pleasantville's staff. However, I didn't realize just how seldom I'd see images of myself. There was a fellow administrator who was also biracial like me. Outside of a handful of teachers, none of whom taught at the building where my office was located; the remaining employees of color worked among the maintenance and custodial staff. Cliché, I know, but true.

In fact, one of the first evenings I was in the complex, I happened to run into my Latino childhood neighbor. What were the odds that two kids from a rundown project community would both end up working for the Pleasantville School District? Even then, I seldom saw him. I seldom saw anyone brown. Before long, I noticed that the brown people might have been working hard not to see me, either.

Imagine having grown up in predominantly brown neighborhoods since birth. Your life's soundtrack, though eclectic, is primarily brown. Your food is brown. Your cultural expression is, in many ways, brown. Imagine you are in love with your culture, your skin and your hair. You are dying to catch the eye of another brown person and communicate, "Sawubona". You turn the corner and enter the drag of the main hallway and to your pleasant surprise, you see a brown person! Fighting the urge to pounce on them like a dog excited that his human is home from work, you anxiously anticipate the coming three-second affirmation. You both walk down the hall in slow motion. And 3…2…1… They avert eye contact and walk right past you. Umbuntu fizzles into a cloud of dust. Then you and they go your separate ways, settling back into the "whiteness" of Pleasantville.

As the song by Soul II Soul goes, "Back to life; back to reality". I once stood in the middle of two flights of stairs and watched a brown boy look back at me three times without speaking once.

This deliberate avoidance, it turned out, was no fluke. It happened again and again and again. It happened with brown and white students. It happened with brown and white staff. Finally, I realized the fluke was me. I was breaking the norm in attempting to speak. I was bringing unwanted attention to brown folk who paid their dues to gain the acceptance of Pleasantville faculty, staff and fellow students. The last thing they wanted, it seemed, was to be a body among a small "gang" of brown people "gathering" – dare I say, organizing – in a public Pleasantville space. Apparently, some of us brown folks had come to Pleasantville, put heads down, went to work or class; and then went straight home. I could not unearth a brown community for me in Pleasantville; most of what I found was brown survival.

In predominantly white environments, brown people have the capacity to avoid fellowshipping together. **We protect white people from their fear of us.** We may cross paths in hallways and give the "black-man-head-nod". We may see each other at the staff meeting, and exchange full conversations in seconds-long eye glances. We may pass fellow brown folk in the concession line at the game; and, we hug like long lost family members. Older brown women's voices go an octave lower in conversation together. They playfully slap each other on the wrist or lock arms with an affirming chuckle and when the conversation settles in that good place, one of the women will look away and simply say, "Girrrrrrrrrrrrl...!" Young and old men heartily interlock thumbs with closed hands and pull into each other with one armed hugs we affectionately call "grip. They ball up fists and hit-the-rock, fist-bump or "give dap". Others may not know what we mean by these gestures, but we do.

Sure, brown folks argue, fight and yes, we even kill each other sometimes. The truth, though, is that we love us. Brown people love brown people. Unfortunately, many of us believe we're not allowed to love each other in public - at least, not in a way where the expression of love can be transparent and sustained. Many of us are convinced that solidarity between brown folks makes white people nervous. Coincidentally, nervous white people can make brown people nervous. Therefore, brown folks exchange just a touch of love with one another. We sneak in a peak, a pinch, a nudge or a scrap of love; then, it's gone. Right before we get comfortable not being "the only", we remember where we are and how brown our skin looks in these Pleasantville places. We come to our senses when we've loved on each other too long in plain sight. We think and half-jokingly say things like, "Let's split up before 'they' think we're plotting or forming a gang." Friends greet each other in white spaces and then split up, whispering, "Don't all sit together; spread out [among the white people]." Brown parents have been known to instruct their brown children when entering predominantly white spaces, "Don't bring attention to yourself" or "Don't cause trouble."

This phenomenon has happened for hundreds of years in brown communities all over the world and is arguably a learned behavior to ensure survival. During the slavery era in the United States, slaves were not permitted to congregate for fear they might organize and form a rebellion against the slave masters. Family members were separated and sent to separate plantations. Slaves were prohibited from reading and writing to prevent them from having the ability to communicate. Instructions for organization were disguised in old Negro spirituals. Runaway slaves used the glow of the North Star to travel out of slavery states to the north. To disguise plans, runaway slaves sang songs whose lyrics told them to "follow the drinking gourd". [In other countries, dippers are sometimes referred to as gourds. The North Star is a star located in the constellation referred to as The Big Dipper.] Communication between slaves could be punishable by whipping, beatings and in severe cases, death.

Coded language and behavior also manifested in the history of South American slavery. There is a Brazilian martial art called capoeira (pronounced cap-where'-uh). This unique form of martial arts emerged to disguise the practice of brown folks communicating with each other. Brazilian slaves were not allowed to practice ways to defend themselves. Creatively, they disguised their martial arts movements to resemble dance steps. Their fighting commands were sung in Portuguese. This Brazilian martial art is practiced to this day. Presently, an observer of capoeira might liken the fighting combinations and movements to that of break-dancing.

Brown folks have grown accustomed to hiding our relationships in predominantly white spaces and "mixed company". Meanwhile, we need each other. We need to see folks who look like us while we're here at school or work – especially here in the Pleasantville School District. We need reminders that we're not alone. We need each other so that we can exist. Instead, we come face to face with the culture of bad, unspoken diversity training. We have trained ourselves to be so appreciative to have just been let *in* to predominantly white institutions; we don't expect to be sustainably and authentically included or culturally affirmed. Have we trained ourselves to not make white people uncomfortable with our brownness? They pretend to not notice we're brown; and, we pretend not to be noticeable or brown. Everybody's happy, right?

Chapter 13

My Eyes Were on the Sparrows

My office was located off the beaten path of the high school hallways. Lunch was "open", meaning that students in the middle and high schools could leave the premises for the lunch hour. This time was either well spent or poorly spent, depending on the degree to which one "fit" in with the Pleasantville culture. As if it were a page out of the films *Grease* or *High School Musical*, Pleasantville Schools were incredibly segregated by clique during the lunch hour. I expected lunchtime to be Beverly Daniel Tatum's book, *Why Are All the Black Kids Sitting Together in the Cafeteria?* personified; however, I found it to be slightly more disturbing than that. At least per the generic stereotype of race and mealtime in public settings those of similar hues gravitate toward each other. Not so in Pleasantville Schools. Race was but the first sift for peer circles. Also, calculated into the equation of lunchtime turf was classism and hobbies. In fact, students who had more expendable income or lived in closer proximity to the school district complex didn't even stay on campus for lunch. They ate at home or at friends' houses or walked to local restaurants in clusters for a quick dine-in experience.

My curiosity was piqued one afternoon when I heard what sounded like familiar "brown girl chatter" outside my office in the hallway corridor. When I had a gander at the owners of the voices, I was pleasantly surprised to find four or five young brown girls sitting outside my door on the floor. Their eyes widened and bodies stiffened a bit when I interrupted their conversation. "Hey ladies. I don't mean to disturb you. I just wanted to say 'hi' and introduce myself." Polite but muted salutations were extended to me and I quickly tucked myself back in the office.

To be honest, I was a little afraid. I needed a reference community that looked and sounded like me as much as those girls did. They had each other and I had no one. To make matters worse, I'd already scared off pockets of brown students and found others in hallways that avoided me like the plague. It was as if I'd discovered the rarest of sparrows feeding on berries in my backyard. Twenty-first century instinct called for me to grab a smart phone and snap pictures, but I feared if I got too close, made too much noise or was too aggressive with my contact, I might scare them and they'd fly away for good.

It took weeks of patience for me to carefully tiptoe around the beautiful brown sparrows that ate outside my office. I frequently turned down my web-streamed music to listen to them talk. After a while, I walked out in the hallway just to make excuses to speak to them. Looking back, I can't explain what I was sensing or how I figured it out, but I knew I could win the sparrows over if they "picked me" first.

One day during the monotonous open lunch hour, something fortuitous happened. No one showed up for an open dialogue session I was hosting about girls, hair and self-esteem. Not a soul emailed me, called me, walked in the hallway or even pretended to find my office by accident. I wanted student feedback on the topic to gauge a grant I wanted to write. Without student voice, though, I didn't trust my instinct to move forward. But the sparrows... Perched perfectly in the hallway outside my office hallway was a flock of beautiful brown sparrows with extension braids, sew-in weaves, twists and relaxers. The hair stories I went searching for were already sitting in the nest by my office door.

Still fearing I might frighten them away, I carefully puffed out my chest and approached them. They were sitting on the gorgeous stone polished floor with French fries, fruit cups and mass-produced chicken nuggets. The hallway reeked of ketchup and cafeteria grease. The girls were sprawled out, as if comfortable in a dark, hallway while dust bunnies gravitated to the back pockets of their skinny jeans. As I approached them, the pace of their conversation slowed and quieted. They were not trusting of people and I understood. I was aware that I'd have to ingratiate myself to them swiftly and sincerely – and I only had one chance to do so.

Where I could imagine some Pleasantville faculty or staff members might see the approaching engagement opportunity as textbook example of when to code switch or change behavior according to the present audience, my intuition communicated an opposing message. Because of who I *really* was, I knew I had to approach the sparrows authentically. I assumed they already had a list full of amiable teachers who didn't understand them. My intention was for them to see the-girl-who-had-changed high-schools-six-times. In my mind, they needed to know I was a real person and I recognized that they were real people, too.

Me: Excuse me ladies. I have a project I'm working on and I could really use your opinions. Do you think you could help me?

Girls: [Apprehensive] Sure...

Me: I'm collecting stories ladies (and men) of all races have about their hair. Good stories, bad stories. Really, anything you want to share. Can you think of some bad hair stories?

The girls turned toward me but paused. Of the four, two were extroverted and comfortable enough to speak. Before opening their mouths, the girls all seemed to look at one student in particular. Her name was Satin and it appeared as though the other sparrows were deferring to her to "chirp" first on their behalf.

Girls: [Giggling and making inside joke eye contact] Yeah, we can think of all kinds of bad hair stories! We see them every day!

Me: I'll give you an example. I used to have a Jheri curl.

[Girls smile and chuckle a bit]

> One month, my Mom didn't have enough money to send me to the beauty salon. So, a lady in our project community named "Miss Jessie" was supposedly an amateur beautician. My mother had Miss Jessie put a Jheri curl in my hair at a reduced cost. Within a month, my hair started breaking off and I ended up having to have *all* my hair cut off. I had a baby 'fro. It was a hot mess!

The girls' body language loosened and they laughed while looking at each other, almost in approval that the space was safe. My mind was moving a little quicker than my mouth could, but somehow, I felt I had picked a story that showed the sparrows who I really was. Though older, wiser and a little taller, deep down inside, I was also a little brown sparrow.

Chyna: What about them little bitty ponytails girls be puttin' in they hair?

Satin: [Laughing] One time, I was fixin' my hair and one of my braids fell right out my head!

Chyna: [Shocked and focused solely on Satin] Oh my God! Whatchu do?!

Satin: [With nervy confidence] Girl, I kicked that braid right across the room!

Me: [Smiling and chuckling] That's pretty fantastic – and smart, too!

Chyna: You know what I can't stand? When girls' eyebrows be lookin' a mess. My mom been doin' my eyebrows since I was in middle school.

Satin: I cain't stand when girls come out the house and they kitchen be lookin' wrecked. ...That and edges. My edges got to look right.

"Kitchen" and "edges" are universal code words for brown women, particularly African American women. A kitchen is the area of hair at the nape of the neck. Edges refer to the hair along the front hairline of one's face. Brown women with coarse, tightly coiled hair who prefer to wear their hair straightened or "relaxed" often have a difficult time keeping the texture of hair straight at the nape of the neck and the front hairline. The desire is for the hair on the front hairline and above the nape of the neck to lie flat, straight, and preferably wispy and "under control".

73

Chyna: Yeah, I like when some of the boys with that "good", curly hair have the baby hair on the edges. I used to do that with gel.

We sat for the remainder of the lunch period that day and chatted about hair until the late bell rang for the next class period. By the end of the conversation, I understood why they were in my hallway instead of the Art Wing, Black Hallway or Starbucks around the corner. Similar to me, they, too, were finding it difficult to "fit in" the Pleasantville School District climate. The sparrows' appearances, attitudes, brownness, manner of speaking, and style of socializing were incompatible with most of the students at Pleasantville High School – both brown and white. I'm inclined to believe these beautiful sparrows grew up like me. I knew what it was like to be on-the-outs of both brown and white people. I recall so many times when it was easier to be alone than to go through the torture of "auditioning" for a clique of girls whose standards I could not meet. Like the sparrows, I had the aptitude to compete, but my income didn't give me access to the opportunities my peers had to widen my peripheral vision. Like the sparrows, when I was in high school, my eyes were wide, my ambition was high and my trust was low.

The sparrows were personable, polite and talented, but didn't have the monetary means to wear the Pleasantville "uniform", which consisted of North Face jackets, black leggings, expensive riding boots, high-priced hair weaves, professionally manicured nails and a designer scarf. They stuck out like sore thumbs and so, they stopped trying to fit in right away. Home may have been an apartment. Refrigerators may have lacked a plethora of fresh fruits and vegetables. Extracurricular activities may have been limited on account of "car trouble". The heart was likely soft, but the exteriors had been hardened.

Meanwhile, my heart warmed because in fellowshipping with the sparrows, I realized I wasn't alone. I saw beauty very similarly to the way the sparrows saw beauty. We spoke similarly. We thought the same kinds of things were funny. We disarmed each other. I spoke more plainly with them and they didn't code switch for me. I saw myself in them and silently committed to do whatever I could to take care of them.

Chapter 14

Head Negro in Charge Competitions

As a child, I recall hearing one of my elders use the term "crabs in a barrel". My mother and grandmother explained to me that sometimes when a crab scratches and crawls her way to the top – and nearly out – of the barrel, another crab will use its pinchers to grab hold of the ascending crab's leg and pull her back down to the floor of the barrel with the other crabs. I didn't quite understand the idiom when I was younger. Why would crabs be in the barrel? And, if so, why would they pull each other down? Clearly, I did not come from the New England seafood culture. And clearly, I was still a bit too young to be jaded. Unfortunately, the older I got, the clearer this idiom became. Sometimes clarity appears in the form of youth calling each other derogatory names, especially within the same cultural community. Girls referring to each other as "bitches". African Americans affectionately calling each other "nigga". Same gender loving folks jokingly calling each other "fag". All state that they've reclaimed the words, as if one can reclaim something she or he never owned in the first place. Better yet, why would they want to reclaim such hurtful words?

Other times, "crabs in a barrel" rears its ugly head inconspicuously. It might be in the form of a negative reference check for a job. Bad-mouthing a colleague who is not aware of her or his criticism. Even bullying bystanders who see someone victimized and say or do nothing to stop it.

Many of us have been guilty – in word or deed - of pulling a peer or colleague down, present company included. What I wonder, when I have distance from the occurrence, is why we do it? Why is it so easy to eclipse someone's ability to shine? Is it that the possession of power and control is so tempting or that not having power and control is so terrifying?

Nearing the midpoint of my first year in Pleasantville, February was fast-approaching. I'd had the opportunity to begin forming relationships with a small amount of African American students – mostly female. In the fall, several brown students shared some of the personal race-related stress-inducing incidents they'd experienced; and, attempted to manage in silence. In almost every instance, they struggled to cope with the pain while having no voice and no adult as an advocate. This was not because the adults weren't willing, but because the adults weren't aware or informed. The adults – teachers, administrators, parents - hadn't earned the trust of the brown students yet. Some of Pleasantville High School's brown students spoke with me about how they were given an opportunity every year to host a Black History Month program. A few students expressed, though, that in doing so, they often felt like "jokes" to their white peers. Instead of white students being curious about the lives and the legacies of their fellow brown students, I was told that white students often laughed at or simply ignored the presentation.

Through past advocacy work at Downtown Community College, I'd planned some rather large MLK celebration events with nationally known speakers, local community leaders and regional artists. Ideas rushed through my head concerning ways we could empower the brown students at Pleasantville to be heard and taken seriously, but, in a non-threatening way. I carefully crafted a plan and presented it to them for buy-in. Once the students were on board, the planning was underway.

A funny thing about working in a predominantly white environment as an administrator of color is that you crave the sight and presence of your cultural group as much as students do; but, you have *less* access. Due to the small population of employees of color in our school district, my best bet at seeing or interacting with someone who looked like me was by speaking with students. There's a line of appropriateness there that must be respected; cannot be crossed. Though our experiences might be mirrored by students, brown professionals are often groomed by our mentors and supervisors to believe we must keep our feelings to ourselves so as to not be perceived as emotional, defensive or reactive.

December turned into January. January turned into February and I heard much of nothing from the students with whom I was working to plan the Black History Month program. I feared we wouldn't be ready for our assembly and being unprepared was not an option. After all Pleasantville's brown high school students experienced on a regular basis, I was committed to ensuring this year's Black History Month program would result in them feeling respected, empowered and affirmed.

Then, one day while warming up my lunch in the break room, a teacher notified me that she had heard my name mentioned in the next room. I peaked in and the student planning team for the Black History Month program was meeting with a guest teacher about the event. It appeared as though they'd been meeting for a while; and, I hadn't been invited. They notified me that they would connect soon with an update – and that, they did.

Within 24 hours, a few students and the guest teacher came to my office and informed me that they wanted to make "a few" changes to the program I had designed. No problem; collaboration is always best, especially when one is new to an environment. As you know, I was well aware of the politics of being "the new kid". Over the next half hour, I learned that so many changes had been made to the program. It was virtually unrecognizable when compared to what I had crafted with the students. I was shocked. Stunned. I felt like a power move had been made on me by my own people – and students at that. To be honest, I was offended and hurt, but I remembered to keep my feelings to myself.

That year, the Black History Month program for the high school went just as it had been planned for the last few years, by one of the high school's beloved student leaders. My program was executed for the middle school. As far as I know, both were decently received by students. However, there was an unexpected occurrence after the high school assembly. A parent was offended at a comment made by a guest speaker at the assembly. The speaker was a brown man with dreadlocks and a warm but sarcastic sense of humor. He had been invited to share information on hip hop dance culture at the assembly and during the program, he made a joke remarking about the lack of knowledge the largely white audience possessed about hip hop. "Most of the audience chuckled," he reflected when we chatted weeks later. What he didn't know was that a parent who was offended by his joke called the high school the next day and complained to Luke, the high school principal. Because the guest speaker was one of my community contacts, I was asked to, "speak with him". I'm not sure what I was supposed to say.

Things went silent after the Black History Month program. The guest teacher didn't speak with me again. Most of the students who redesigned the program didn't speak to me again. The little communication and dialogue that had been established between the larger group of brown students at Pleasantville High School and I fell apart like a Jenga tower. Our conversation was over; and, the tension between handfuls of brown students and I had just begun. Maybe this occurrence wasn't about the success or failure of the Black History Month program. Maybe the tension was more about who, of the brown folks who weren't afraid to be brown in Pleasantville, was the brownest. Had I moved in to Pleasantville too hard and too fast? Had I presented myself to be too light in pigment to be this behaviorally brown? Had I been alienated by the folks who felt most like me on the inside but couldn't bring themselves to share a movement with me?

I own no kentae cloth or authentic African garbs. I do not speak Swahili. I am not Muslim. I do not strictly adhere to or annually celebrate the seven principles of Kwanzaa. No matter how I slice or dice it; and, no matter how passionately I live my life identifying as a brown woman, my father is still white. My blood is only half brown. For some, that means "the struggle" is only half mine. I have no proof that my fair skin played a role in the coolness of the air between brown students and me after the ordeal of the Black History Month program. I bore my heart early to the students. They did not accept my invitation for a relationship with them. I extended an open-door policy to the students. They did not come to me.

The thing about invitations is that they reserve the right to be declined. I asked to have a relationship with brown students at Pleasantville and in many cases, they replied with a resounding, "No." In psychotherapy, a great deal of work is invested to grasp the concept that "no" is an acceptable answer. It doesn't mean that accepting the rejection hurts any less, though. And so, the tone was set for the remainder of the academic year.

This unexpected turn of events made it obligatory for me to let go of some hopes and wishes I was still holding on to. I realized I may not be able to grow close to the brown families in the personal and familial way to which I had aspired. These students wouldn't get to know my daughters as had been the case in past higher education institutions where I'd worked. There would be no graduation invitations personally addressed to me or walked down to my office. No white - or brown – students would request me as their person to hug on a hot May afternoon, sweating under a graduation cap and gown. My daydreams of being a little piece of refuge for students of color were over.

Painstaking detail had been invested into the décor of my office. I'd brought in lamps for warm lighting. My office table was covered with crayons coloring books, Play Doh, cards and other knick-knacks. My eight-foot-long white board was decorated with doodles at the margins. Inspirational quotes were taped to my office door. Nearly all hours of the workday, cultural music could be heard streaming from my computer. I wanted to make my office feel like a home-away-from-home for "all of us". Instead, I'd built a perfect haven for me.

Visits to my office from the more powerful brown students ceased. Hellos in the hallway by brown students who so personally confided in me in the early fall quieted. My emails to check in and touch base with students were not responded to. The relationships I was so excited to foster with brown students ran dry. It seemed that I had been excommunicated. The hallways were a little icier. My existence got a little lonelier. In some strange way, I became a little browner. What I was learning is that in a predominantly white environment where the notion of cultural affirmation is newer, being browner is a very bad thing.

Chapter 15

The "How Are You?" Test

I'd survived the first year at Pleasantville and had already told myself I would not complain. My salary was higher than it had ever been. My office was Zen-like. On paper, I held the perfect job in a "destination school district" where many educators desired to work and I was, according to many outsiders, "living the dream". Colleagues and community members had attempted to show me what I preached to be the foundation of my job – to create a safe, welcoming and sustainably inclusive environment. All of the attempts were not successful, but we all seemed to be trying to "play well" with each other.

If my purpose in Pleasantville was to diagnose and treat the school climate challenges, I felt like the first year of work adequately prepared me for the next leg of the journey. Year one was all about conversations. Between one-to-one meetings, community dialogues, staff and community conversations, I literally had a shelf of qualitative data. After a year of studying multiple sources of pre-existing quantitative data as well as my new qualitative data, I knew what my focus would be.

Going into year two, my driving mission was to address all non-academic barriers to learning and achievement. Written into my position description was my duty to accomplish, "home, school, community assimilation; diversity and cultural competence; dropout prevention; health/wellness; drug and alcohol prevention; graduation awareness; and adherence to federal and state statutes, professional development and practices." It was an impossible task to complete in a two-year contract, but I had always loved a challenge. I was positioned by Dr. Springsteen to serve as the district's catalyst in the development of a safe, welcoming and sustainably inclusive learning environment for Pleasantville students and somehow, I had to figure out how to get the faculty and staff on board – and quickly.

I'd only had a chance to meet colleagues in large groups during the first year with the exception of a handful who made it a point to introduce themselves to me early on. The structure of my appointment with the school district made it incredibly difficult for the collective staff to learn about me, my job and my approach to attain social-emotional wellness for Pleasantville's students. Thanks to the leadership of Dr. Springsteen, my supervisor and number one supporter, though, I would soon have a moment to share my vision with colleagues at an all-staff convocation. Here was my plan for the coming academic year:

1. Develop an internal system of care including school-based behavioral health services

2. Create non-traditional advocacy and engagement opportunities for students and families, especially students of color
3. Provide personal and professional development opportunities for faculty and staff

Professional development in education can be very mechanical. There are so many legislations, assessments and legal parameters that guide the work. Though it is absolutely a relationship-heavy career, educators don't always get the opportunity to professionally develop those relationship muscles. Not the case this year. I was the proud new owner of an entire day of professional development (also known as in-service day) for the entire district staff and the focus would be social-emotional topics and soft skills.

This year's in-service day would be about getting healthier as a staff to reduce non-academic barriers from turning into adverse conditions for our students' success. We needed to teach our system how to fight our non-academic barriers, which were showing up in the forms of mental illness, substance abuse and "isms" such as racism, classism, and sexism regarding different diversity lenses. Our tools and truth would be empathy and compassion, implicit bias awareness and behavioral health. We were going to take a deep dive into the *messy* waters of social-emotional issues and explore wading in the water without drowning in the heaviness of the task at hand. Believe it or not, the entire body of work would be based on two simple questions we hear every single day: "How are you" and "Are you okay?"

Let's see if this scenario resonates with you.

You are in the grocery store and you see someone you know. He isn't a close friend; just an acquaintance. As you two cross each other's paths, he smiles and asks, "How are you?" and I'll bet five dollars you say, "Fine" or "Great" or at least, "Pretty good".

Now, my truth is that I am often not "Fine" or "Great" or even "Pretty good". Maybe this is true for you as well. Sometimes we're angry or aching or depressed or grouchy or fatigued. There is the general polite assumption that it would be rude to express our true sentiments. I once wrote a poem joking about this phenomenon. Can you imagine asking a colleague how she is and her responding to your inquiry with details about marital challenges or struggles to pay the bills? A portion of us will wait until the honor of old age settles in our brains almost to the point of dementia before we feel we have earned the right to speak freely.

Where's the opportunity to practice empathy and compassion in that, though? What if someone's health – or life – depended on an accurate and honest response to "How are you" or "Are you okay?" In my role as a Director of Student Services, my general assumption was that students were *not* okay. Chances are that if we knew of a student who was abusing alcohol, cutting or was a survivor of sexual assault and we asked that student, "How are you?" the student would respond, "Fine". The truth is, that might be the most dangerous "fine" we'd ever hear.

I culminated a full day of social-emotional professional development staff training with an open question and answer session. There were few questions; and, of those asked, there were expressed concerns and doubts about a teacher's right to nose around in students' personal business by asking questions like, "Are you okay?" I feared that we were either in the habit of not asking the tough questions or worse, not wanting to know the answers to those questions.

Let's unpack questions like "How are you?" or "Are you okay?" for a minute. Is it too presumptive to admit that some of us hope and pray the folks to whom we direct those questions will give us generic, affirmative answers? When we inquire about a person's well-being whom we do not know very well, we hope they're "Fine" or "Great" or "Okay". From time to time, the truth may be that if she or he is okay, we are absolved of responsibility to have to do anything.

Responsibility and accountability can feel burdensome. So many of us already feel overwhelmed with home and work life. At times, it may feel like we can barely manage our *own* lives, let alone the fragile life of a child who does not belong to us. I believe it is a fair statement to say we all want children to be socially-emotionally well. Not only that, but hopefully, we want adults to be socially-emotionally well, too. I often wonder if part of the reason why we want folks to be well is because there are those who cringe at the idea of having to "fix" folks who are in need of repair. That said, is it our responsibility to "fix" each other or is one responsible for the health and well-being of oneself?

When I gave this charge to teachers, I was later told that some privately complained, "I didn't go to school to be a counselor." I, too, heard exhausted educators complain that students need to be more self-sufficient. Hand-holding takes too long. There's too much to do in the long list of endless, mounting demands on educators. The pervasive theme I heard, second only to a fear of liability, was a concern about lost time. If teachers are asked to provide students with social-emotional support in addition to instruction, teachers lose time to teach. They lose time to prep for assessments and grade papers. They lose time to complete paperwork.

I knew my personal perspective on human suffering heavily influenced my charge to the teachers. I believed it was a reasonable request to ask teachers to form more personal relationships with their students. The fact of the matter is that my position did not require me to be in a classroom. Maybe it's true that I didn't fully understand what I was asking of them. Still, student holistic wellness was paramount based on my objectives in the Pleasantville School District. The challenge was extended to teachers to educate and nurture Pleasantville students. By that, I meant I wanted teachers to stop, think, feel; and, be mindful by being "in the moment" with students in crisis. There's no supplemental contract for that. I wondered if resistant teachers were uncomfortable with feeling students' pain because it might require them to be vulnerable, too. There are some who come from the school of thought that power and vulnerability cannot exist in the same space at the same time. The only way the student-teacher relationship works, in the opinions of some, is if the teacher possesses the power. Generally speaking, whoever has the most power feels safest; and, whoever has the least power feels threatened. Was I wrong to advocate for students to feel safer and be given more power? For some, the answer to that question was, "Yes."

Chapter 16

That Black Girl

In year two of my two-year contract at Pleasantville, I was still "one of the only" brown administrative leaders. I had begrudgingly accepted that brown faces would likely not stop to say hello to me in the halls. Pleasantville's brown folks had grown to understand that we defined survival and self-preservation differently. Apparently, there was more than one way to make Pleasantville's brown folks feel safe, welcomed and sustainably inclusive. We brown folks were having entirely different Pleasantville experiences and our inclusion needs varied considerably.

For some brown folks, survival and self-preservation in Pleasantville is accomplished by suppressing cultural behaviors as much as possible to mimic white culture, white preferences and "white behavior". Some refer to this as "acting white". Keep in mind that this behavior, for certain folks, is not indicative of an authentic desire to be white, but is a legitimate survival tactic. "Behaving white" minimizes the experiences of some people of color from having unconscious biases directed toward them.

Another approach to brown survival and self-preservation in predominantly white environments is achieved by fully embracing and personifying everything about brown culture, preferences and behavior. Inside of the community, this is sometimes referred to as "keeping it real" or remaining loyal to the brown community.

Imagine, then, that "walking out" brownness is more of a continuum than a binary concept. There is also a middle path to survival and self-preservation, which involved being brown but not "too brown". There were Pleasantville students and parents who identified with brown culture; however, these brown folks did not include me as one of their affiliates. I assume in these instances, being marginalized by white folks was less painful than accepting me as "one of them". Maybe I was too brown. Maybe I wasn't brown enough. Either way, the only way I knew to survive and attain preservation of self in Pleasantville was to be the most authentic version of myself possible at work and at home. I decided to be and stay unequivocally brown and that was a tougher trail to blaze in Pleasantville.

Being authentically brown at work meant accepting all parts of my identity. I gave myself permission to be brown in white spaces without excessively culturally code-switching. While a certain degree of behavior modification is necessary in order to be perceived as "professional", I postulated a reality that existed where I could be both brown and professional. The two terms weren't mutually exclusive. I made a choice to stay as true as possible to what I believed was my authentic way of speaking, dressing, behaving and feeling. Brownness made me feel safe and I desperately needed to remember who I was when I was at work. Colorblindness – often expressed in statements like "I don't see color" or "I don't care about what race you are" – sounded threatening to me. I *wanted* people to see that I was brown; I just didn't want the honesty of my brownness to be devalued by others. I sought ways to live and work truthfully while telling the truth. My Pleasantville survival and self-preservation required me to be honest even when my honest choices painted me to be incompatible with Pleasantville's historically white culture.

My style of dress had a surprising impact on my Pleasantville experience by year two. My clothing was an honest expression of my youthful personality. Like some of Pleasantville's favorite teachers, I was casual in attire. I was regularly adorned with low-top converse sneakers, skinny jeans, printed button-up tops and a long, dreadlocked pony tail that swished west and east behind my back when I walked briskly down the hallway. I rejected "suits" and "click-clack" high heel shoes. Wearing pantyhose was out of the question. I interpreted the suit and blouse "uniform" as a type of culture that made me feel inauthentic. Nonetheless, the consolation prize for my jaunty attire was looking like and being mistaken for a student. Everyone wants to look younger until seniority matters.

There are only a few stereotypes that position brown folks over white folks. Dancing is a stereotype that works to the advantage of brown people – black people in particular. All of us can't dance, but there is a disproportionately large amount of brown people with rhythm. We don't just win in dance, though. Brown folks are also particularly proud of being brown when classrooms have lice infestations. Fun fact: we can't get 'em. The coarse, tightly coiled hair of folks with African American heritage is so dense; lice typically can't survive in it. When lice letters go home during school outbreaks, we flippantly throw them away. Conceivably, the favorite stereotype of brown folks is age ambiguity. Brown folks' skin typically ages like Dorian Gray. We wrinkle in slow motion, if at all. Genetics with regard to melanin and photoaging has been scientifically proven to benefit brown skin; and, the healthier we are, the younger we look as we age. As an older brown female mentor of mine once told me, "Baby, black don't crack".

Another way I maintained some authenticity was building and maintaining networks outside of my administrative leadership peers. Many know that the lifelines of organizations - the eyes and ears – are the administrative assistants and support staff. They see everything and they know everything. Support staff members, from receptionists to custodians, see an institution for what it *really* is. In a school district, particularly one within a small community, administrative assistants experience an institution through the lenses of its community members. Their friendships and perspectives are invaluable.

One of the women who worked on a main desk in the district was always kind enough to ask, "How are you?" but in a way that communicated to me she was looking for my real answer. I appreciated Candy. I was affirmed in knowing that Candy saw me; she noticed me. There are few sensations as cold and isolating as feeling invisible. Since the opportunity for me to find a "family" within the larger brown Pleasantville community dissipated, I accepted friendliness wherever I could find it. This kind, older white woman couldn't quite give me the cultural endearment I so longed to have at work, but I felt cared for by her, so I was receptive to her good will. Decades ago, I found only partial acceptance of my biracial identity within certain brown and white peer circles. Now, a similar sentiment had re-emerged. I did not have full acceptance in Pleasantville from the brown community or the white community. Yet, Candy extended an offer of friendship, albeit on a basic level; and, I needed a friend, so I accepted.

On my way entering the building one morning, Candy waved me over to chat. She was always a source of fun gossip and neighborhood rumors. It seemed there was recent chatter that involved yours truly. She stalled and we fumbled upon entering into conversation. Candy seemed troubled and vacillated before sharing. Her eyes looked away as she began.

Recently, she had been socializing with a circle of women in the higher income bracket of the school district. In between cocktails and small talk, someone shared thoughts on the new diversity and inclusion efforts that were emerging in Pleasantville. "Why was the district talking about diversity?" they pondered. There were, after all, no diversity issues, from the public's vantage point. "Well, they hired that black girl..." another responded. The words hung in the stale air of Candy's tiny office like a frumpy sweater. Her cheeks blushed as she conveyed the ignorant conversation to me. She looked appalled, as if those three words were regurgitated bile in her mouth. "That. Black. Girl...," she repeated. "I couldn't believe it. If you were white, they would have never referred to you as *girl*", she fussed. "They would have called you a young woman."

Maybe I should have been shocked; but, I wasn't. Candy looked more uncomfortable than me and apologized for repeating the bias-laden conversation to me. Well, at least they didn't call me "colored", right? So, the myth had been busted; white people do see color. I laughed it off, as brown people tend to do when we are overwhelmed and outnumbered. Unfortunately, some of us have grown accustomed to microaggressions – dismissive or insulting treatment – by white people in predominantly white environments.

Though I thought I was unscathed during my conversation with Candy, for the rest of the day, her words echoed in my head. "If you were white, they would have never referred to you as girl." Perhaps she was right. Who knows if my race factored into the equation? Maybe all women are "girls" in their lexicon. Maybe my youthful appearance influenced their word choice. "Maybe", in this moment, was one of my survival words. It is a word I use to buffer the discomfort when I've been offended. Maybe makes microaggressions hurt less in the moment. "Maybe they didn't mean it the way it sounded." "Maybe they don't realize how old I am." I had too much time left on my contract to think, "Maybe they don't respect me or my professional expertise in this field." Self-preservation would not allow me to contemplate, "Maybe I'm not as welcomed as I thought."

Chapter 17

Looking the Part

When I first joined the Pleasantville School District, one of my social justice mentors who was born and raised in Pleasantville gave me a metaphor to better understand its foundation. "Imagine," she suggested, "that Pleasantville's cultural history is a huge tree with a broad base and deep roots. The work you're preparing to do is going to shake that tree. You may not be able to move it. Things might fall out of the tree that you don't expect. Just be careful of what happens when you shake that tree."

I had reached the second September in the district and learned that I was working in a "cocktail community". Swanky parties were a dime a dozen. Entertaining guests was a regular occurrence and drinking was just part of the experience. Eat dinner with a glass of wine. Cookout while sipping on imported beers. Host an upscale event and sip a flute of champagne. The drinking didn't stop there. I heard stories of high school students drinking in the basement. An alumnus told me tales of vodka hidden in plain sight in water bottles in study hall. There was so much alcohol in the community; we needed to redefine what constituted a "drinking problem". Pleasantville was suffering from convenient "blindness". Just as it didn't see color, it couldn't see addiction, either.

Furthermore, where there is alcohol, there are drugs. Where there is money, there are better quality drugs and more access points. Where there are absentee parents with financial means, there are more opportunities for youth to use. Again, this scenario was not unique to Pleasantville. Around the larger metropolitan area, other suburbs just like Pleasantville faced the same severity in substance abuse issues.

We were facing community sickness and I believed Pleasantville would benefit from measures to ensure the entire community pursued holistic wellness. The Substance Abuse and Behavioral Health Services Administration (SAMHSA), an agency within the U.S. Department of Health and Human Services, approaches its work with an eight-dimension of wellness model. This wellness model includes social, emotional, physical, spiritual, environmental, occupational, intellectual and financial wellness. I wanted to test this model in Pleasantville.

The legendary tales of drinking, drugs, and partying hard were inherited and kept alive from one generation to the next, per the stories repeatedly told to me. As an outsider, it seemed that folks placed a higher priority on pretending they weren't sick and hiding dysfunction instead of pursuing authentic wellness. It was going to take a series of bold moves to interrupt the party culture of Pleasantville and get the attention of the community members. I felt it was time to shake the tree and I was willing to do it alone if I was the only one who could see what was happening. How would my wellness work be perceived by Pleasantvillians? I was an ambiguously young brown, female outsider; and, I was preparing to boldly tell a historic wealthy, upper-class white town that it had some behavioral health issues and needed to seek rehabilitation and recovery. I wasn't just planning on shaking the tree; this news flash would essentially cut the tree down like a chainsaw-toting arborist.

The time had arrived. Pleasantville needed to come face to face with its wellness truths for the sake of the students' social-emotional wellness. Around this time, I learned that a neighboring city was home to a sports hero whose abuse-influenced fall from grace happened in front of the camera just ten or more years ago. Thanks to incarceration, diagnosis, medication and a wellness program, the star athlete was now on a road to recovery. I thought, "This is a story Pleasantville needs to hear." Among some of my committee members and administrative colleagues, it had been mentioned that one of Pleasantville's biggest liabilities was its dependency on having a "perfect" image. **Looking well was more important than being well.** It was implied by Pleasantville residents themselves that the biggest hurdle to wellness might be the perception of a fall from grace. I wanted the community to know that, like the star athlete, owning a recovery story could be just as honorable as wealth and upper class status.

Collaborative decision making is essential in a school district. After getting funding partners, I took my proposal for the sports hero and recovery speaker to the school board to seek approval. The speaking engagement was set and ready to be advertised to the community. I was proud of my preparation on the initiative, not only because of the wellness and recovery message, but also because the speaker was a person of color.

I expected questions about logistical things like cost, partners, time and day of event, etc. I was *not* prepared for the questions I received when I stepped up to the podium to field inquiries from the school board. Inquiries about my proposed speaker were veiled in implicit bias and microaggressions. A board member asked, "Don't we know of anyone else who could speak on this topic?" She went on to add, "I don't want *him* representing us. He doesn't *look* like Pleasantville." Maybe the fact that the speaker was a big, brown man was inconsequential. I did wonder, though, what exactly does someone from Pleasantville "look" like? I feared I already knew what the board member was implying. She did not speak the words, but what I heard was that Pleasantville doesn't look **brown**. However, I was brown; therefore, if the proposed speaker didn't properly represent Pleasantville, neither did I. Moreover, the brown students who attended the Pleasantville School District didn't "look like Pleasantville"; nor did the five percent population of brown folks employed by the district.

Since when does wellness belong to a certain cultural community? Whose wellness and recovery story is more acceptable and accessible than another's?

Again, the question of "fit" had entered the conversation. If it is assumed that there is a "right" way to look in the Pleasantville zip code, then one must assume that all else is wrong.

The votes passed – with one "nay" vote - to bring my brown speaker to share his recovery story and the event was an overwhelming success. There were folks of all colors, religions, ages and classes who were wowed by his transparency. I was well aware that some came, hoping to witness a possible debacle. What they found, however, was absolute inspiration. In his story, the Pleasantville community could see and hear both their own addiction and mental illness stories as well as a different cultural perspective on the journey of addiction, intervention and recovery. Every heart was touched that night. After the speaking engagement, tons of white folks stood in line to purchase the speaker's book, get his autograph and take pictures with him. Despite some growing prickles, even Luke congratulated me on a job well done and took a "selfie" with our star athlete speaker in the high school hallway. After the conclusion of the event, all I could think about was how invisible the speaker's brownness was once he became a three-dimensional person.

If my star athlete was eventually accepted by Pleasantville, could acceptance ultimately be possible for me and Pleasantville's brown folks, for that matter? If I kept plugging away at the social-emotional initiatives, maybe both brown folks and white folks could be accurate visible representations when considering the "look" of Pleasantville. Maybe there existed a future where we could all – together – not only "look" well, but we could *be* well.

Chapter 18

Too Black, Too Strong

Labor Day had come and gone. The albatross of advocating for students who didn't even speak to me in the halls was growing to be cumbersome. I fretted over how to communicate – and make real – stories of pain and discrimination to predominantly white leaders and educators while protecting the identity of people who had confided in me. I grappled with new ways to tell the truth about the ongoing community dysfunction I had discovered without polarizing myself from those who I needed as allies.

Over the past school year, I gained *one* brown parent colleague who was quickly becoming a friend. With four (soon to be five) children in the district, this mother had her finger on the pulse of student conversation. I was appreciative of her for sharing with me a conversation she had with her very wise high school son.

"What's the deal with the brown students and Mrs. Brazwell?" she inquired. As one of only two employees of color accessible to high school students, the young man's mother was curious as to why brown students seemed to avoid a brown adult role model in the building. "They think she spies on us. She just came on too strong, Mom." Students were suspicious of my salutations. The familiarity in my tone was off-putting to them, as a deeper relationship had not been established. They didn't know me and their willingness to let me get to know them had not increased after a year of my employment in the district. The bottom line was they didn't trust me and they didn't see me as part of their community.

This might be a good time to mention that I am an extreme extrovert. I have never met a stranger, as the saying goes. I am instantly friendly and familiar with people and this trait does *not* always work in my favor. In fact, I received professional constructive criticism on this trait in the early days of my very first job in education. I was told that I needed to be "more reserved"; "more formal". Add a little more polish to my demeanor. In my world, that translated to overcasting my sunshiny personality with a little partly cloudy so my light would be less offensive. Since when did enthusiasm become a bad thing? What I was learning from my Pleasantville experience is that there was no frame of reference for understanding the "motives" behind a spritely professional brown woman. They didn't know what to make of me. At the same time, there was little benefit, if any, in being perceived as the "angry black woman" or the stoic brown woman with an attitude. It wasn't who I was.

So, what are the benefits to being a professional brown woman?

One of my worst attributes may be my poker face or lack thereof. Often, I display strong emotional reactions on my face clearly and vividly like colors on a mood ring. It's part of the extroversion package deal. When the mother shared brown students' perceptions of me, I prayed my voice didn't give away the plunge of my heart into my small intestines. Perhaps she knew how disturbed I felt. She quickly responded by affirming me and explaining that the kids were still young in their cultural identity development. True; but, psychological theory didn't make me feel any better. I was a new girl in school all over again and I was struggling to make friends. By being unapologetically comfortable in my own skin, I had essentially repelled brown students. How was that so? My coping mechanism had somehow alienated me from a reference group. I felt as if my cultural pride had impeded my ability to be a role model.

It's true that I am fair-skinned and have freckles. Maybe it's true that light-skinned brown folks sometimes have a propensity for being extraordinarily passionate about their brown heritage. Had I entered the district with a dashiki and a "black power fist" hair pick climbing through my afro, I would have better understood being perceived as coming on too strong. Had I greeted the brown students with "all power to the people" salutations, I could see being perceived as coming on too strong. Had I solicited anyone brown and walking in my direction with as-salaam alaikums and warnings of the evils of pork when they fed their bellies in the lunch line, yes, that would have been too strong.

I contemplated over being too brown and too proud – even though I am half white. I often joked that sometimes I wanted to pull brown students aside in the hallways and remind them that the Civil War was over and brown people were free. In my opinion, Pleasantville High School's brown students bit their tongues when treated poorly. It pained me to watch what I labeled, perhaps harshly, as modern-day indentured servitude. Brown students had a right to the same learning environment and experiences as white students at Pleasantville, but in many ways, I imagined it didn't feel much different in these hallways than it felt when school segregation was overturned in the landmark Brown v. Board of Education case in 1954. I wanted brown students to believe they could listen to their music proudly instead of shying away from hip-hop inspired school programs. I silently willed the beautiful brown sparrows in the "Black Hallway" to embrace the spread of their noses, the fullness of their lips and the roundness of their bottoms with near smugness. I prayed the brown folks in the Pleasantville School District would see that they were beautiful and brilliant, not despite our brown skin but **because** of our brown skin. Taking nothing away from white identity, I just wanted us to believe and internalize that there was nothing wrong with owning the identity of brownness …or so I thought.

I wanted to say all of these things on loud speakers in the school buildings, but I didn't. I thought I'd done a good job of approaching culture softly. Somewhere between George Washington Carver and W.E.B. Dubois. I just wanted to show them their worth. I invited them to experience cultural affirmation, but I am not confident they knew what I was doing. On many occasions, I asked both brown students and brown employees, "How would you like to tell your story?" "How would you like to do a Black History Month program?" "What do your white peers need to understand about you?" "Have you ever retraced the steps of the civil rights movement?" "Would you like to join me for a conversation on race and class?" Perhaps in opening my mouth, I had already said too much.

As mentioned before, the thing about invitations is that they operate on the framework of free will. Invitations are subject to receive one of two acceptable responses – yes or no. The answer to my invitation to fellowship in brownness felt like a resounding, "No."

Chapter 19

My Life on the Agenda

As a social justice advocate, I am a walking agenda item. When I sit in a room full of my white peers and I am the only person whose ancestors were owned by my colleagues' ancestors, it changes how I sit in the meeting, especially if the "d" word comes up. Diversity. Educated adults are smart enough to look forward and make no sudden movements when diversity as a topic "rears its ugly head" into previously pleasant conversations. Less polished folks fight themselves to not dart eyes at me when diversity and inclusion is on the agenda menu and I'm the only one in the room who looks like a menu item.

Leaves were falling as was my emotional energy to fight bias and privilege. I had put so much of myself into my work, assuming working harder would reap improved progress. In my opinion, it was disingenuous to ask colleagues, parents and students to display behavior that I myself didn't model. The community needed to see that I was willing to invest my own blood, sweat and tears to get the work done, too. I wanted to be vulnerable with them so we could go through the experience of getting well *together*.

Four years prior to arriving at Pleasantville, I created a diversity learning community. Based on the original design, I adapted a similar program which I facilitated for a cohort in several monthly sessions. My supervisor at Pleasantville graciously sacrificed half of his leadership meetings to create an opportunity for the district's administrative team to have tough conversations about diversity as well. Since the structure of the learning community focused more on "implicit bias" than outward talking points, the growth opportunity was tremendous. The leadership meetings and diversity conversations were my first efforts at browning the thinking for our top level of leadership.

Session one was on race and ethnicity. What better way was there to start an inclusive academic year with colleagues than to learn each other's race and ethnicity identity stories? No doubt, it was acknowledging the elephant in the room but I planned carefully and worked to ensure that we would feel safe enough have an honest dialogue. I knew what initiatives I had planned for the coming academic year and the conversations I'd facilitate fell right in line with the plans. Homework leading up to our first meeting was for all participants to make a life timeline through the lens of race. Their prompt was: "How do you know you are the race that you are and what clues made you aware of your identity?"

The thing about educational leadership is that once educators transition into to administrative roles, they frequently hide more of their personal side. They can be moved to emotion, but not in front of others. They should be passionate, but not biased. They must be human, but not at work. Administrators in education have a uniform that transcends blazers and loafers. There is a "professional" way to dress. There is also a "professional" way to look, act, speak and behave. I suppose this is a good thing (for others), but in the space of diversity and inclusion work, political correctness and professional politeness can regress meaningful dialogue. People can become so concerned about saying the "wrong" thing that they don't say anything at all. For those brave enough to speak, they often censor themselves so intensely; the honesty of their statement is tempered by a fear of saying something offensive.

As my colleagues, Dr. Springsteen and I began our conversation on race and ethnicity, I could already sense reservation in the room. No one appeared to want authentic dialogue. Often, in conversations where folks aren't ready to share but the conversation is intended to be inclusive, people have "go-to" answers. If a professional has been well mentored or well groomed, she or he has "canned" responses that are honest enough to fulfill the requirement of a dialogue prompt but not authentic enough to push the conversation into a learning space. Honest responses are true but not deep. Authentic responses are both true and reveal a deeper level of vulnerability.

Here's an example. I will often start diversity dialogues in my learning community by asking participants to do "Honest Introductions". By this, I mean that one should use multiple identity lenses and a personality descriptor to (re)introduce themselves as who she or he *is* as opposed to what she or he *does* occupationally. [In the United States, we often define who we are by what we do. I always push back on this in conversation by challenging participants to describe who they are while omitting their job titles.]

> Typical introduction: My name is Kim and I'm a diversity practitioner.
>
> Automated response: My name is Kim. I'm biracial, a middle child and a mother of two daughters. I'm an extrovert and I'm interested in Buddhism.
>
> Authentic response: My name is Kim and I'm a creative with attention deficit disorder. I am biracial but understand the world as an African American woman and my curious personality shows up by way of chattiness.

Which introduction version helps you to best understand me?

My leadership colleagues entered the race and ethnicity conversation and it was quickly understood that we brought the safest versions of ourselves into the room. We were "holding our cards close to our chest". We knew what our authentic responses were, but I assume the room and the "company" didn't feel safe enough to be more vulnerable. That meant the learning and growing would be minimal if it happened at all. We weren't seeking a transformative experience. We were checking the box which confirmed we had a diversity conversation. Checked boxes mean status quo. I'm a trained facilitator, so I knew I needed to push the group a bit; but, they weren't budging. We couldn't talk effectively and that was a bad sign. There was no evidence that we trusted each other as leadership colleagues. So, how could teachers and students embody a culture of trust and dialogue engagement that we as leaders can model?

I pushed. I pulled teeth. I bled my story. I affirmed other nibbles of stories that were shared. As a team, we had clearly not hit a groove of trust and we needed to – fast. The entire room was mastering the practice of cultural code switching and likely had no clue what was happening. I gave them an example of the threat of code switching.

I posited the leadership team to consider the African American church community for an example I was trying to make. There is a phenomenon in the black church affectionately known as "call and response". The preacher or pastor says something that touches you and you respond to him out loud to let him know you affirm his statement. An appropriate response could be anything ranging from a moan to an "Amen" to a "Yes, Lord" or even clapping.

Now take the brown child who faithfully attends church every Sunday and place him in a fourth-grade class in a predominantly white environment. The teacher plays a video clip for the class to differentiate instruction of a language arts lesson and poses a question to the class. The young brown boy who frequents a church with traditional "call and response" might blurt out the answer. He may repeatedly do this by force of habit. Subsequently, he may be perceived as a "disrupter" or a "troublemaker" in class by his teacher. The truth is that he's not a bad kid; on the contrary. He's likely a great kid. He's just not yet mastered his cultural code switching. Church set a culture that welcomed talking. School set a culture of being silent.

The example drove the message home for some and left others foggy. Regardless of the results, the session was over and based on Dr. Springsteen's praise following the session, I naively felt good about it. The depth of participation was not ideal, but it was a start. We did it; we held a conversation about race and no one died. There would be more diversity conversations to follow. Every journey begins with one step.

Later that evening, I received an email from a colleague who was present for the morning session on race and ethnicity. He informed me that he was disappointed with our leadership team's conversation. It didn't meet his expectations, he claimed. I, too, was disappointed, but likely for very different reasons. He was anticipating a more research-based information presentation and a list of race-based resources. Instead, I facilitated a discussion session. I wrote a quick and curt message back to him explaining that our session was intended to build empathy and work on implicit bias. I spelled out that some conversations of race are not simply exchanges of intellectual and witty banter. After I clicked "send" and the message zipped away into cyberspace, a deeper wave of concern rushed over me.

He doesn't get it, I feared. They don't get it.

Chapter 20

Ask Me No Secrets; Tell Me No Lies

Do you remember the first secret someone ever told you? Do you remember the first secret you ever kept? How about the first secret you ever told someone else? Secrets are a pretty big thing. We have a brief and finite amount of time in childhood innocence before we depart from the value proposition that honesty is the best policy. And somehow, secrets and lies become related in the process.

I promise not to tell; then I do tell. One of the emotions that cuts to the core is betrayal when confidential information is shred without permission. A secret requires you to trust someone with something your vulnerability. A secret is like giving someone a tiny piece of your soul and making them vow to keep it protected in the center of their cupped hands forever. It's one of the most precious things we can give each other and one of the most egregious of hurts when the trust is broken.

Secrets have everything to do with safety. Secrets have everything to do with power. The one with all the secrets wins. She or he has the ability to breathe life into or destroy the foundation of safety in the other person. You have to love or, at least respect the keeper of all those secrets. Giving them your secret(s) means taking care of them for as long as the two of you draw air on this planet.

Pleasantville, though lovely with its mature trees and numerous 1960s-like throwback small businesses lined along America Street, had plenty of secrets. Due to the nature of my position with Pleasantville Schools, I knew many of its secrets. While most of the neighbors in the community were "salt-of-the-earth" folks, there was a small subsection of the population with dark, twisted roots. These folks – and they exist in every community – didn't reflect Pleasantville's public-facing image. These folks were drinkers and drug addicts, rapists and batterers, drug dealers and thieves, manic depressives and many, many others with mental illnesses and mood disorders. In the crevices of the neighborhoods, there were both poverty-stricken households and homes of legacy wealth. Residents represented old blood, blue blood as well as blood, sweat and tears. Therefore, in the schools, we served students with old money, new money and "hood passes". Though it was not public knowledge to the untrained eye, Pleasantville was home to a broad cross-section of America. The town's diversity was not quite the same richness of the nation as a whole; but, the diversity was here, none-the-less.

Though I was newer to the community, I had been entrusted with stories Pleasantville preferred and pretended to hide. The town's least desirable narratives walked their way right into my office through its own residents' mouths. However, Pleasantville was the kind of place where you could make your secrets "go away" if you had enough money. The wealthiest of the wealthy and the most powerful of the powerful knew who to call to make noise of spectacle and dysfunction go "silent". If Pleasantville as a community was a big, beautiful home, its owners had carefully swept all of the dirt, soot and carcasses underneath a most exquisite Afghan rug. They had cleaned their hands of the unpleasantries and asked its guests, "What mess? Pleasantville doesn't get messy."

This is how secrets become lies. This is how the truth becomes a thing you only discuss over a martini – or four – when the dinner party gets a bit too real. Though I had seemingly worked my way over the moat and into Pleasantville's city limits, I was learning that access to Pleasantville functioned in layers. Getting "in" the town was but a first step. I was not yet "in" the houses or hearts of the residents with the most social capital.

I would argue that it gets easier to lie as we become older. Truth becomes relative. White lies are but a little deception if they keep everyone comfortable, I guess. Why do certain lies feel better coming out of our mouths and landing on the shirts and blouses of our acquaintances than truth? Sometimes we don't even have a reason for lying. We lie to friends as well as enemies. We lie to our parents and to our children. We lie to our spouses and best friends. We even lie to ourselves.

The notion that Pleasantville was "pleasant" was beginning to feel like a lie to me. Within one school year, I seemed to be falling out of good graces with community and faculty members who previously "couldn't wait" to work with me. Their past welcomes were present lies of collegiality. My teams were smaller. My volunteers were few and far between. All of that great engagement and involvement, too, had fallen away. That I felt a "slight concern" was a drastic understatement. My undertaking was not possible without support. As the saying goes, "Many hands make the load light". I had a premonition, though, that the task at hand was about to get much heavier. More than bodies participating, I needed to know that the district constituents and I were on the same page. Did they know I was on their side? Did they realize my sole purpose was to support and advocate for *them*? The foundation of my position was built on trust. I needed to test the waters to see if I was earning it.

Ever the nontraditional thinker, I decided to analyze each school building in the district for their perception of their school's climate. The bigger revelation this examination would show was the degree of trust our staff family felt toward one another. In order to win long-term buy-in, I thought it would be important to start with the teachers. Educators are the lifeline of the schools. Our trust lies in them to have the most important relationships with the students. Could I get a snapshot of how trust lived in our school buildings? Still feeling new, I was searching in the dark for a way to tap into the energy of the school culture. It was like wandering in a dark field on a summer night, trying to catch lightning bugs in a glass jar.

Secrets - that's how I decided to measure our district-wide culture of trust. Around 2005, a brilliant man named Frank Warren dreamed up a project called "PostSecret". He created a post office box and invited strangers to anonymously write and decorate (if desired) a notecard of a secret that they wanted to get off their chests. The secrets could be light and airy. They could be dark and twisted. Whatever the sender wanted to share was permitted and welcomed. Each week, Warren posted pictures of the anonymous secrets on his blog website. The project was vulnerable, human and beautiful. It did an excellent job of linking individuals from all over the country, who, through each other's anonymous secrets, felt connected.

My thought was to bring the PostSecret energy to the district on a small scale. If the flavor of the month was role-modeling which requires authentic trust, I thought PostSecret could jumpstart the positive energy. It would be charming, inviting and confidential.

Over a weekend, I decorated jars, bought index cards, markers, pens and assembled the items in little PostSecret stations – one for each school building staff lounge in the district. At our next leadership team meeting, I gave one explanation poster and PostSecret station to each principal and explained the task. I then sent an email out to all staff members, inviting them to be part of the project. The prompt was for them to anonymously share any thought they have on living and/or working in the Pleasantville community. "Practice makes perfect," I thought. I intended for us to practice trust by sharing our thoughts and feelings as a way or reminding ourselves that we were both professionals *and* human beings. That way, when it came time for us to be human for our students in need, we would already be in practice. I had plans of assembling our staff's anonymous "secrets" into a summary story I'd share with them.

Posters, cards and jars were taken back to school buildings and placed in a station inside of teachers' lounges. In my previous work at Downtown Community College, I had done PostSecret projects, and they were always well-received. I had no reason to expect otherwise in Pleasantville. One week passed and I didn't hear anything from principals, nor did I receive any postcards from school buildings. Two weeks passed and still, nothing. Since my office was located in the high school, I checked our PostSecret station in the high school lounge. To my disappointment, there were nearly no secrets in the boxes. I thought I'd aid the process along by submitting a secret or two of my own. Something was going wrong with my plan. Maybe I needed to go first and lead by example. Maybe staff didn't get the point of the project. Worse, maybe they *did* get it, and they didn't trust me as the sole visionary of the project and the harvester of the secrets.

On three different occasions, staff members came and talked with me to clarify my intentions behind the PostSecret project. I could ascertain by their questions that they were suspicious. Apparently, there had been teacher chatter. Something about the word "secret" implied something negative to them. They also felt "forced" to participate in the project. It wasn't the first time I caught wind of teachers' opinions that I forced them to engage. I was told that a few staff members even felt as if they were being "forced" to speak negatively about their experiences as Pleasantville District School employees. Never had it occurred to me that this project could somehow diminish trust among colleagues and me, but it did. I attempted to send a clarifying email to staff explaining that any private thought was welcome in the PostSecret stations. Submissions were required to be anonymous and they didn't even have to be related to Pleasantville. Those who spoke with me in person seemed reassured; therefore, I aspired to hope again.

For approximately six weeks, the PostSecret campaign took place and I highly anticipated the return of the boxes of secrets like a Christian child delights on Christmas morning. Already, I'd learned so much about the district and its families through formal and informal dialogues. The missing voices, however, were teachers' voices. The PostSecret project was designed to fill in the missing link – and I couldn't wait to get to know our teachers better through their stories.

Programs I'd planned came and went, but teacher bodies weren't in the room. By now, I had developed the habit of making excuses for their lack of attendance. "They're busy." "They have lives and families of their own." "They didn't know about the event in advance." "They have papers to grade." This was the era of Core Curriculum and a million and one assessments. Through interactions here and there with teaching staff, I was learning that they suffered from just as much anxiety as students behind testing. My empathy grew for them in thinking about the numerous measurements, rubrics and unrealistic expectations mounting on the educators. I understood that they needed breaks. I believed all teachers – including and especially our Pleasantville educators – gave 100% to our students. Teacher expectations were even more intense as a high-performing district. Our faculty needed a break and in many cases, that meant teacher bodies weren't present for afterschool events.

I understood. I got it; honestly, I did. Perhaps I was just being a dreamer by imagining that I could support teachers' efforts inside of the classroom and teachers could support my efforts outside the classroom.

Then, a random email blipped on the radar of my inbox that I randomly happened to open. This email included notes from a council of parents that advised Luke. In the notes, I read that there had been a complaint. Per the text, teachers expressed discomfort with the PostSecret project. They didn't understand it. Though I tried to clear up any lingering confusion, the PostSecret campaign was still received as a prompt from "the new diversity lady" to force them to say something negative about the school. I had, again, been misunderstood.

Fearing the damage had already been done, I knew I needed to pull the project. One by one, each of the school building principals sent their PostSecret stations back to me. Each box I opened was more disappointing than the one before.

In total, after a couple months and across five school buildings, less than 15 "secrets" were submitted. One staff member later told me that she contributed a story, but fearing someone might pull her story from the jar, she took her story back, typed it and resubmitted it so her handwriting couldn't be recognized.

While the secrets were few in total, one big secret had become glaringly obvious to me. **Pleasantville was a community with a lot of secrets and very little trust.** The obstacle of mistrust pressed on my bruised convictions like a cold compress. It chilled my spirits.

Year two of my charge was about implementing an action plan for inclusion and holistic wellness. It relied on the school district community's ability to trust me, to trust each other and to establish authentic trust with students. How on earth could we get the students to trust us when we didn't even trust each other? I wanted to deny it, but I couldn't. We were in trouble.

Chapter 21

Being Joe Clark

The movie *Lean on Me* came out in 1989. I was thirteen years old and in the 8th grade at the time. The transition from eighth grade to ninth grade was critical for my racial identity development as was the film. Though prickly and polarizing, the on-screen depiction of Joe Clark, the lead character, was but a mentor wish and prayer for a kid like me.

For those who don't know this cult classic, let me do the honors of describing the film. *Lean on Me* is based on the true story of fledgling urban, inner city Eastside High School. The staff is arguably incompetent at managing a group of largely minority, low income and highly troubled and traumatized students. The school is at-risk of closing unless their test scores in the coming year can display the basic level of proficiency.

Having reached their last resort in attempts to manage what many consider a "lost-cause", the superintendent reached out to a radical leader, colleague and friend who had a stellar past with the school decades ago. When he returned to be the high school's principal, he discovered a nightmare environment with young adults fighting to survive the mean streets of their neighborhoods as well as the high school hallways. Yes, as you might imagine, Joe Clark came into the scene with incredibly controversial and atypical leadership practices. He polarized many in the school and community. In the end, though, he became a beloved leader of the students, won over many of the faculty and was able to lead efforts to produce passing assessment results for the students.

Hindsight being 20/20, especially as an education administrator, I see the flaws in this story now. In my opinion, his leadership tactics and interpersonal skills were nearly traumatizing. Through my grown-folk wisdom, I think his ego could have destroyed the "greater good" plan and his narcissism flowed with reckless abandon. Be that as it may, as a skinny, golden biracial girl with a white father and a brown mother who was educated in a parochial school, I was aching to have an "authentic" brown cultural experience (that was not a poverty experience). As a child, I had convinced myself that being Catholic, educated and biracial made me less brown. I believed I needed more exposure to brownness and I selected *Lean on Me* as a lens through which I could vicariously experience urban inner city life. Additionally, *Lean on Me* was superb before-and-after story and I have always been partial to comebacks and transformations. At thirteen, I believed that every brown student needed a "Joe Clark" in his or her life to be a "crazy" advocate for students.

Joe Clark was the definitive change agent for Eastside High School's culture of apathy. I wanted to be led by a person or a movement that brown and bold when I was thirteen. The St. Therese Catholic School teaching staff was predominantly white and in all seven years, I had only interacted with one educator of color. Many of my role models were white. My teachers were white. My school principal was a white Catholic nun. These women were kind to me; in fact, a few took me under their wings as if I was a "pet project". My teachers were kind, but there is no comparison to having regular interaction with a person in a position of power that looks like you.

The closest I came to having Joe Clark was my second-grade teacher, Ms. Gene. She was firm but kind and incredibly "familiar". She looked like a family member, down to her freckle-faced brown skin and honey-blonde dyed hair. She talked to me like an auntie or a grandmother. I accepted her sternness. I understood her love. Ms. Gene *looked* like people who cared about me; hence, I wanted to give her my best as a student. It mattered that my learning was in the hands of "family". I knew that not only were her expectations of me high, but she would accept nothing less than excellence because she knew I was capable of delivering excellence. Let me be crystal clear - Ms. Gene was *not* a sweet teacher. She didn't give out hugs simply because it was Tuesday. Still, when second grade was complete, I knew my math facts. I could write paragraphs in perfect D'Nealian cursive handwriting. I also knew that indoor recess meant we could listen to Michael Jackson's Thriller album. She was overt in stating what she needed from me and I knew what I'd get in return. To know Ms. Gene was to understand that you give Ms. Gene what she wanted.

Here I stood, over thirty years later, an education administrator in a predominantly white school district. I wonder what Ms. Gene would think of my endeavors in Pleasantville. Further, what would Joe Clark think of my endeavors in Pleasantville? The first year of my contract had been fulfilled and I had a laundry list of things I wanted to accomplish in this next year. Pleasantville would need a catalyst to ignite the transformation story for marginalized students and staff in Pleasantville. I was trying my best to make myself "fit" in the district, both figuratively and literally. Though my job encompassed so much more than brown students, they were, of course, near and dear to my heart. Just like Ms. Gene came to school every day to teach every student in her class, I'm certain every little brown girl reminded her of her daughter. How can that *not* have an impact on an educator?

My social-emotional bucket list was overflowing and it would be no easy task to bring my position aspirations to fruition. After 365 days, it felt like the load had become more elephantine. By mid-fall of year two, I was learning that teachers weren't so trusting of the environment with their personal thoughts and opinions. I'd already been iced out from the brown student community. Folks weren't happy that I was sniffing around the community to learn more about Pleasantville's drug and alcohol stories. To make matters worse, unless I'd interpreted my first community meeting incorrectly the year before, the Pleasantville Police Department and I weren't going to frequent gluten-free donut shops and swap family stories, either. Still hopeful, but much more cautious now, I imagined being at the foot of the hill and beginning a steep climb. Working at Pleasantville was beginning to feel like a burden rather than a privilege.

At this moment in time, my supervisor, Dr. Springsteen, re-emerged. Dr. Springsteen and I had developed a warm relationship and I respected his mentorship and care of me. He spent the first year positioning me to get to know the "who's who" of Pleasantville. There was little to no friction between us and I brought little to no complaints his way. Until recently, my optimism toward the potential of being a change agent had blinded me from the conspicuous occurrences during the past school year. Something felt different now. I desired his insight to help me make sense of things and to prevent me from doleful thinking about year two of my contract.

Though Dr. Springsteen was not "familiar" to me in the way that Ms. Gene was, there was something I recognized in Dr. Springsteen that felt familial. He reminded me of a bolder version of my father. Dr. Springsteen was decisive and smart, but still rather quiet and reserved. At any given occurrence of him capitalizing on a moment to speak, one could be certain his tone would be opinionated and his words would not be minced. Both Dr. Springsteen and my father were emotionally as cool as cucumbers. They possessed some other-world ability to be placid. I needed that kind of serene advocacy. I needed a tranquil truth-teller in an environment where mistrust sometimes felt like tempestuous "Pleasantville nice" cover-ups and lies.

During the season of annual reviews, Dr. Springsteen made a point to meet with his subordinates in their own office spaces. He believed it made the reviews less intimidating and he was probably right. I had no clue or expectation of how my performance review would transpire. My entire job description was quilted together with fluff, dreams and a few wishes. Oh, and did I mention that my job description was *three* pages long? The requested deliverables that accompanied my position was a stew cooked up by committee members who campaigned for their personal interests. My assigned priorities were authored as mostly abstract and insanely ambitious promises with no real road map. Because I had learned a long time ago that perfection wasn't possible, I was not nervous about my annual review. In fact, I don't know if any of us were certain about how I would be reviewed, evaluated and measured. How could we be? My position has been created and staffed for the first time ever and there was no equivalent position that we knew of in the entire state for comparison at the time; we checked. Neither the board nor I was entirely certain I was doing my job correctly. We were all "winging it", but with good intentions.

Turns out, my abstract job was not the main focus of my first performance review. Lean on Me was the focus. Joe Clark was the focus. The role of Joe Clark as played or interpreted by Kimberly Brazwell was the topic of discussion. Dr. Springsteen and I had two parallel conversations in my performance review meeting. One tangent was about me as a beloved leader of brown students and the other tangent was his interest in "dynamic tension". Dynamic tension, as Dr. Springsteen explained, was the discomfort and friction of disagreement that could, at times, create higher level thinking. Unbeknownst to me, both brown leadership and dynamic tension were in play.

I was unaware of the extent of dynamic tension surrounding me. Dr. Springsteen shared confidentially that some of my colleagues had been in conversation about the needs of Pleasantville's brown students – and how I wasn't "getting the job done". Per thoughts shared with Dr. Springsteen by my peers, I had not kept support from brown parents alive and I allowed these supportive efforts to die without an attempt to revive or recreate them. Brown student needs were great academically, socially, and emotionally; they were Pleasantville's lowest-performing students.

I was in agreement that the gap in achievement was cause for immense concern; no dynamic tension existed there, right? Actually, there was. Thanks to Dr. Springsteen's love for dynamic tension and his uncanny ability to tell the truth without "beating around the bush", I was informed that there was a feeling from one of my administrative peers that I wasn't doing "enough" for brown people in Pleasantville Schools. The feedback pressed on my eardrums like speaker reverberation. Reverb that I wasn't "Joe Clark" enough. Reverb that I hadn't created enough brown programs. Reverb that I hadn't displayed enough brown activism. Reverb that I hadn't given enough brown administrator face time in the hallways. I just wasn't being brown "enough".

It wasn't the first time I'd been told I wasn't brown enough. This time, though, it was different and much more disturbing. Peers told me I was "gold" before I figured out I was brown, too. The recurring caveat to *my* membership in the brown community was that as a biracial person, I could never be as brown as '*they*' were. I was never brown enough. With that being said, I was used to this message coming from **brown** people. I had never heard from a white person that I wasn't being brown enough – until now.

I assume upon my hire into Pleasantville Schools, there was discussion and a belief that the needs of the brown students could and would be supported and met by me. Now, it seemed from Dr. Springsteen's revelation, I was not meeting the expectation of my service as a brown person to brown students in the district. My blood pressure rose. When I finally found the words to respond, my voice rose. Perhaps my defensiveness rose, too. I had worn my "spiritual armor" into school buildings, but I did not shoot the messenger. Dr. Springsteen *never* stated that he believed I should be Joe Clark. He never expressed that I would be tasked to manage brown students in Pleasantville as if they were wayward students at Joe Clark's Eastside High School. He did advise me, though, to look into addressing some possible dynamic tension coming my way from Luke.

I was angry. No, I was fuming. No, I was pissed. I was also aware and awake now. Forewarned is forearmed. I appreciated Dr. Springsteen for being "a little birdie" in my ear. Unfortunately, a seed of resentment tool root in my belly. Anger began to grow. I wanted the feeling to be wrong, but the inference I detected was that because *I* am brown, I should lead *all* efforts to support brown students. The message I fought hearing was, "Take care of our brown people problem." That I even uttered the thought sickened me.

In recent history, district leadership on the secondary level had already put forth great efforts in partnership with minority parents to support students of color. The programs struggled to gain traction, though. By the time I joined the Pleasantville administrative team, the efforts – albeit noble and fueled with love – were dead on arrival.

I should be fair about this and a bit more transparent. Dr. Springsteen never mentioned the film *Lean on Me* nor did he sit down in my office with a storyboard of the movie and ask where and how I might re-enact critical film scenes for the Pleasantville School District's brown students. To be honest, I'm not even sure Dr. Springsteen has seen the film Lean on Me. What I *am* sure of is that on a very implicit level, some educators and community members knew there was a problem at Pleasantville and they knew it involved the brown students. What I am uncertain of and hope I'm wrong about is if I was brought to Pleasantville – in part – to be their brown answer to a brown problem.

Our quantitative data clearly showed a disparity in achievement between brown and white students. If we had earned the trust in the brown community to talk candidly, their qualitative data would have likely supported the dismal achievement gap quantitative data. Pleasantville was a high student achievement factory – one of the best in the state – unless you happened to be brown or poor or learning disabled. God forbid, a student identifies with all three of the lowest performing student categories. The truth is Pleasantville is not alone in these specific achievement gaps. Most school districts show an achievement gap between brown students and white students. My suspicion is that this gap increases in suburban school districts where, speaking plainly, there is a greater struggle for cultural competency.

The challenge and the tension was the expectation that I, alone, was responsible for "saving" the brown people. By virtue of the fact that I was brown, it was assumed that all of the other brown people would anxiously anticipate developing a relationship with me. It was also assumed that I had the answers to all of the "brown people problems". Was the hope that my brownness could be so powerful, the sheer magnetic pull of my brown genes would create a gravitational force and literally drag brown folks in my direction?

I quip, but this was no laughing matter. This implicitly-biased assertion leaned heavy on my pressure points. It activated some of my older race pains. My peers wanted more for the brown students; so did I. They wanted me to do more for the brown students; so did I. They wanted me to be more for the brown students; so did I. They wanted me to be browner; Joe Clark browner – and I only knew how to be as brown as me. They wanted the brown kids to lean on me. The fact of the matter is that I desperately needed somebody to lean on, too.

Chapter 22

Denying the Negro Whisperer in the Garden of Gethsemane

My second September in Pleasantville began like a stealth migraine headache. The climate – at least around me – seemed to be changing rapidly with more dynamic tension than I ever anticipated receiving. Pleasantville was less aware of its microaggressions than I thought, but I felt them everywhere. What's worse, Pleasantville, it seemed, expected me to give my "stamp of approval" that they were, indeed, advanced in cultural responsiveness. Twice in year one, an administrator recounted a story of a brown boy sharing a warm hug with a school counselor. To them, I wonder if that singular hug was proof that Pleasantville was racism-free. I now realized I was going to have to tell Pleasantville things it didn't want to hear about itself. I felt the only way to get at the heart of the matter sincerely was to put a mirror up to Pleasantville and let them see themselves without any smokescreens. This would require bolder and more consistent advocacy on my part. In year two with Pleasantville, my warfare armor would become a daily uniform rather than a rarified costume and the thought of war on home soil distressed me.

Identity and advocacy are capricious bedfellows. In the spirit of acceptance, we can say things that are ridiculous, untrue or arguably insulting. "I don't see your gender." "I could care less if a person is straight or gay." "I'm part of the human race." Though human beings sometimes claim to be "blind" to identity descriptors like skin color, gender, sexual orientation or other forms of identity, what we're really trying to imply is that we do not assign weighted value to identity. That, too, is, unfortunately not true. We know when we're looking at identity and in the blink of an eye, our subconscious has already decided what that identity means and what its value is to us. And what if I <u>want</u> you to see my gender? What if I choose transparency about my sexual orientation? What if one of the things I'm proudest of is my race? **It matters** – particularly when one is fighting on behalf of a specific identity lens. When someone says to me, "I don't see [blank]", what I am hearing is that a person wants their values and behaviors to be congruent. Who of us does not want to be an advocate for all people? The truth, however, is that our behavior gets much more fierce, passionate and personal when our own identities feel like they're being threatened.

As a formerly low-income and presently biracial woman who happens to live with attention deficit disorder, it absolutely impacted me on a personal level to learn that Pleasantville Schools' data showed it had the lowest success rate for African American students, low income students and students with IEPs (individual education plans). I would have been a "triple threat" student in Pleasantville Schools. Aside from my personal biases toward identities that reflect my own, I am still incredibly passionate about the equity and inclusion of folks whose identities may *not* include minority race, low income, female gender and mental illness. In fact, because of my lenses and my natural strengths in empathy and compassion, I am able to passionately advocate for many different disempowered lenses and constituency groups.

Now let's complicate advocacy and passion with a nasty little word called, "defensiveness". If you are passionate about a cause that looks like you, then I would like to welcome you to the Land of Defensiveness. Please sign in and get your anger name badge at the registration table.

What does defensiveness look like? How does it sound? What does it feel like when the label is assigned to you in conversation? Do you fear for your personal, emotional or physical safety when defensiveness enters the room? Does it serve a purpose or have any effective function? Further, if you find yourself floating in it, would you recognize it quickly enough to swim out or would you drown in its accusation? Could you stop your "defensive" behavior? Further, would you want to?

It has taken a while, but I think I have figured out what defensiveness feels like in my body. It became important for me to know its biological warning signs for my own peace of mind. When the scarlet letter "D" is pinned to my chest and I am labeled defensive, I feel fire. In my body, the accusation of defensiveness feels like the wrong kind of fire in my belly. It burns my face, just below the surface of my skin. My cheeks get hot and I can feel saliva droplets form in my mouth. Acid churns in my gut. The adrenaline gasses up the tank of my fight, flight, freeze or fawn responses. Should I attack? Should I run away? Should I petrify like drying cement? Should I go limp and acquiesce to make the pain stop? In my case, my muscles constrict and a thousand little prickles pierce my skin as if I am getting a tattoo on my entire body, all at once. Defensiveness makes me a fire-breathing dragon – with ADD.

I felt my scales forming during my meeting with Dr. Springsteen when he informed me of Luke's complaints regarding my relationship management with brown Pleasantvillians. When my cheeks flushed, my voice volume increased and my tongue began to fork, Dr. Springsteen told me not to "be defensive". I don't know how not to be defensive when I feel like my character is being attacked, but that's what I was expected to do. He encouraged me to talk with Luke directly, but to "not be defensive"; I froze.

Days later, the district leadership team met for one of our monthly meetings. The meeting conference room was slight with walls decorated with student art. A large wooden conference table swallowed up space. One by one as we filed in, we poured into the narrow confines of our chairs. The late-comers borrowed chairs from an adjacent room and scooted into space crevices. Careful to not position myself as if it was my meeting, I avoided chairs at either ends of the table. My manila folder was stuffed with handouts of coming programs designed for Pleasantville's marginalized students. I should have been excited to share my developments, but instead, I was tense. This meeting was different for me than previous meetings. I was different this time. I wasn't angry, but I was ready to breathe fire if needed.

My medieval suit of armor rattled when I walked in the room; the armor and I barely fit in the chair. Less than a week after Dr. Springsteen told me about the perception that I was dropping the ball of brown student support, I found myself in a leadership meeting and I was ready to defend myself if I was "attacked".

During the meeting, I was disengaged and in survival mode. I scanned the room as my colleagues talked about agenda items that had nothing to do with my job function. In linear fashion, we ticked off talking points of basic school administration items of importance – curriculum, facilities management, assessment, scheduling, programming and the like. Though we were all peers, I felt like I was sitting in *their* meeting. Social-emotional well-being of students was important, but not as big of an emergency as, say, gifted education or district technology updates. That morning, Dr. Springsteen was not able to attend the meeting; nor was my biracial colleague. I was the only person of color in the room. I had no back-up or reinforcement. Though my complexion is fair, at that moment, I felt very brown and very alone.

My attention was distant and I wrote notes to myself on the bottom of the agenda. As the meeting drew to a close, my ears perked at a concern raised about district achievement gaps. Lo and behold, the topic of brown student support and success presented itself and that meant I had been called to the carpet. Luke spoke up on concerns about the current lack of programming for and relationships with brown students – my lack of relationship with brown students. It was the same story that Dr. Springsteen told me, only this time, Luke "said it to my face", as we'd say in the old neighborhood.

Luke: We're not closing the gap in achievement for our African American students. The programs we had for them are gone and you haven't created anything in its place.

Me: It's been one year. …And I didn't kill those programs. They were dying before I arrived. I spoke with the black students and they didn't even know what they were supposed to be accomplishing in those programs.

Luke: Well, they're gone now and you haven't produced anything. We have less now than we did a year ago.

Me: That's not my fault…

Luke: I don't see you talking to our African American students. I expected you to be walking the halls and developing relationships with them.

Me: There is a reason why the black students and I are not close yet, but I'm not going to sit here in the meeting and divulge personal cultural information here in a staff meeting. It takes time to build rapport with communities that struggle to trust authority.

Luke: All the more reason for you to be walking around and getting to know them. They need to see you more. Have more exposure to you.

Me: It doesn't work that way for us. As a person of color, you're just going to have to trust me.

Luke: I've sent some students to you and haven't heard anything else as a follow up. Nothing's happening.

Me: The truth is that the black students don't talk to me. They don't trust me yet. They need to trust that I'm here for them as opposed to just being another administrator in Central Office.

Luke: We have relationships with the African American students. I've seen a young African American man hug one of our counselors. I guess I'm just frustrated and disappointed. I thought we'd be further along than this by now.

Me: Do you trust me to do my job or not? I'm so angry right now! I cannot and will not rush black students to have a relationship with me. It has to be their decision. They have to set the pace to get to know and trust me. I know what I'm doing. The scope of my job is broader than just brown students and if we all don't understand that, we have an entirely different issue to resolve.

Kelly: So, if we shouldn't be referring African American students to you, how would it be best for us to utilize you?

You could cut the tension in the room with a butter knife. The administrative staff at Pleasantville Schools heard their most popular and beloved principal say I wasn't getting the job done. In his opinion, not only had I let minority programming die, but I had yet to make any attempt to revive or recreate it after a year in my position. Right there in a meeting among my peers and the Lord Almighty, Luke stated that support for African American students was regressing and the regression was my fault. He was resolute. I thought Luke was bold and I thought my colleagues were either shocked or cowardly for not uttering a sound during the entirety of the exchange.

Besides feeling enraged and hurt and incredibly vulnerable about my own racial identity and history of intra-racial relationships, I was disappointed in myself. Dr. Springsteen would have said I was defensive. I actually said, "I am so angry…" out loud. I confirmed (to them) that I was an angry black woman. Wafts of steam sprouted from my nose. Fire singed the edges of my handouts. Acid gurgled in my belly. I was a dragon in a suit of armor. When provoked, I didn't keep my cool. My face caught on fire in an administrative team meeting and all because of those pesky brown kids. If I could just save all the brown kids, my face wouldn't catch on fire. I wouldn't get defensive. Pleasantville wouldn't have an achievement gap and all would be fair and right in the land.

Exactly how does one navigate this type of confrontation in a non-defensive manner? As a brown female professional – and especially in environments where I am a tokenized brown leader - it's way too easy for me to lose in attempts to keep my professional dignity and credibility. In a room of all white colleagues who have very little experience working with someone like me, I had to imagine that implicit bias and all of my stereotypes were in the room with me. To defend myself and my credibility against Luke's accusations meant to fight not just him, but all of my stereotypes as well.

I can't get loud.
I can't get personal.
I can't walk out the room.
I can't use foul language.
I can't speak with my body or with my hands.
I can't get emotional.

So how am I allowed to defend myself when battle occurs? Better yet, am I allowed to defend myself?

In the meeting, I attempted to explain myself (as if I should have been put in a position to do so in the first place). I explained that social-emotional work is about trust, which takes a while to develop. I told snippets of stories I was living, getting to know parents and students on a one-to-one basis. I described, again, the timeline of brown student programming at Pleasantville and that the beginning stages of its death preceded my hire. To an older, white male colleague with seniority over you, I can only assume that sounds like defensiveness. Out came the armor and weapons when Luke pushed back on me in the meeting in front of colleagues. Our administrative peers were so stunned, they sat in awkward silence. There was barely any breathing in the room as sonic boom pin drops on carpet floors ricocheted off the walls.

Due to the complexity of brown folk culture, I didn't explain my race relations with brown students to my white peers. Nonetheless, I knew what the problem was between Pleasantville's brown people and me. That conference room, however, was neither the time nor the place to divulge more brown secrets. My credibility felt like it was on trial. My ability to have a relationship with brown people felt like it was being cross-examined. Kelly's question, in all of its sincerity, helped to crystallize the issue. It was like a red silk blanket had been dropped from the ceiling, revealing the elephant in the room. What I heard my colleagues asking me was, "Are you the 'Negro Whisperer' or not?" My fate as a credible brown person – in their eyes - depended on my answer. The conference room was the Garden of Gethsemane and my credibility was contingent upon me confessing to the complex and sometimes dysfunctional elements of brown psyche in terms of relationship-development with other brown folks.

I was in an incredible amount of emotional pain, sitting in that meeting and being questioned about my lack of ability to relate to, support and be supported by brown people. Yet, when weighing the two options on the table, I realized it would have hurt worse to give my white colleagues – even those who were sympathetic and well-intentioned – the truth about internalized racism and brown folks' ability to be inhumane to other brown folks.

I couldn't do it; I denied addressing our cultural challenges in the meeting. I denied speaking about brown suburbanites who struggle to support brown programs in suburban schools and communities for fear it will make them look too African, brown and un-American. I denied the fact that in predominantly white communities, when a brown leader enters the environment, the brown community takes a significantly long amount of time trying to determine if the brown leader is a "provocateur" or an informant of the white people or an authentic advocate for the brown people. I denied the truth that some brown folks simply trust brown programs and initiatives more and take them more seriously when they are created and/or initiated by white people. Some brown folks aren't confident in other brown folks' ability to be professional, sharp and detail-oriented.

The anguish I felt about being in my fourth decade of life and still struggling to prove my brownness to brown people left me defeated and depressed. The anguish I felt about being perceived as too brown by brown people also cut like a knife. My hair was too nappy and yet not nappy enough. My skin too brown and yet not brown enough. My gestures were too sassy and yet my head didn't roll around on my neck enough. The freckles on my face distracted the dogs from my "Negro" scent. I was already trying to cope – in private - with having no cultural reference group in Pleasantville. The surprise of being expected to prove my brownness to middle class white colleagues was profoundly incredulous.

Do I know how to have a relationship with brown people? Do I know how to whisper to brown people? In the Christian Bible, there is a story told that one of

Jesus' followers, Peter, denied knowing Him three times. In this meeting, I denied knowing dark truths of brown folks and internalized racism four times.

Chapter 23

Detonating Bridges in the Name of Diversity

All while Pleasantville students jaunted to and from school seemingly oblivious to a world outside of black and white reality, something unique and entirely different was beginning to unfold around the nation that autumn; and, all school year, really. Evening news programs conveyed an impression that a pattern was developing of brown men dying in the hands and on the watches of officers of the law. In several incidents, these officers, stressed from having accidentally killed a brown person, were exonerated.

I pondered over the most recent killing at the time – Michael Brown – and thought that the city of Ferguson, Missouri was drastically different from Pleasantville. Yet, I could imagine "Ferguson" happening, perhaps to a lesser degree, in Pleasantville. In my mind, the comparison begged the question, "Could Ferguson happen in Pleasantville?" What a powerful community conversation we could have on that topic, I mused! I was already planning to host four new community dialogues during the academic year and what a fiery start "Ferguson" could be in getting us to talk more about racial implicit bias in action. Upon further reflection, I figured I could get more bees with honey than vinegar if I renamed the presentation to include the larger metropolitan area. An authentic conversation would have to include "the powers that be" and it was imperative that they did not feel threatened by the conversation. The superintendent arranged for a meeting so I could personally and cordially invite the mayor and police chief for a conversation.

Word was beginning to spread about my bold social-emotional efforts, but in all the wrong ways – as if my program was a social justice cootie, if you will. My style was rather counter to Pleasantville's culture and I thought that was a good thing. "Pleasantville Nice" meets "Keepin' It Real". My immutable truth-telling was like kindergartner sneezes that weren't shielded by the insides of elbows. Truth was getting onto all sorts of surfaces. My honest reputation was spilling out of the school district and into Pleasantville's residential areas. It crept into homes through tiny crevices in the broken window seals of old homes built in the 1930s. It trickled through sewer pipes and even found its way to city hall. I was under the impression that honesty would be a refreshing start to deep healing. Some, though, perceived my style to be more egregious than honorable.

There is this odd thing that occurs now and again in conversation among people of low-income heritage. We sometimes half-jokingly compete over "street credibility". Who grew up the roughest? Who was the poorest? Who knows the most about the "school of hard knocks"? Whose friends were the "gulliest" or the rawest and gangster? There is a secret to deciphering the winner and it is a subtlety that others don't notice. When one has a true impoverished upbringing, she seldom wants to talk about it. She understands that poverty is a unique "badge of honor" to those who survive and succeed.

Like many, many others, I have "U.S." poverty war stories, which cannot begin to compare to second world and third world poverty. Those of us with "American poverty" experiences have a few recurring patterns in our stories. One, our households experienced a lack of some of the basics in Maslow's hierarchy of needs. Two, we dabbled in exploration and manifestation of "cool pose" or a physical and attitudinal presentation of toughness. Three, we likely have a strained relationship with or a negative perception of law enforcement. Either we don't know any police officers or we know police officers all too well – and not the good, helpful ones.

I grew up in some of my hometown's rougher inner city neighborhoods. Though cliché in the media, sceneries from my childhood do include row-house project communities, streets with boarded up houses and duplex homes with no front or backyard. I recall playgrounds where children were forbidden to play because neighborhood drunks and drug abusers had taken them over. My family and I have shared a community with gang turf, prostitute turf and wonderful gray-haired characters that have lived in their homes since before the street "changed". I know and understand that life. In fact, there was one odd thing I discovered from living in a poverty-stricken neighborhood. In rare instances, if the block is rough enough, police may not regularly patrol its streets. Think about that for a second. Somewhere, neighborhoods that are inflicted with arguably the most threatening and violent behaviors may see police officers the least when theirs is the 9-1-1 call.

Contrast this experience with Pleasantville. My truth, per stories told to me by community members of all ages and races, is that there were four Pleasantvilles when it came residents' perceptions of the police department.
1. There was the perception of Pleasantville police to the community's middle class white people.
2. There was the perception of Pleasantville police to the community's brown and poor people.
3. Finally, there was the perception of Pleasantville police to everybody else traveling along the town's urban fringe.
4. Finally, there was the perception of Pleasantville police to Pleasantville police.

I think back to my mother's consistent advice to stay out of the Pleasantville of her youth. I remember her instructions to me and especially to my browner older brother to, "Drive through Pleasantville with your hands on the steering wheel at 'ten and two'." She displayed a near-maniacal willingness to drive longer routes to avoid traveling through Pleasantville. That fear was passed on to my mother from her mother. That fear was also passed on to my siblings and to me. Yes, in case you were wondering, negative perceptions can be inherited in both brown and white communities.

Though I was given a framework for understanding police – particularly suburban police, I wanted to discover and rewrite the narrative for myself. I believed my clean criminal and driving record made me different. I'd like to think my sweet disposition, sense of humor and engaging smile made me, well, pleasant! While I'd had a bumpy start with Pleasantville's police chief, I had confidence that I could still win him and the other Pleasantville folks over. My view was so tightly focused on one teeny zip code, Pleasantville's; and, I was hyper-focused on making my Pleasantville relationships right.

Then the lens with respect to brown folks and law enforcement got bigger. Local issues broadened to become state, regional and national issues of injustice. In the midst of everyday life, a huge story began emerging in the news media and the stars of the show were police officers and brown folks. Jordan Davis, dead. Renisha McBride, dead. Eric Garner, dead. John Crawford, dead. Michael Brown, dead. Tamir Rice, dead. Tony Robinson, dead. Walter Scott, dead. Freddie Gray, dead. Words from an old Negro spiritual stirred in my soul.

Over my head I see trouble in the air.
Over my head I see trouble in the air.
Over my head I see trouble in the air;
There must be a God somewhere!

Something was happening. The elephant in the room had been awakened violently from a nightmare. He was frightened, stirring and thrashing around. His flesh was pierced by bullets and his ivory tusks, sawed off, stolen and sold. The United States had hidden something ugly for a long time and thanks to a serendipitous use of cell phone cameras and social media, the whole world discovered a thread of our dirty little secret all at once. We had to take notice and we needed to talk about it frankly. Race dialogue reared its ugly head in a venturesome way and some folks' fears became a tangible reality.

How, then, does a national crisis of brown men dying while unarmed and in police custody connect to a place as 'perfect' as Pleasantville? Well, it depends on who you ask. In my first year on the job at Pleasantville, I gathered a great deal of stories. I heard many wonderful tales of police officers bringing used bikes to Pleasantville's low-income children. I heard about the great work Pleasantville had begun with community policing. Unfortunately, I also heard about the disproportionate number of drivers with brown skin who were pulled over on a regular basis. In fact, I heard stories about brown marathon practitioners stopped by the police while jogging. I heard stories of brown students stopped by police while running to football practice. I learned of stories where brown teachers from within the school district had been stopped by Pleasantville's police while coming from or going to school. To be perfectly clear, not every Pleasantville police department story I heard was negative. The problem lied in the fact that a pattern could be presumed from the negative stories.

The nation was absolutely torn up and polarized over the issue and the value of black lives. In fact, three brown women began efforts that became a movement called "Black Lives Matter". The country and the world was a buzz – *outside* of Pleasantville. Race dialogue had not yet found its way back into the Pleasantville school buildings about the deaths of the brown men. Pleasantville finally had a critical mass of brown students, though. We had a moral imperative to talk about it. I invited more targeted race dialogue inside Pleasantville; not unlike inviting a vampire into my house. I could feel the need; the national, regional and local tension was palpable. We had to do it.

I created a community conversation and planned to facilitate attendees carefully through very sensitive talking points. The dialogue inquiries were questions likely in the minds of Pleasantville's brown residents – could "Ferguson" happen in Pleasantville? Or even the greater metropolitan area? Further, had it already happened? The planets had aligned in a very frightening way. Were we ready to boldly address our own best practices and transgressions? Were we aware of our safeties and our threats? There was a national dialogue taking place about implicit bias and I wanted to capitalize on the moment for voices in the district that had not yet been provided with an opportunity to tell their stories.

Brown stories weren't the whole story, though. I knew the other side of the story, the stories of Pleasantville police and Pleasantville white folk, had to be in the room. Together, we needed to practice having compassion through tension. I needed a miracle to happen. Somehow, I had to get the Chief to accept an invitation to be in the room when this conversation happened. Dr. Springsteen's wisdom helped me to understand that the invitation extension was going to be much more multifaceted than I first anticipated. It would require smooth talking and a great deal of social capital that I had, quite frankly, not yet earned in Pleasantville.

Moments like this called for a supervisor who trusts and understands your work. While I prepared to have a community conversation on Ferguson and implicit bias, I was aware that some of my diversity and inclusion colleagues at other educational institutions had been silenced. Not only did I have Dr. Springsteen's support, but he agreed to broker the deal to help me get the right people in the room.

Ingredients for an invitation extended to police to attend a community conversation on race included: Coffee, donuts, humility, a tough chin, a good morning mood and hot seats in Pleasantville's police department.

I was the last to arrive at the meeting and had to wait for an officer to escort me upstairs to the police station conference room. Behind the glass, I gave the officer in the reception area my name and swear I felt a bit of instant negative energy between us. The lobby was frigid. I paused for small talk, but was met with nagging silence. Waiting patiently for an officer escort, I pretended to be interested in the wall art. I felt eyes on me, perhaps mistakenly, but did not feel quite safe enough to look over and meet the eye contact scanning me. Finally, a female sergeant appeared from behind one of the neutral-painted doors. I looked up and smiled. "Come with me," she asserted with an emotionless face. Her behavior and tone reminded me of my mother when I had displeased her. Had I upset the sergeant? Is that what the coldness in the lobby was? Had I disappointed the police staff, too?

The sergeant walked me up a flight of stairs and led me into a larger, sterile room of rectangle tables and blue, plastic chairs. Dr. Springsteen already had a box of donuts sitting in the center of our table among several cups of coffee. Pleasantville's mayor, police chief, school superintendent and I sat down and got the formalities out of the way. I couldn't help but notice my brownness, comparative youthfulness and womanness among this group of mostly older white men in power positions. I was a collage of dreadlocks, full lips, relative inexperience and breasts in the presence of some of Pleasantville's Good Ol' Boys. As if deferring to seniority, we all paused until Dr. Springsteen began the meeting.

Dr. Springsteen sat to my left. The mayor and Chief sat beside each other, adjacent to Dr. Springsteen. We sat in "L" formation and I leaned into the table, showing my interest in connecting. The meeting began with Dr. Springsteen sharing why my position was created with Chief and the mayor. He spoke of my focus and skill set as a value-add to the district. Numbers, anecdotes and theories poured like the coffee into the center of our group. It was a sales pitch. His words sounded like a reassurance that my addition to the Pleasantville Schools staff was a good thing.

Dr. Springsteen told stories of what he was learning at my quarterly community dialogues or town hall meetings and how the "dynamic tension" of the conversations was good for the school community. I smiled and nodded, offering my softest possible face. The mayor's eyes looked curious. Chief sat in his chair, arms folded across his chest. I swear he didn't even blink. You see, folks – particularly white folks in positions of power – were nervous, apprehensive and feeling great trepidation about joining vocal brown people for a race conversations in the Black Lives Matter era. At the time, the police officer who killed Michael Brown was just acquitted and Dr. Springsteen and I had the audacity to ask Pleasantville's chief of a predominantly white police department to be part of a mixed-race conversation about implicit bias.

After laying the foundation, Dr. Springsteen had me explain the structure for the conversation I planned to lead. Though brown folks struggle to admit it, the narrative of police officers was a stereotypical overgeneralization just as the narrative about brown folks, particularly brown males were. My hope was that the conversation could be approached from all sides through the lenses of safety, fear and humanity. We all longed to feel safe. We all experience fear. We all seek to be received as human beings by others. I explained every nook and cranny, leaving nothing to the imagination. More than anything, it was imperative for me to emphasize that no "attack" was coming. There was no intention to set up the police officers as racists. The conversation was designed to be exploratory on all sides.

I'd rattled on a bit as I tend to do. So excited, I was, I hadn't realized I never paused for questions. When done, I turned the meeting back over to the superintendent. He glanced back at me with his usual satisfactory eyes like a proud papa. Pleasantville's mayor seemed pleased as well. I looked in the faces of each of the powerful white men, seeking their approval and hoping for their trust. The mayor replied to my glance with a perfect politician smile and asked the police chief, "So, what do you think? Do you have any questions?"

Chief's body was pressed to the back of his seat as if he was a passenger on an amusement park ride that was about to shoot out from the base of the coaster. His jaw was clenched so tightly, I imagined blood dripping from his nose and onto his uniform. He slowly leaned forward, released the crushing grip of his hands on the arms of his chair. His face was flushed and the tendons in his neck peeked from the top of his collar. His neck and face were burning embers, like he'd been holding his breath since I walked into the room. If someone told me the police chief had the ability to spit venom, I would have believed them – and would have ducked when he spoke.

"Questions?" the police chief replied with a sarcastic chuckle. "No, I don't have any questions but I have a few things I want to say," he asserted with a smirk. The stereotype threat of me began… "Here's what I think, Kim. I think it's all about race with you. Black vs. White. I think your work is divisive and I think you tear down more bridges than you build."

I was always told honesty is the best policy, but his honesty burned like pepper spray on my face. The superintendent, mayor and I wore incontestable discomfort on our bodies as we sat in shock at the willful delivery of Chief's astringent words. This was not a criticism of my work with the Pleasantville School District. This was criticism of me as an individual.

All my life, I had been the person who could make friends with and win over nearly anyone. My mischievous childlike smile, jokes and my propensity for hugging were all genuine characteristics in my toolkit. None of those qualities would be effective in this room. The chief's cheeks were crimson now and his fingers were vice-gripped on the arms of the chair again. His white-knuckled hands squeezed blood out of the arms of the conference room chair. A thick mustache covered what I fabricated in my mind to be a snarl. Had his body grown any more strained and rigid, he would have been the cause of his own constipation. He seemed to have not blinked in several minutes. I knew then and there I could never make him like me. His spirit had already made a decision about me. I was a troublemaker and his words confirmed those sentiments. His staff followed his lead and his influence was in opposition of me. I was labeled an enemy.

I took notes on his commentary and feedback of me so as to respond properly and concisely to his criticisms. I eloquently picked his argument apart, but it didn't matter. I smiled at the irony of his statements, but my smile didn't warm him. At the end of the day, I was the one who left the meeting with bruises. My white flag of truce lay on the altar with the coffee and donuts unaccepted. I had come seeking peace but left with a sneaking suspicion that my presence was a declaration of war.

Chapter 24

On Putting Your Black Girl in Check

If you can believe it, as turbulent as my second autumn had been, I was still hopeful that the academic year had promise. I'm a competitive person and now that I was aware there were doubters, I was driven to prove my naysayers wrong. Pleasantville Schools and I were one year and three months into our relationship and the honeymoon had begun to wear off. The initial connection I thought I'd detected must have been infatuation. The excitement had faded and now, we were getting used to living with each other.

In my position as Director of Student Services, the task of leading social-emotional wellness was like herding cats. Everything about my function was irregular. My schedule was all over the place. My objectives were vastly different than those of my peers. I had no baseline data to measure the soft-skill start to the work I was doing. Because community matters spill over into school buildings, I made it my business to meet community folks including the mayor, the police department, business owners, parents, students, teachers, principals and elected officials for input. My key stakeholders and constituency groups included everyone. On a good day, these meetings were planned and not pop-ins. If the odds were in my favor, the content of the meetings were about collective work and not grievances about my forward approach to addressing Pleasantville's social-emotional issues.

Once I got some footing in place about the kinds of programs that might work in Pleasantville as well as ways to use the infrastructure to implement the programs, I believed I had found my groove. I was starting to get the hang of the Pleasantville system and its processes like discretionary funds, grant-writing and utilization of the school culture team, which I oversaw. I also learned about the educators with the most influence and social capital. I needed to get "in" with the faculty and staff who owned some emergent power in the school climates. The trick there is that they were not just going to let me in. I'd have to learn the "secret knock". I needed to ingratiate myself to them so we could support each other.

It almost felt like old-fashioned courting, which would make sense for Pleasantville culture. You check them out and they check you out. If they initially like what they see, they test you out first. They investigate to see if you're worthy of follow-up interaction. After all, you're new to this side of town and they're never interacted anyone quite like you. Anything not native to Pleasantville is exotic, which is not necessarily a good thing. You are a different breed than they're used to. It takes a while before they "knight" you as an affiliate. If you're not born and bred Pleasantville, it takes a long time to get approved and to be deemed a "Pleasantville fit".

Fit is a nebulous thing, virtually impossible to define. It's a moving target, seemingly changing moment to moment and person to person. It's hard to "get in" and much too easy to be cast out. Moreover, God bless you if you attempt to "fit in" a k-12 school district for a high-impact job – particularly in the suburbs – without ever having taught in the classroom. In a K-12 environment, educator specifically means **teacher** – period and the end. Even if you have worked at an educational institution, if you do not have certified classroom instruction experience.

You, non-teacher, are coming in with a deficit. You have not been trained in the Shaolin ways of the teacher ninjas, and for that, you will eventually have to pay your debts in a currency to-be-determined. Your degrees, world views and value system are all under scrutiny. You are permitted to have different thought processes than the Pleasantville teachers – as long as your perspectives *ultimately* align with what they already believe and practice.

It was common knowledge that I was still learning the ways of the Pleasantville School District. Pleasantville was very much an anomaly. It was historically wealthy but very small. In fact, the school district was so small; there was no human resources department. There was an orientation and onboarding session for teachers, but not for administrators. I was hired into a new district that had created a new position whose practices were new every day. No one could help me figure out what I was supposed to be doing; I had to figure everything out on my own. How do I take kids on a field trip? How do I schedule a room for a meeting? How do I take time off for myself? How do I attend a conference? It would have been incredibly helpful to have some assistance such as a partner or a mentor with whom I could touch base on a regular basis.

Social-emotional work in educational systems is relatively new and the nature of the work is designed counterintuitive to how educational institutions function. There are no rubrics or assessments. It is not possible to be a subject-matter expert. Social-emotional work, in many ways, cannot be operationalized. At its core, it is messy. Its solutions are person-specific. You can only imagine how challenging it might be to step into a position with a whole community expecting you to have all of the answers to their unsolved mysteries and you are not entirely certain how to request office supplies or if you are permitted to send a document to print in color on the high school library copy machine. Mundane tasks are just that, but cluelessness about completing mundane tasks can take the wind out of your empowerment sails.

Dr. Springsteen had already given me my performance evaluation by my second September in the district. Since his investment in the position's success was so great, I was pleased he thought I was doing a stellar job. He and a few board members communicated to me that they believed we were further ahead in the social-emotional endeavors than they thought would be possible in one academic year. Luke's sentiments about me not doing enough for brown students were still an irritant to me as were Dr. Springsteen's advice for me to not be defensive. I needed to practice active listening. I wanted to get better at walking away from fights.

I would be lying if I said I had no interest in finding a way to be myself and fit into Pleasantville in my own unique way. It was important for the success of the social-emotional initiative to be accepted by Luke, Pleasantville and the students of the district. Since it was believed that I wasn't doing enough for brown kids, I decided to first work with students who were open to working with me. My theory was that the brown kids would see other students reap benefits and would seek me out for their own benefit. I started my outreach with young teenage girls and incorporated the lenses of race and income.

There was a totem pole of "teenage girl social capital" in suburban schools that was entirely different than an urban school district. Here's how it was explained to me many times by brown students.
- White guys date white girls
- Brown guys date white girls
- White and brown guys may "hook up" (to be physically intimate with) with brown girls.
- Brown girls date guys from different schools – if they're lucky.

Horrified at this plucking order, it was painfully clear we had all kinds of teenage girl drama. Brought to my attention were pervasive matters of slut shaming, esteem issues based on weight, income, class, race, religion, absence of father, hair complexes, etc. I thought there was promise to do some empowering work by unifying several of the Pleasantville High School girls who all felt, in one way or another that they didn't fit in. The challenge was that many of these girls were hiding and presenting as if everything was fine. There was no strength or presence in numbers; no critical mass. My thought was if I could somehow get girls in a room together to share and be led through a self-exploration experience, the effect could be phenomenal.

I hustled and networked to identify the perfect consultant and facilitator for this project. Fortunately, one of the region's premier experts on factors negatively impacting teenage girls and especially brown girls was available and interested in working on my project. She and I met and put together a spectacular outline of a program. All I needed to do was secure the funding, which I hoped could be fulfilled with a pocket of money identified as the principal's discretionary funds. I propositioned both the middle and high school principals for funding and provided them with the consultant's report, a draft form letter and a tentative program agenda. After emailing back and forth, Luke finally agreed to meet with me. Aside from my personal feelings about Luke, I was cautiously optimistic about moving forward with the initiative.

My office was serene with music playing quietly from my desk speakers. My papers were organized as I waited for Luke to stop by. The moment he entered the space, the energy changed. What was tranquil now felt like doom. Perhaps my lighting was too low. Or I wasn't settled in yet. Something was wrong in the air. Only briefly did we discuss the consultant. Luke drew his line quickly that unless I had a troop of girls lined up and banging on my door, he wasn't comfortable supporting the initiative with his discretionary funds. Why, what if only a handful of girls showed up for the conversation event and we'd paid for this consultant to do this work? Before I could get my flying geese in a "V", Luke shot them out of the air.

Luke wasn't done. In fact, he hadn't really started yet. He sat back in one of my office chairs across from me and said, "Perhaps Dr. Springsteen isn't giving you any feedback, so let me give you some feedback." Here is where the sliding doors concept entered the story. The reality that was about to unfold could have gone one of two ways. I could have listened to what Luke had to say and debated with him, point for point or I could practice active listening and just see what he had to say. I was already particularly sensitive because Dr. Springsteen has recently told me to not be defensive. His words were echoing in my head. So, in this version of reality, I sat and listened to Luke.

Here's what I learned from Luke that afternoon in my Zen-inspired safe space:
- Teachers think I'm unapproachable
- I come off pushy
- I'm not being assertive enough with the black students
- My efforts may have worked in college, but they're not translating to K-12
- I'm going too fast
- I came on too strong
- The poetry events I keep pushing aren't getting traction because people aren't interested …and maybe I should let it go.

This unsolicited feedback went on for about 20 minutes. In the first few minutes, I reminded myself that I was just going to be a listener. By the middle, I was shocked and absolutely pissed. By the end, I was heartbroken and empty. Meanwhile, Luke's belly was full from feasting on my dignity. After having relieved himself of his frustrations about me in *my* office, Luke simply got up and walked out without requesting any response or feedback from me. You would have thought it was his office.

Once Luke left, I closed my door behind him and sat in the room in silence for several minutes. I was used to being the new girl. I was used to being the hippy girl. I was used to being the free-spirit girl. But it never occurred to me that I could be the unwelcomed, unwanted prickly girl. This image was such a far departure from my normal style of fellowshipping. It was clear as day that Luke had no idea who I really was; nor did the teachers who complained to him about me and on whose behalf, he represented. My spirit had been bruised for the first time in a very long time. And something else rare happened; I cried. Before Pleasantville, I never cried. Ever. I called my mother and cried into her ear with enough hurt that she begged me to go home.

I sat in my office with my skin morphing from yellow to blush. Crying makes my nose, eyes and lips red and my face puff. So, I waited for my flush to leave, my eyes to whiten and my puffer fish face to relax. It took a couple hours; but, when the coast was clear, I booked out of the building and drove home with a two-day leave request already en route to Dr. Springsteen. That was the first weekend during my tenure in Pleasantville that I contemplated if I was going to return to my job the following Monday. I don't know how Luke did it, but he had really done his research on how to make sure a pawn knows its place on the chessboard.

Chapter 25

Being the Inside Joke

Another October had arrived in Pleasantville. Autumn in Pleasantville was lovely. Everything in Pleasantville was lovely, even as I was growing to hate its picture-perfect surroundings. Everything was cute from the perfectly matched families to the arboretum trees to the coiffed squirrels. Even their systemic dual diagnosis dysfunctions were picture-perfect.

Maybe the push I was starting to feel on the job was just fall fatigue. I tried to convince myself that the new strain might be community noise for more agitation, but I knew that was a lie. I wondered if the challenges I was facing in year two of my position were flukes or the beginning of anarchy. Was I to be the recipient for any treats at all or should I prepare myself for a year full of tricks?

Homecoming was near and I knew that meant our high school student drinking might spike. The principal and I had agreed that I would oversee several of the high school morning assemblies and we collectively decided to have a yearlong theme of wellness. I wanted to be consistent in providing messages that centered around intervention and recovery. Dialogue on prevention was a complete waste of time in this school community once kids hit middle school age. Pleasantville was no different than any of the other well-to-do neighborhoods around town. Kids with means often lived in homes where liquor was present – even when the parents weren't.

Adults model all kinds of things and one of the things many upper middle working class folks model is a culture of having a drink (or four) to relax. Seems harmless, right? Grown adults who can control their alcohol consumption should not be picked on for having a drink or two after a long day at the office. I could live with that argument if it were true, but I suspect there's a different and more accurate perspective of what young, upper middle class suburban kids see at home.

The children sometimes internalize unhealthy stress management. They reap a privileged lifestyle and thus, desire to have nice things and live a good life like their parents. They know Mom and Dad get stressed out from their jobs. And the truth is, high expectations have the kids, stressed out, too. Over time, the children observe that Mom and Dad seem to relax and calm down when they drink. Therefore, they infer that drinking might calm them down, too.

How many times was I told that Pleasantville was a "cocktail community"? Virtually any activity you can imagine can be upgraded in class and buzz with liquid spirits. By the time the Pleasantville kids become middle school aged young adults and start having parties of their own, they mock what they've witnessed for the last ten to fifteen years of their lives. For example, some kid in the neighborhood has a nice home that is always absent of adults, so her peers establish that house as the hangout spot. The next step is making the cut for the invitation list. Yes, there's a list. There is exclusivity because exclusivity equals power and privilege. When one possesses a certain amount of social capital, there can't be fraternizing with Pleasantville's "regulars". For all intents and purposes, consider that Pleasantville has a caste system. The royal scroll states that one may only party with peers in the appropriate level within the caste system.

The perplexing convenience about suburban parties is that the drugs and alcohol are generally already on-location. We mean *real* drugs and alcohol. No one is impressed by marijuana or beer. Those gateways have been seen, heard of and tried so often, beer and marijuana are essentially apple juice and aromatherapy. Mix in some pills and you've got yourself a party. In fact, in some circles, even pills aren't that big of a deal. ...Maybe a little more intense than Skittles. That's the social life of a well-to-do teenager in Pleasantville. You study hard. You serve time in your co-curricular or extracurricular activities and then you party on the weekend with your friends. Playback and repeat for years and for generations. Then you go to college. Then you come back to Pleasantville, have kids of your own and they do the exact same thing you did. Playback and repeat.

Imagine, then, the community reaction to a position like mine. I was given an impossible four-part task. Part I: address and resolve behavioral health issues in Pleasantville as they present themselves in the school district. Part II: address and resolve drug and alcohol issues in Pleasantville as they present themselves in the school district. Part III: address and resolve world issues in Pleasantville as they present themselves in the school district, such as hunger, homelessness, etc. Part IV: address and resolve diversity issues – if any exist – in Pleasantville... you get the idea. That was my charge and I took it very seriously.

Remember those regularly scheduled morning assemblies for the high school that I mentioned? I programmed several of them to have speakers who addressed issues of addiction or trauma and recovery. One or two speakers in particular were pretty hard-hitting about their experiences. What was the result? On three different occasions, students made appointments to meet with me 1:1 or 2:1 and told me about how much they disliked the assemblies. They were *over* the speeches about drug use and recovery. In fact, one student mentioned on a survey that the message he and his friends were learning from the speakers is that if they continue to do drugs, there shouldn't be too much of a concern because the speaker convinced them that they can fully recover.

This was not going as planned.

One afternoon, I met with an incredibly introspective student who was in recovery. He shared not only his perspectives, but those of some of his close friends as well. The general message was that I was a joke. You read that right. To my face, a student (and he was not the only student to deliver the humorless joke that quarter), told me student opinion on me was that both I and my job were "a big joke". Stopping the drug and alcohol use in Pleasantville was impossible, they all believed. Anyone who thought they could even make a dent in the cocktail community culture was fooling themselves.

There were those delusions of grandeur; I could feel them weighing heavy on me now more than ever before. I *did* believe I could make a difference. I was telling myself that if I could help only one person, it was worth it, but that, too, was a lie. I wanted all the under-18 alcoholics and drug abusers to have a recovery message resonate with them. Even while thinking it, I knew it was impossible. But to hear that I had been busting my butt for students who found my passion to be laughable was an inexplicable bruise to the soul. Not only did the students feel like I was wasting my time preaching about intervention and recovery, but there was even some underground chatter that some of the young Pleasantville drug dealers were irritated with me and my message.

Can we take a moment and unpack the psychological impact of being called a "joke"? Of people having no idea what you do and further, having no *interest* in you explain your job to them? Can we digest the impression students had of me, being the brown lady in the abandoned hallway, kicking her feet up on the desk and doing nothing all day? Can we process my experience walking down a crowded high school hallway, convincing myself that I'm starting to make a difference? Meanwhile, in my hallway walk, I am virtually invisible to students. Moreover, those who can see me get a chuckle when thinking about how dumb I am for thinking I could stop Pleasantville from a future tragedy of alcohol poisoning or a lethal drug overdose. Stupid. What a joke!

Chapter 26

Megaphone Throats in Math Class

By October, the Ferguson and racial implicit bias conversation had come and gone; and, indeed, the community showed up to talk. It was as if they were ready, willing, able and <u>waiting</u> to have a community forum about race. Parents of brown children who had rarely come to the school buildings (except for a fight) affirmatively received and accepted the invitation to talk. We somehow even made good in getting the police chief of Pleasantville to attend – and he brought the chair of the police advisory board with him - again. Fine, I declared to myself. The more, the merrier. The town mayor stopped in and of course, Dr. Springsteen was present, as always.

Community dialogues are a peculiar thing. They must be carefully led. Conversation moderation is an art form, particularly when the subject matter has the potential to be a volatile topic. I constructed only three questions to ask and tried to pose them in a way that afforded all attendees the opportunity to enter into conversation bravely, curiously and in a space of appreciative inquiry. Thankfully, most people in attendance accepted my invitation as host and facilitator. In fact, a great deal of trust was established that night. We discovered a wealth of thoughts, experiences and reflections together in the room.

One of the most profound stories we learned that evening came from the mouths of two students. They shared their personal experiences as brown students of Pleasantville High School's Math Department. An instantaneous image of numeric signs ricocheting off brown children emerged in my mind. The two students went on to share with the audience how they felt Pleasantville math teachers don't call on students who were not perceived to be bright. The young voices expressed embarrassment and fears that they had, somehow, annoyed their teachers by asking too many questions and requesting help too frequently when they felt they needed more singular attention to comprehend the math lesson. We sensed in their voices that instead of being affirmed and willed into having math ability, they intuited a belief that they were less than. Their voices were hesitant and their eyes avoided those of the adults in the room as they fidgeted with their hands and the corners of papers while they talked. I recognized possible sentiments of inadequacy regarding their mathematical abilities. They expressed feeling inferior to the bright students who already seemed to be excelling in class – students who also happened to be predominantly white.

According to our guest students' viewpoints, the Pleasantville math teachers had a more outwardly expressed willingness to support enrichment for students who were already above level as opposed to getting students who were still struggling to reach a level of proficiency. I feared that if math teachers heard those stories, these students' truths would be debated, shut down or vehemently denied. Good ol' Sociology 101 notes from my college days sifted themselves from my brain dust as I recalled that **perception is reality**. Whether district teachers and administrators believed there was truth in the students' statements or not, was of no consequence. The only truth that registered with me was that the students *felt* othered. Therefore, district leadership had a responsibility to consider the culture of the Mathematics Department. Speculation of lower-performing students being underserved needed to be settled right away. After the community dialogue session was over, the superintendent made a "b-line" to me and asked if I'd follow up with the Mathematics Department for Pleasantville High School. I concurred, "I'm already on it."

Within days, I connected with Darryl, one of the emerging leaders of the Mathematics Department who also had a natural predilection for diversity work. He and I sat together and discussed what I'd heard from students at the community meeting. Their perceptions hurt him as was evidenced by his quickened blinking and blushed cheeks as I retold their stories with anonymity. Darryl had already been participating in my monthly diversity training sessions and had the idea that I could facilitate a mini-session with his department colleagues. As it turns out, their department was close-knit. I kid, only slightly, that only in the Pleasantville School District would the high school Mathematics Department already have a habit of eating lunch together every day. Darryl and I decided the best strategy was for me to drop in on a lunch session and lead them in a brief facilitated dialogue on race and ethnicity awareness.

As a social justice nerd, I was looking forward to the interaction during the session. Every human interaction I have teaches me something and I knew I still had a lot to learn about Pleasantville. The diversity training sessions I'd developed nearly four years ago were some of my favorite practices to lead. From the visual make-up of the room when I walked in for lunch about a week later, the group size and demographics were ripe for a rich discussion. With only 45 minutes to host intellectual dialogue on a conversation that could, in theory, last for years, we jumped right in. Time was limited and my hope was that we might make progress on at least opening the conversation of personal implicit bias.

I began by asking everyone:
- How they identified racially and ethnically and,
- How they learned or perceived the race and ethnicity with which they identify

Already, I sensed the conversation would either drift in a space that was so "politically correct", it would be ineffective or it would get honest to the extent that the discomfort would be suffocating. Further, need I say I was the only brown person in the room?

The teachers and I took turns sharing in linear fashion around a large wooden table. A few struggled through the prompt, but gave what I believed to be honest answers, which was a good sign. We were beginning to establish some trust; and, that helped as we dug into some memories about race. The directive was to think about moments in our lives when our experience of race identity – particularly our race identity in *comparison* to someone else's differing race identity – showed up during a significant event in our lives. Again, some toiled through the reflection, but others had no problem responding in a rather thoughtful way to the inquiry. A couple folks even took the prompt further and began applying the lessons learned to present-day experiences as teachers in Pleasantville. Excellent work, I thought. That's exactly where I wanted the conversation to go.

As a diversity practitioner, facilitator and social justice advocate, my hope and dream is always to get the room warm enough that we trustfully balance the act of not holding back *and* not harming each other. The Math Department meeting seemed to be headed in the direction of openness.

One of the math teachers, a large white man in stature, shared his story and it was challenging for all of us to hear. His first interaction with brown folks was unpleasant and literally painful. His giant-like frame shifted in his seat; large hands now fumbling with the edges of his sandwich. His body language screamed discomfort. I imagined he thought he was "over" the anger from his negative incident with brown folks, but he wasn't.

It's not uncommon that our first experiences with people from other identities and walks of life are not ideal. The key is to remember that groups are not monoliths. There is not one experience or one reality that can be assigned to an entire racial group – and that's a very good thing, especially if the first interaction with an "outside group" is unpleasant.

Once we gave the teacher permission to feel something about his negative initial experience with brown folks, he then became more liberated than my safer space guidelines had intended.

Hank began the second half of his story by telling me – directly - that he felt like I was, "shoving this diversity stuff down his throat". That comment took me off-guard. I'd always assumed resistant sentiments might sound like that; I never actually prepared myself to be **in the room** when someone *confessed* the sentiment. Hank and I were sitting directly beside each other. We were in close enough proximity that his perceived disgust and fatigue landed on my handouts. Just as I was trying to readjust myself to wear his last statement, he raised a question about brown kids to those of us – and particularly me – in the room. "I guess I just don't understand," he pondered in frustration, "why the black kids are so loud, entitled and attention-seeking."

139

The boldness of his probe pierced through my chest like a clean bullet. There was nothing but silence in the room and my prayer was that the other teachers had enough wherewithal to be uncomfortable by what he said. My deeper fear was that there may have been another teacher or two who was thinking, "Thank you, Hank! I was wondering the exact same thing!"

I thanked Hank for his honesty and did my best to briefly respond to what was essentially a complaint about the brown kids at Pleasantville High School. In truth, though, I felt like a defense attorney who accidentally got the accused to confess to his crimes. "Ah," I thought. "This is what's happening in math class." The brown kids of Pleasantville are culturally code switching like nobody's business to simply function in the school environment vs. their home environments. There is often a natural, pre-existing misunderstanding of brown culture in predominantly white environments. Then, we have the added element of bravado, which many brown students exert as a survival skill to thwart threats that may subconsciously be perceived as hostile. The whole cycle is a big mess.

Folks with brown racial identity seem to be at the bottom of the "social capital" totem pole in Pleasantville. They're not expected to be smart. They're not regarded as being quite as attractive. The only real prize many can claim that can't be taken away from them is their bravado or "cool pose", as scholar and psychologist, Dr. Richard Majors, terms it. Pleasantville, too, had the kind of brown folks who brought their swagger and posturing to class with them. Some brought bravado to the lunch line. Weekly, one could hear bravado coming down the hall. What many white teachers may not realize is that all that bravado can be negotiated. Much of the "loud, entitled and attention seeking" behavior can be brokered with a little respect. If that's all a teacher sees in the brown kids, he will spend the entirety of the class screaming, "SIT DOWN; BE QUIET!"

As a former brown student, especially one who was also low-income and may have had an individualized education plan for Attention Deficit Disorder (or any other issue that may have interfered with my comprehension of math), I had little power at school. I sometimes felt like I was worth nothing. The very last battle to be lost for a brown kid in a predominantly white environment is "respect". If only teachers like Hank saw each kid's individual stories as they entered his classroom instead of a choir of thugs…

Now enter into the equation that we're talking about mathematics classrooms, which are high-stakes learning environments. What if the students were already nervous about math? What if they already felt "stupid" before they came in the classroom? What if they already were told that they can't learn math? If any of these "what ifs" had occurred, then ideally, a dose of affirmation could be an empowering response for the self-doubt the students might be experiencing. These same bravado students are treated, in extreme instances, as if the teacher is herding dangerous animals at the zoo. Can a student learn from a teacher who thinks the presence of his student is threatening? If you were a student struggling with math

140

and Hank was your teacher, would you feel comfortable asking him first, second or an eventual trail of questions about a subject you're fighting to understand? Would you believe that teacher cared about you?   I wouldn't.

Neither did his Pleasantville the students.

Chapter 27

A Red Line Between Love and Hate

One of the most challenging things I presume a doctor must do is determine which medicine to prescribe for her or his patients. As the pharmaceutical industry becomes more and more powerful and science gets more technologically advanced, I imagine the choices in medicine are nearly endless. What is the magic potion? What does the patient need to be healed? Will there be any side effects? Will the patient abuse the medicine? These same questions were on my mind as a diversity practictioner. Now that New Pleasantville and I had spent a year in conversation in an attempt to "diagnose" the problem, it was time to start thinking about treatments and solutions.

Professional development. The phrase conjures either tears of joy or stabbing needles into your eyes. No one is just tepid about professional development because it tends to be either really good or really bad. I wanted to steer clear of that polarization of experiences once I learned I'd have an opportunity to provide professional development to the Pleasantville faculty and administrators. Instead of providing some impersonal consultant to do a training session that no one would remember, what if we took the time to have candid conversations and grow together?

There were three major themes rising to the surface regarding nonacademic barriers to student success: implicit bias, behavioral health and finally, empathy and compassion. All three topics are incredibly abstract concepts. Before a sincere conversation about any of the three can take place, everyone involved must commit to be open to the topics. It had to feel personal. The trick was figuring out *how* to make it personal.

Perhaps the one thing teachers have in common, regardless of varied identity perspectives and walks of life, is a care and concern for students. No one wants to see a student fail, struggle or suffer. I figured I couldn't go wrong with the topics of implicit bias, behavioral health or empathy and compassion as long as I could tie it back to the students. So, contrary to how I might have been advised (had I been advised), I thought there was no time like the present to push the envelope and really challenge teachers and leadership to dig deep. The truth is that I was the only one in the district whose job it was to worry about warm and fuzzy stuff all the time. I needed a way to capture folks' attention quickly while they weren't swamped and bogged down with all the other exceedingly unrealistic expectations of educators these days.

A critical symptom of the behavioral health issue in our school district was drug and alcohol misuse and abuse. It seemed to me that we might gain some perspective on how the lifecycle of addiction begins and how folks hopefully and eventually find paths to recovery. Remember, Pleasantville was a community known for its veneer-like appeal. Bright, shiny, white and eerily perfect. Stepford Wife perfect. Donna Reed and Jane Cleaver perfect.

One of my challenges as the district leader regarding social-emotional issues was, in part, convincing folks that we even *had* a drug and alcohol problem. Can you imagine the challenge of selling the town folk on some parallel universe reality that Donna Reed snorted a little nose candy after the husband and kids went off to school or work? Or that Jane Cleaver made herself a hot toddy that was a little more hot than toddy? Why, shut your mouth and smack your lips! The problem with presuming that some of the kids in Pleasantville had substance abuse issues – as is the case with many kids in many suburbs across the United States – is that the parents automatically are at fault. The obvious questions bubble to the surface. Where would Johnny get alcohol or cocaine? Where are their parents while they're using? Didn't anyone notice that Johnny was drunk or high?

In addition to the film, Pleasantville, the town of Pleasantville also reminds me a lot of movie Fight Club. The first rule of Fight Club is that no one talks about Fight Club. The second rule of Fight Club is that no one talks about Fight Club. Well, many times it seemed like becoming part of the Pleasantville culture was like being initiated into a special club. The first rule of elite suburbs is that no one discusses its residents' dysfunction. The second rule of elite suburbs is that no one discusses its residents' dysfunction. The problem was that I, too, had a set of rules I followed; however, they were a little different than the Fight Club model.

I fancied "Rule Number Six", which is referenced in *The Art of Possibility* by Rosamund Stone Zander and Benjamin Zander. It ruins it if I tell you directly what "Rule Number Six" is; you have to read it for yourself. Here's my favorite passage from the book.

> *Two Prime ministers were sitting in a room discussing affairs of state. Suddenly a man bursts in, apoplectic with fury, shouting and stamping and baning his fist on the desk. The resident prime minister admonishes him: "Peter," he says, "kindly remember Rule Number 6," whereupon Peter is instantly restored to complete calm, apologizes, and withdraws. The politicians return to their conversation, only to be interrupted yet again twenty minutes later by an hysterical woman gesticulating wildly, her hair flying. Again the intruder is greeted with the words: "Marie, please remember Rule Number 6." Complete calm descends once more, and she too withdraws with a bow and an apology. When the scene is repeated for a third time, the visiting prime minister addresses his colleague: "My dear friend, I've seen many things in my life, but never anything as remarkable as this. Would you be willing to share with me the secret of this Rule Number 6?" "Very simple," replies the resident prime minister. "Rule Number 6 is 'Don't take yourself so*

144

damn seriously.'" "Ah," says his visitor, "that is a fine rule." After a moment of pondering, he inquires, "And what, may I ask, are the other rules?" ... "There aren't any."

Sure, my background and upbringing was leagues apart from that of the Pleasantville culture. I'd hoped, though, that once I got to know them, they would become more human than mannequin to me. In most cases, that proved to be true. There were some amazing and sensational folks in Pleasantville. But there was also a definite segment of the population who took themselves rather seriously; and, I'm willing to wager they weren't looking to enter a "confess, repent and be saved" community conversation. I wanted to notice and acknowledge the elephant in the room. Name her, introduce her to the group and make friends with her so we could lower our risk of being trampled by her if she felt threatened and became afraid. Those who had more to lose, more skin in the game, may have felt that pretending the elephant was invisible was the better way to go. God help us, if the elephant stirs, shoot her immediately with a tranquilizer dart.

Professional development took place for secondary schools in the fall. Since I was inviting the faculty and administrators to have conversations we'd never had before, I thought it might help if we had new conversations in new ways and formats. I crafted the three topics with three entirely differently-formatted designs.

For the behavioral health professional development session, I invited a colleague to come in and do an improvisation workshop. In the past few years, I had researched different unconventional but highly effective uses of different art forms. For example, there was a school in Detroit who utilized improvisation and spoken word poetry to decrease risky behaviors of kids in schools. My thought was that the professional staff in Pleasantville could use the art of improvisation to practice having conversations with students in crisis. Improvisation, I hoped, could be used as a de-escalation skill for students who were experiencing trauma. Research had already been done on the approach and since we were a forward-thinking school district, I thought we were ready for forward-thinking approaches on social-emotional issues as well.

Let's be honest about something and air out the dirty laundry right away. Nobody wants to talk about being prejudiced, biased or bigoted. The fact of the matter is that everyone –yes, even the brown, gay and estrogen-heavy folks – have the ability to exhibit those ugly behaviors. Conversations around this topic grow increasingly dicey with new vocabulary words like "microaggressions" and "implicit bias". We all want to believe that we're good people. For the most part, maybe we are. The truth, though, is that we all think, say and do things from time to time that aren't as warm, welcoming and inclusive as we'd like. It's easy to be in denial about this. Therefore, science was the best way to approach this topic, I figured.

For the implicit bias session, I leaned on ivy league-supported data. Thanks to good ol' Harvard, there's a beautiful tool called the Implicit Association Test. In just 15 minutes, anyone can go to a free website and take a test to measure their bias toward and/or against folks based on a specific identity lens. Fascinating stuff. The plan was for us to start a conversation on implicit bias by first taking the assessment and then using a storyboarding process to walk through our own experiences of race and class.

The final topic for professional development that the faculty and administrators needed to practice was empathy and compassion. These two virtues just might be the pinnacle of warm and fuzzy sentiment. How does one tap into the virtues of empathy and compassion, let alone practice them? Thanks to grad school, I remembered a powerful exercise called the "Fish Bowl". In this exercise, a few people sit in the middle of the room and the rest of the larger group sits in a circle around the individuals. The group then watches the individuals in the middle of the circle have an uninterrupted conversation while they observe in silence. At the end of the Fish Bowl, observers are welcomed into the conversation only through clarifying questions. The plan was to go deep in a feeling-based conversation with a few brave souls who were willing to bear all while teachers watched and ideally felt the conversation unfold.

I invited a brown alumnus and two brown current high school students as my Fish Bowl speakers to discuss their honest, lived race experiences as Pleasantville students. I knew how huge of an ask this was and felt an inexplicable amount of responsibility to protect these three souls who agreed to share their stories. Their vulnerability behind this request was so visceral; I had to personally ensure the mother of the current students that she could entrust her children's emotional wellness to me. The alumnus, a successful businesswoman in the city, was still so traumatized by her Pleasantville experience that she cried before working up the courage to join the Fish Bowl conversation. One by one, they poured their hearts out to a large gathering of Pleasantville staff. As they spoke, they nervously stared at their shoes and held the microphone with quivering voices and shaky hands. The hurt of their stories brought some to tears.

After the speakers finished sharing and left us to process, the room was so silent; some teachers hung their head in shame. White guilt was corporeal in the large room. After sharing their painful stories with the teachers, I opened the floor for staff to ask questions. One of the most profound questions asked was, "What can we do about it now?" I explained race issues for Pleasantville were much older than current staff of the district realized. To better understand how to resolve the issue, I suggested it might help to understand where it began – and the answer to that question was "redlining".

In the early 1950s, the practice of redlining was alive and well. According to the redlining practice and de facto segregation, laws had already done the guesswork for folks and told the citizens where they could and could not live as well as to whom they could sell the house.

Redlining laws were organized by race, class and gender with the best land being saved for wealthy white men. And as one may have guessed, the least valuable land was rendered to poor (and) brown folk. I shared in the professional development session that Pleasantville had, for many years, been a redlined community. Ironically, the same Pleasantville that was, in its origin, never intended to be home for black, LatinX and Jewish families now had enough diversity that brown kids were identifiable in its schools.

Most Pleasantville residents had no clue of its history of redlining, but the discrimination didn't stop there. I went on to further explain that once redlining became unethical and illegal in 1968, race-related deed restrictions kept many high-valued areas white and wealthy. Eventually, deed restrictions became unethical and illegal, too. Without legal backing, many suburbs relied – both consciously and unconsciously – on their historical reputations and the slow tides of change to stay wealthy and white for as long as possible. When enough so-called minority archetypes found success, and demanded homes in nice zip codes, the browning of communities like Pleasantville became inevitable. Very slow, but inevitable.

During professional development conversations with teachers on an in-service day, we discussed the moral imperative of race dialogue. We talked, too, about the relevance of race dialogue specifically in Pleasantville. Though the community resident turnover had been incredibly low over the decades, it was surprising how few of its residents knew about the cultural history of Pleasantville. To put the race dialogue into context, I walked teachers through a timeline of how we got from redlining to predominantly white schools with a small but steady increase in minority enrollment. This session had been dedicated to increasing a skill set for empathy and compassion. Though the information was ugly, I hoped that I'd hit a nerve and got teachers in the room to feel *something*.

Well, indeed, they did. Some didn't feel the emotion I'd hoped, though.

The week following professional development, I returned to my office and was met straight away with an impromptu conversation with my administrative colleague, James Peep. Apparently, he got word that some of the stories shared at the in-service day from the brown students "may have been jaded". I also received word about a conversation that rattled some of Pleasantville's educators about real estate. Word on the street was that some teachers took the confidential content of the empathy and compassion dialogue session home and in their personal households, expressed being put off by my *alleged* comments about redlining and deed restrictions. Perhaps it was too dark to be a truth of this perfect and peaceful village.

Before I had a chance to catch my breath from the fact that the "safe space" had been violated, I received concerning correspondence from Dr. Springsteen. He'd received an email from a very important real estate leader in the community who'd heard about the bold statements I'd made with teachers just a week prior. In an effort to be fair, Dr. Springsteen contacted me with open, curious inquiry as to what I said and let me know that the esteemed real estate leader had also requested a meeting.

It's easy to say race doesn't matter and is not a factor in a conversation when everyone involved is the same color. The challenge is that no one understands the intricacies of an entire race of people better than its own people. The old adage says that things are "business, not personal", but that couldn't be further from the truth. Those two worlds are constantly jumbled together. We bring all of our conscious and unconscious experiences, sensitivities, red-button topics and emotional scars on the table. We say we won't do it and then we pack all of our race-related emotions in our book bags and briefcases.

In preparation for my meeting with Dr. Springsteen and the real estate leader, I did serious homework on redlining and deed restrictions for the local area. I had no idea what kinds of things I'd find. I scoured and scoured, but I couldn't find the smoking gun. ...Until my white father stumbled upon an entire book chapter that documented how the greater city's suburbs were created.

On the day of the power meeting, I brought proof of redlining and deed restrictions. Heaven forbid the folks in the room take my word as bond. We settled into the chairs at Dr. Springsteen's table and I know Dr. Springsteen imagined he had provided a safe, non-intimidating and comfortable environment for us to meet. Maybe *they* felt safe, but I didn't. Though I knew Dr. Springsteen was an ally and had set expectations to ensure my success, what I saw and felt was that I was a young, brown professional female in the room with two older white men who absolutely knew the password to be admitted into the Good Ol' Boys Network. It didn't matter if they used the privilege or not. The point is that they had the access.

The round table was a lie to me. Circles suggest that everyone around them has equal power, but I knew that wasn't the case. I had the least amount of power in the room. I was present to "explain myself". I was there because I told Pleasantville that their lineage had participated in and benefitted from systemic racism. Pleasantville was a beautiful suburb from its inception. Lovely and lily – as in lily white.

Chapter 28

Guilty by Association

Still meandering in the month of November, I was struggling to be thankful for being gainfully employed. My second school year in Pleasantville was off to a rough start and I craved a quiet moment away from school premises more than the students. The rougher terrain during fall quarter cajoled me to show more assertiveness, more advocacy and more restorative practice than I had anticipated in my wildest dreams. I had battle fatigue. What I anxiously anticipated was the fresh start that a new academic quarter would bring. I needed a "control-alt-delete" and a clean slate or perhaps more drastically, a new beginning.

When students and teachers leave for break and school buildings get quiet, administrators feverishly go into planning and paperwork mode. These are the rare moments when we can concentrate and thoughtfully plan our work. Calendars are finalized. Forms are signed. Reports are written. Things get done. Though I'm more abstract than linear, I *do* like moving projects along in the process timeline. I want to see things get done and the paperwork is simply a method to the madness; a means to an end.

Among the many odds and ends that were included in my job responsibilities, I also over saw a grant process and a pool of money that was tied to one of the district's top initiatives – school climate. Teachers had the ability to write grants and if approved, to receive school funding to improving social-emotional needs or providing international and multicultural engagement opportunities for students. Oddly enough, this grant pool was also the only source of funding for personally-designed initiatives from my office. Unlike the other administrators, I had no discretionary fund. The thought was that writing a grant for my programs would automatically stimulate support and buy-in for my work. Completion of the paperwork for the grant included the acquisition of a host of committee and administrative signatures. Naturally, the understanding was that each signature indicated buy-in for the grant. While the process was a bit of a headache, I appreciated the intended collegial approach. It was a novel idea.

Afternoons were cold by this time of year. Letting teachers know that their grants were approved was a warm, bright spot in the day, though. My notifications were prompted by receiving confirmation from Central Office that all necessary signatures for respective grant applications had been acquired. As I fired out affirmation notices, it occurred to me that I hadn't received word about two of my own grants. That was rather odd, seeing as the grant process required my signature for approval. My curiosity was further stirred when the district public relations coordinator contacted me to verify my winter programming calendar. I couldn't confirm any dates because my calendar was contingent upon the approval of my grants. It was time to do some investigating.

Dr. Springsteen was a pop-up kind of visitor, which was fine by me. One afternoon during the break, he popped into my office with some familiar paperwork in hand – my grant applications. Sympathetically but plainly, he alerted me that Luke refused to sign off on my grants. Not only did he refuse to sign them, but he walked them to Central Office and notified the treasurer and superintendent of his lack of approval as well as why he disapproved. My visit from Dr. Springsteen was provoked, as it unraveled, by his curiosity to better understand the motivation and implementation plan of my grants. Apparently to the naked eye, the programs didn't appear to be substantive. To my mind's eye, the flank appeared to be influenced by cultural incompetence.

Grant number one was an attempt to link the culture of hip hop to potential student engagement. Having collaborated with hip hop DJs in the past, I envisioned inviting a DJ into the schools to work with students on academic links to the four elements of hip hop – MCing, DJing, breakdancing and graffiti art. The grant was based on a program I had created and administered at Downtown Community College a few years ago. My hope was that I could use the incredibly popular culture of hip hop to unite students of varied backgrounds while demystifying the negative stereotypes of hip hop. No signature; no buy-in.

Grant number two had been pitched to principals and guidance counselors in the district prior to it being written into existence. In response to the differing needs of minority females and self-esteem, this grant was based on hair as an entry point to an ongoing conversation about body image. "What if," I thought, "we could bring together a racially diverse group of girls and have various community partners give workshops on esteem and grooming?" Understanding that a predominantly white environment also has a predominantly majority standard of beauty, the workshop plans were designed to empower the "otherness" in beauty. No signature; no buy-in.

Icy winds blew outdoors but winds of indignation blew fiery embers of frustration inside my office. How could my grants get blocked?! How could a peer prevent my initiatives from coming to fruition with a single refusal of a signature? Immediately after learning what had taken place, I requested a meeting with Dr. Springsteen, the district treasurer and Luke, the high school principal. It took all of my home training to calm down, prepare for and enter the meeting as if I had some sense. I was ready! …Or so I thought.

On the day of the meeting, the four of us gathered in Dr. Springsteen's office under the direction of his facilitation. One after the other, we walked through the grants and the items in question. Early on, the treasurer, Craig, identified himself as a neutral party. He stated repeatedly in the beginning that he had no opinions on the grants; he was only present to verify that there was or was not money in existence to pay for said grants. Got it; he wanted to be a neutral bystander. His declaration clarified for me that there was only one person in the room who was against my grants.

Luke's handling of me felt patriarchal and ageist. He spoke to me like a teacher educating one of his slower students. He put me on the spot and quizzed me to make sure I knew what I was talking about. I became well trained to be prepared at all times when in meetings with him and this meeting was no exception.

"Fear of a lack of student participation" was the reason given for not signing off on the hip hop workshops grant. Luke stated that he'd seen a workshop I'd done earlier in the academic year and only about five students were present. He noted that they were just standing around and no one seemed to be engaged. I was afraid he'd say that, so I brought pictures and videos of the event. Based on my evidence, I proved that the DJ and I served an estimated 45 students at the event. I gathered that he likely peeked in on the first few minutes before students had congregated around the DJ. Still, buy-in was not achieved. I hadn't convinced him. The negotiation made between Luke and Dr. Springsteen was to fund my grant at one-fourth of the amount for which it was written. Instead of planting a mighty oak tree, I would receive trial seed money. "Let's see how things go," I was told. If I could prove that the initiative was successfully implemented, I could try to get additional funding to continue the program.

What just happened? How, as an administrator over an area where I was thought to be the subject matter expert, did I get minimized and silenced? My mind was whirling and my heart was racing. I could feel the fight, flight, freeze or fawn instinct welling up in my spirit. As gravity pulled on me in my chair, I wanted to scream. Looking around the table with older, upper middle class white men in all directions, I had never felt browner, younger, more female and more low-income-rooted than I did at that very moment. I just tried to sell hip hop from a social justice lens to my cultural opposites and in one fell swoop, my attempt was preyed upon and failed. I was dumb-founded. Conscious of being misunderstood, I pressed on in the meeting and felt the reaper slip into the room, waiting to take my hope with him.

"Fear of not passing future levies." That was the reason given for not signing off on the hair-themed body image workshops. The internal dialogue and self-doubt began. They didn't get it. They didn't understand brown girls. They couldn't connect with or receive the reality that our self-worth and self-esteem is heavily rooted in our hair. The notion seemed asinine to them. Beyond weight, skin issues, income levels or other image barriers, if a brown girl's hair is "right", all is right with the world. That's the sentiment I had attempted to write in the grant. But Luke and Craig articulated what they heard and read in my words. "We can't pass a levy if the community thinks we're paying for girls to get their hair done."

Oh, my God... I knew at that moment that I was in the room alone. With no levy even on the ballot for the next year or two, I heard an entirely different kind of fear in their voices. What I heard and felt – particularly as a brown woman – was that Pleasantville wouldn't tolerate the district financially backing and blatantly affirming brown culture. Heads would roll, I assume and no one was willing to put their neck on the line for girls who looked like me.

"I support your efforts in concept," Luke explained. "I just don't want to be associated with them." The statement was so bold and audacious I wasn't even offended at first. I assumed I misunderstood what he said. But he repeated the statement over and over; frequently enough that Dr. Springsteen himself noted the crassness of the phrasing. As its sting settled in on me, I was barely able to speak through my anger, frustration and hurt. I breathed I slowly and responded, "I feel unsupported. What if I told you that I supported you as an administrative leader in concept, but I didn't want to be associated with you. Would you feel supported?" I hoped that my inquiry would be received as an invitation for a little empathy and compassion. Instead, I was asked to "distance" myself from the word "associated" and hear that I was being supported. I assure you; by then, couldn't hear anything.

The silence in the room was deafening. Even more so as Luke asked Dr. Springsteen to <u>change the verbiage</u> on the grant application form under his signature line to say that he supported the program proposal "in concept". The former grant was funded at one-fourth the asking amount and the latter grant, after verbiage was changed, was approved – at one-half of its original proposed amount. Unbelievable. Inexplicable. Every girl in the district who looked like me was failed that afternoon. In my mind, the district just told me my brown community was only worth 25% and 50%, respectively, of its asking value.

As my young, brown, female skin boiled in the room. Luke then excused himself to go home for the weekend. Once he confirmed that his presence wasn't required anymore, he got up and walked out of the meeting. Craig, Dr. Springsteen and I sat in awkward silence, looking silly. No one knew what to say or do, but we all knew that the meeting hadn't gone well. Craig made a feeble attempt to apologize for and excuse Luke's behavior, but the damage was done. We all knew it. Perhaps I was expected to have perceived the meeting as a win because my grants were now live, but as far as I was concerned, my advocacy efforts suffered a great loss that day. Healing suffered a great loss that day. I'd hoped that my grants would support wellness with a little culturally affirming healing, but in my mind, what had transpired in the meeting demonstrated clearly that the district just got sicker.

Chapter 29

Break a Leg ...Seriously

Pleasantville was living life like an undiagnosed mental illness. Little did they know I was acutely aware of the difference between folks who are sick and folks who want to be well. My mother is one of my most important gifts. She lives with and fights to manage multiple mood disorders including borderline personality disorder, suicide ideation, Post-Traumatic Stress Disorder and social anxiety. You can imagine that these behavioral health conditions were challenging at best for her to manage as a single head of household. Thankfully, my mother has always been a model client and a star patient for her psychiatrists and psychologists. She takes her meds regularly and as prescribed. She regularly attends her therapy sessions. She is an avid student and lifelong learner with regard to her diagnoses. Watching her navigate the realities of behavioral health gave me a solid framework for patience and understanding.

I've seen what happens when behavioral health is still mental illness. I know what it looks like when people's brains lie to them. I've witnessed the struggle one has when living is excruciating and ideation over death conjures feelings of peace. I call them the "dark and twisted" places. We all have them, but those with mental illnesses and mood disorders feel them in a bigger and stronger way than others. My mother explained mental illness to me like an allergy. "Imagine having an allergic reaction to stress," she told me. I thought about all the things the average person stresses over. Homework. Jobs. Social interaction. Money. Health. Then I juxtaposed anaphylactic shock over the average stressers and I saw a glimpse of what she was trying to illustrate. There's no epipen for her condition. We just hope she'll survive her allergic reaction every 24 hours.

Wouldn't it make sense? If every stress you experienced felt like you were suffocating, vomiting up your small intestines, lighting your skin on fire and spinning in circles, wouldn't you do almost anything to find relief? Is it so strange, then, to understand why people drink themselves into blackouts or pop so many pills, they drown in their own drool? By no stretch of the imagination am I saying that I agree with or condone substance misuse and abuse, but I certainly get how it happens. I can absolutely sympathize with the desperation of wanting pain to cease.

The unfortunate thing about mental illness is that it is the great equalizer. Mental illness cares not about a person's race, class, gender, religion, sexual orientation, marital status, intelligence level, ability, or any other identity marker. While folks talk about their "spirits being low", mental illness is a very tangible and real thing. Even for faith-based folks, managing mental illness requires a "supernatural practicality" of sorts. Pray, yes. ...And then remember it's a chemical imbalance. It required therapy and medication. For those who have never seen mental illness close-up, it can be a painful experience for everyone involved. No one is immune; not even Pleasantville.

Upon my arrival to Pleasantville, I was handed a story of its secret dysfunction nearly every day. The common theme was crystal clear to me – mental illness. There were so many stories of human beings in pain. So many stories of alcohol and drug abuse. Sure, this folklore was the exception; minority tales in an ocean of functional, "normal" stories. However, I was hired to address the needs of those who were in the social-emotional *minority*. I needed to be partial to stories of hurt and pain. What I heard was a cry for help. Instead of focusing on the surface-level issues, I thought it best to go to the heart of the problem. We needed to go to the impetus for the bad behavior; the root causes. We were in a behavioral health state of emergency.

I'd been researching a new approach to behavioral healthcare for youth called school-based mental health. Its premise was that students, now more than ever, have increasing social-emotional needs that can't wait to be addressed after the school day is over. When the crisis of trauma hits, learning stops. School-based mental health presumed that behavioral healthcare can be directly imbedded in schools to help students in the moments when they most need clinical assistance. I was sold.

My next move involved reaching out to colleagues in the behavioral health advocacy industry to see what programs existed in the local arena for school-based mental health. Thanks to my network of mentors, I learned of a grant that could place a behavioral health clinician directly in Pleasantville's schools – and luckily, we were eligible to apply for the grant.

Winter break of year two was dedicated to conversations, baseline data sharing and conferences calls to complete Pleasantville's grant for a clinician to be provided by the metropolitan area's children's hospital. We were fortunate Children's Hospital was willing to partner with us and our collective team authored a beautiful grant proposal. Based on our needs and their programs, they planned to provide us one clinician with a specialization in trauma and another clinician with a specialization in substance misuse and dual diagnoses. This provision exceeded our highest expectations! It met the very needs we were deficient in providing to students with the greatest behavioral health and social-emotional needs. Not only was help on the way, but it was slated to be in place by the first of the year. The grant would cover everything. All we needed to do was provide office space for the healing to unfold.

To my relief, school-based mental health was one of the rare points on which Luke and I could come into agreement. The district's administrators supported the coming grant-funded initiative. After careful and thoughtful discussion at a couple leadership meetings, it was decided that the clinicians might best be housed right beside my office – the current home of the drama teacher, Bethany Mellow (AKA my hospital ambulance driver). We knew, however, that it would be no easy feat to transpose her and reclaim her office territory in the name of behavioral healthcare.

Our corridor was perpetually silent. Only two offices were housed in our hallway; Bethany's and mine. We were off the beaten path. If a colleague, student or parent stopped by to visit, it was understood that they were not "in the area". We had destination locations. One had to intend to come to us. For that very reason, the location was ideal, especially for private, sensitive matters. There was little chance at being seen or heard. There was privacy, seclusion and confidentiality in a little hallway dedicated solely to the mission of social-emotional wellness. It seemed like an easily agreed-upon point of interest.

Luke was the one who delivered the relocation plans to Bethany and as you can imagine, she did not take it well. News of the office acquisition was delivered in a couple doses and eventually word of the pitch trickled its way back to me. Once during an event of mine that was hosted in Bethany's black box classroom, she approached me for conversation. I was taken completely off-guard that she and I were speaking. After all, I'd tried to establish a working relationship with her for a year with no luck. We'd bonded over a trip to the emergency room and there had been no follow-up on her end since then. Naturally, I was incredibly intrigued about what inspired her to talk to me now.

The office. She was upset about having to leave her office and she wanted to talk with me about it. My medical emergency hadn't warranted further conversation, but an office move demanded immediate discourse. I could tell she was in the thick of conversations with her supporters and momentum from the supporter conversations led her to me. She thought I conspired against her, I figured. She must've reckoned I was a modern-day Christopher Columbus. ...A stranger to the new land, rewriting Pleasantville's history to fashion myself as a hero when, in fact, I'd attacked and dishonored the culture of the Pleasantville natives. Perhaps she deduced that I'd embarked on some suburban adventure, stumbled upon some awesome turf (her office) and simply reclaimed it in the name of, well, me.

It would be biased of me to say that thespians are dramatic. I will say, though, that she was not successful in masking her strong feelings about the move. In fact, she articulated them on more than one occasion. Weeks after her "carefrontation" in the black box classroom, she came to my office to talk – again. I'm not certain she'd ever stepped foot into my space before that moment. Her emotions were, again, palpable. She told me she hadn't been able to sleep. She'd cried over losing the office. Her parents were upset. Her students were upset and that, folks, was bad news. Bethany had a faction following with her drama kids and drama parents. In fact, she forewarned me that some students were preparing a petition for her to stay in her office, but she stopped them.

Having recently completed a grant battle with Luke and Dr. Springsteen, I was numb to what I discerned as someone picking a fight with me. A wave of passive-aggressive energy poured out of her and into the space between us. However, my numbness washed away any potential I had for anger or threat. "I know you have a large student following," I admitted. Bethany concurred, "Yes, I *do*." Her statement was uttered like more of a threat than an agreement. I lacked the energy to play chess. With apathetic eyes and arid voice inflection, I encouraged her to keep fighting for her space and she informed me that she would continue to do so.

Forget that Bethany laid claim to three or four spaces in the school. Disregard that her office's new purpose would be to house behavioral healthcare clinicians. Overlook that perhaps theatre kids – who might need some counseling as much as other students- might benefit from the new service. Bethany's prevailing emotions in that moment were threat and loss.

I acquired the office space, but at a cost. Those were our first and last full conversations. I was Christopher Columbus. I'd sailed in and reclaimed inhabited land. I'm sure the maneuver seemed cold and calculated. At the end of the day, I had to decide whether to appease one teacher or to house our district's forthcoming school-based mental health program. My objective was to be obedient to the moral imperative of the holistic wellness of students. I thought about my mother, who was a leading thespian in high school. What would she have asked for in retrospect? What would the high school version of my mother have needed? Without flinching, theatre lost but the future of school-based mental health for our students won.

Chapter 30

Rewriting a Bronze Renaissance

Professionals who claim to keep personal and professional matters separate are lying to you and themselves. It is impossible to separate the two. Humans are complex creatures. We don't have singular identities. Our experiences make up who we are and we tote all of them around every day into every situation. This phenomenon is also referred to as intersectionality of identity. Having the ability to keep business and personal separate is not unlike one's ability to mindfully choose to leave a limb at home. Unless one's limb is literally a prosthetic, this feat is impossible.

Midway through my second year with Pleasantville, I was finally able to admit I had absolutely brought all my identities and history with me into the new job, but I wasn't alone. Along with everyone else, my past experiences were playing out before my eyes. My implicit biases were alive and well. I didn't even *attempt* to keep my personal and professional lives separate. Jordan and our children, Charlotte and Paris, could attest to that.

During my senior year of high school, after attending five previous high schools, I made a promise to myself to be the same Kim everywhere and to stop assuming aliases. I made a commitment to always try to be authentically me. This promise was a double-edged sword. The blessing and curse of this promise is that I am the same Kim everywhere. Prideful Kim. Sensitive Kim. Activist Kim. That same uncensored Kim was present in every aspect of my job – and that may not have been an ideal approach, especially not in Pleasantville. I'm not sure I could have prevented it, but I had not yet mastered adjusting the volume of my authenticity; it was a skill I desperately needed.

After a year and a half of seeing invisible students – particularly brown and poor students – fading into nonexistence in Pleasantville's hallways and classrooms, I was growing sick to my stomach. In reviewing reports from the year before, I recalled a data point someone shared that Pleasantville's students were engaged at a rate of nearly ninety percent. That's incredible! However, when I looked more closely at the disaggregated numbers by race and then removed athletics, I discovered that our students of color were engaged in non-sports related activities at a rate of eighteen percent. That's appalling. I knew there was a story behind it. These disengagement stories reflected sentiments of those who were disenfranchised from Pleasantville's culture and community.

The first thing many teachers and administrators did when I shared the low percentage of minority student engagement with them was tell me how they had personally tried to recruit students of color into their programs. I heard about the "dog and pony show" class visits and infomercials of programs pitched to every student in the room. What they didn't realize was that different students with different experiences need to be invited differently.

We have become languid and unindustrious with our invitations. We don't want to customize and personalize anything anymore. We look for life hacks – even for sincerity. If you reflect on culture, though, it's easy to see why a slothful approach won't work. Brown men, for example, have had a long and arduous history of being marginalized, hurt and betrayed by systems. In many cases, invitations to them from systems were insincere. To marginalized folks, systems are often perceived as dangerous.

The Tuskegee Studies were an invitation from a system. The men who trusted scientists for a little money and a science project ended up becoming intensely ill and dying. Systems led to slavery. Systems outcast men from voting. Systems sent many, many men to prison. Systems split men from their families. This is just a demonstration of systems in relationship to brown men. You could likely find similar stories within any marginalized community. Hispanic and LatinX peoples. First Nation peoples. Asian peoples. And yes, African and African American peoples. What all these groups have in common (besides being brown) is a track record of being harmed by systems to which they did not belong. The current result is that these communities struggles to trust systems.

It takes exponentially longer for a white person to form a relationship with a person of color because people of color have inferred – either directly or indirectly – not to trust white people. Therefore, when an invitation is extended by a white person in a white environment in the manner by which a white person would normally expect to receive an invitation and said invitation is being extended to a person of color, we instinctively believe the invitation is a lie or at minimum, not intended for us. We don't accept invitations from people we don't trust. Simplified translation: If this invitation isn't from my people or brokered by one of my people, then the invitation is not real. It's lip service.

When you are already part of the group and new information is presented to you, it is understood that the invitation is yours. When you are or perceive yourself to be "other", it is understood that the invitation belongs to those who are part of the group, which you understand to *not* be you. For an invisible or othered student, an announcement of a club or a program means you can take a timeout from listening until folks are talking to you again. You eventually learn that invitations are not for you.

I saw the impact of a pervasive lack of belonging in othered students' eyes and body language. During the day, othered students moved through the building as if they were borrowing the space and working to ensure that they stayed in their lanes. **They weren't attending Pleasantville schools; they were surviving them and that is two very different things.** I'd lived that existence, myself and I knew how surviving something felt. For them, school had become a place to put your body until three o'clock. If there was life left in the body, true living would resurge at home. Where, then, were the opportunities for these othered and invisible students to engage?

I was fed up with employees of color, students of color and parents of color behaving as if Pleasantville didn't belong to them as well. However, I acutely understood it wasn't their fault. What they had not received – to date – was a sincere and targeted invitation. None of the engagement opportunities presented felt like they were for Pleasantville's brown folks. I wondered what would happen if I created an opportunity that was unequivocally designed and intended for students of color. And what if the invitation reinforced it? There were plenty of programs, speakers and events that were crafted with a typical Pleasantville student in mind. White, upper middle class, highly intelligent and highly privileged. So, what if the target audience, for once, veered off that path?

My state of mind reminded me of some of my darkest days in high school. Current times were reminiscent of when I used creative expression to "feel" when my heart and soul couldn't. I wondered if that might be the case of some of our students of color. We were, in so many ways, so similar. I, too, had battled school and a jury of my peers in brown skin, poverty and a disability (although the diagnosis of A.D.D. didn't exist yet). What I needed at the time was a direct, blatant and sincere invitation to be creative. I had an art teacher who knew something else was going on in my life that warranted distraction. He invited me into the visual arts – and more importantly, I believed his invitation was for me. Over twenty years later, I wanted to return the favor of that very special gift.

I had a bold idea for our district's education foundation and decided to work on writing a grant to them during the winter break. We needed to shake up Pleasantville with something bold and invigorating. Students and families needed something in which they could believe. Brown students needed a vehicle for authentic and creative expression. Students of color in Pleasantville needed their very own Harlem Renaissance. I'd name it the Bronze Renaissance.

I tried leaving no stone unturned with the grant idea. Go big or go home, right? I threw everything but the kitchen sink into the grant. I courted and recruited brown, male community artists who would serve as creative mentors to guide the grant program. According to my vision, the grant would consist of a monthly student creative workshop followed by a monthly open mic to showcase student talent. The workshops were to be managed by a brown, male actor and the open mic would be overseen by a DJ as a program and event host. As a finale, all brown student participants would finish the experience by attending a creative conference for artists of color that was founded by a local brown male visual artist and entrepreneur in the city.

As I spoke with potential vendors for whom I was planning to write into the grant, they could barely contain their excitement. One meeting with my brown male thespian resulted in a conversation for hours in my Pleasantville office. I was flattered at how impressed he was with my idea. It felt good to know I had done good work. More importantly, I was proud to have created something whose design components alone authenticated the intentionality of requesting the presence of brown students. I wanted them to know I wrote this grant with them in mind. I wanted them to see the opening showcase, application and flyers for the program and know that finally, an initiative had been birthed especially and specifically for them.

Weeks after submitting the grant, I received a call from Paula, head of the foundation office, as well as one of the foundation board members. Unlike year one, this wasn't a quick call to let me know that my grant had been approved. I heard in her voice that a follow-up conversation needed to take place – and I was right. I was told that the foundation wanted to support me. Yet, I was asked to explain myself. Thankfully, I trusted the relationship I had with Paula enough to have the meeting. If I had not done a great job of making my point, perhaps I could do a better job of convincing them in person that this was the way to increase brown student engagement in the arts to a number greater than an abysmal eighteen percent. This, I figured, could be an easy sell if I could effectively articulate my cultural intentionality and approach.

Paula, board member and I met a week or so later and they first articulated to me that they were on my side. Then they let me down easy. I was told in the gentlest of terms that they could not fund my grant as I had submitted it and Dr. Springsteen backed their decision, as its approval required his signature. From their lens, the problem with my grant was that it was written to be too exclusive. Alas, by developing an arts engagement program specifically for brown students, I'd made folks uncomfortable about not intentionally inviting the white students. Apparently, my bias reared its ugly head, but not against white people. My bias crept up in its desire to want to advocate for brown kids in Pleasantville who were implicitly and explicitly excluded from programs on a regular basis. None of those programs were halted, reprimanded or asked to change their policy and language. My program, written specifically for brown kids with an omission of a blatant invitation for white kids, was not supported.

Maybe it was me. Maybe I was being sensitive. Maybe I was wearing the meeting again. Maybe I looked too much like the grant's target audience. All I knew was that the news landed on me funny.

This was a sticky wicket. The reoccurring challenge with my Pleasantville colleagues and I was that I looked like the stakeholders for whom I was advocating. By wearing my work, often was received as defensive as opposed to being passionate. I felt the discomfort in my meeting with my two foundation colleagues from both sides. It seemed they didn't understand – as much as they wanted to –

how it felt to be brown in the walls of Pleasantville Schools. I suppose they feared I wouldn't make any progress in creating more inclusive environments if I was perceived by funders as being too brown. So, what was I supposed to do? I was brown; therefore, I understood what Pleasantville's brown people probably needed. Yet, I felt restricted from giving it to them.

I was given the "opportunity" to re-write the grant so the wording was more inclusive. In other words, rewrite it so white students would have just as open and clear of an invitation to participate as the brown students. What my foundation colleagues didn't understand is that by doing this, I effectively went back to Pleasantville business-as-usual and inadvertently communicated to the brown students, "This program *seems* diverse, but it doesn't belong to you, either." I knew my colleagues meant well and I understood their position as funders. I also knew that until Pleasantville was ready to intentionally speak to its brown folks, the awful eighteen percent student engagement rate for minority students wasn't budging anytime soon.

Chapter 31

Black Lady in the Back Room

I am allergic to my own lactate. Lactate (otherwise incorrectly referred to as lactic acid) is responsible for that burn you feel in your muscles when you've had a hard work out.

Over the ten years that I ran track, I noticed a pattern of having pain in my legs and experiencing a deep itch that I couldn't seem to get rid of. Worse, the harder I scratched, the more painful the itch became. After the itchy pain subsided, my body would be temporarily scarred with an intricate series of whelp patterns over the surface of my skin.

In my sophomore year of high school, my family practitioner diagnosed me as having an allergic reaction to my own lactate when I exercised at a higher rate. Essentially, every time I had a solid work out, my body broke out in what was identified as hives. The itch was originating in my muscle tissue, which is why scratching made the itch worse.

Though I knew that suffering was imminent, I continued to run track and to play volleyball in high school. I had long since fallen in love with track and field and I knew it was something from which I couldn't walk away. On the bad days, I suffered through attacks of hives and prayed that the endurance work outs would be few and far between.

Finally, however, priorities demanded I stop running track during my freshman year of college. Though my track and field days were behind me, I came to discover that hives weren't. The hives that were once only triggered by intense physical exertion became much more prevalent. As a child, jumping rope in the basement for a little exercise triggered hives. As a young adult, my sensitive body became more irritated by my lactate. Activities like walking too swiftly in the grocery store or briskly walking through a parking lot to go to a music concert had produced hives. What was once a stress reliever was now becoming a source of stress and physical pain. I lost exercise as an outlet.

After battling hives for the better part of 20 years, I found myself in a dermatologist's office with eczema-related questions. The topic of my hives came up and after a small but kind interrogation, my dermatologist was confident that she could not only repair my recent skin issue, but she had an idea on how to address the hives as well.

That month, I began taking daily allergy medicine. Though I had no seasonal allergies or even home-bound allergies to pets, dust or other stimulants,

Allegra became my new best friend. Within a week, a simple daily block of my histamines gave me back the power to walk my dog. I could chase my daughter in the backyard without an hour of itching. I could exercise again without dermatological pain. It was like a small but decades-long prayer had been answered; and, how simple of an answer, it was.

So what the heck does this have to do with Pleasantville? *Everything*.

I only half-jokingly rationalize to myself that the brown kids in Pleasantville were on some kind of "racism antihistamine". I imagined that each morning, they woke up, would pour a bowl of cereal while listening to music and took their daily vitamins. Along with the vitamins, they would also pop a "racism antihistamine geltab" to block all the usual nonacademic bad vibes from penetrating their psyche. These meds prevented the brown students from being able to see, feel, hear or sense, in any way, that they were being negatively impacted by racism at school.

Due to the "magic" of my antihistamine, my body can attempt to do all kinds of crazy things while I exercise, but thankfully I won't feel it. If I can't feel the reaction, then I can't suffer from it. I believe the same thing was happening to brown students in predominantly white school systems like Pleasantville. To tell the truth, I'm not sure if an inability to feel racism was a good or a bad thing for these children.

Prior to my arrival in Pleasantville, I had this nonsensical idea that I was going to be the answer to some secret subconscious prayers of the poor and brown students. Once I was offered and accepted the position with Pleasantville Schools, I deducted that the main reason why I was the right fit for the job was because I, too, was brown and had grown up poor. It was a no-brainer in *my mind* that I would be able to form a unique bond with Pleasantville's brown students. I figured they'd never had someone like me who worked for the schools and knew their experiences so intimately. I wasn't just a sympathizer of blackness and its accompany reality, I was living it right along with them.

Instead, something strange happened. When I arrived in Pleasantville, I discovered that many of the brown students – in particular – didn't seem to feel what I was able to feel. They didn't even appear to be in pain. It was almost as if they had been given something that hampered their ability to be able to feel race and class related oppression. Every time I walked down Pleasantville hallways in the school buildings, I sensed the tension. I watched students changing classes or in the cafeteria or walking home from school and see that the brown students were having completely different experiences from the white students. The painful part, though, is that I'm not altogether certain that the brown children could sense or see what I did.

After a considerable amount of time trying (unsuccessfully) to form relationships with the students via their own free will, unexpected conduct issues brought brown students to my office. Substance abuse. Though the Athletic Board (on which I sat), we implemented a substance abuse policy that first went into effect for athletes. Some of the first students who received discipline for substance abuse policy violations were male students of color. The new policy required that I work with the students and then recommend them to outside agencies to complete a series of community service hours.

During one meeting after school, I had the opportunity to meet with a young brown male student. He was new to the district and had come from a town that had a higher rate of diversity than Pleasantville. Waiting to finally form a connection with a fellow person of color, I began the conversation.

Me: So, how has your experience been here at Pleasantville?

Student: Fine

Me: What's your peer circle like?

Student: Good

Me: Have you had any issues?

Student: Nope.

Me: Have you ever noticed anything different about how they [white students] treat you?

Student: Nope. There are no race issues here. Everybody seems pretty cool.

Me: So, you haven't felt any discomfort re: race here?

Student: Nope.

Me: Do you know what my job is?

Student: Nope

Me: Are you curious to know what my job is?

Student: [Doesn't answer; just awkwardly laughs.]

Me: You have no idea what I do, do you?

Student:	[Again, doesn't answer]
Me:	What do all of you think I'm doing back here? Do you think I just sit back here in the dark with my feet propped up on a desk?
Student:	[Embarrassingly laughs as if I nailed his answer in my first try.]

My hope is that my jaw was only dropped to the floor in my mind. Here, sitting in front of me, was a handsome young brown student who apparently had no racism "detection system" at all. In fact, unless he wasn't being forthright with me, he seemed to think he was living in a post-racial society – a society of altruistic equity where the rights of each individual were honored and there was no longer any need for strong effort to enforce the laws written to grant them. He had friends who were from all different races. Everyone treated him kindly and fairly. The teachers had no ill will. The president of the United States was black. Racism was over and apparently, the real problem seemed that I was trying to re-create tense race relations where none existed in his estimation.

Yet, I knew what *the truth* was. I had been advocating for students like this young man behind closed doors for over a year. I had a front row seat to what adults inside and outside of the district really thought of people of color in general and especially, of black people. If I were to walk through the hallways of the middle school or the high school for instance with my arms outstretched, I believe I could actually pick up on their subconscious knowing that the school didn't belong to them. These schools belonged to the white students – and especially to the white students of privilege. The brown students just had some classroom chairs on lease. So how, when I could see, hear and feel all this every single day, were there brown students who talked about race in the same way we talk about cassette tapes? Like it was something folks *used to* have before we got rid of and moved on to something more sophisticated – like "implicit bias".

The very students I had been brought to Pleasantville to advocate on behalf of had *no clue* who I was, what I did or why. Further, they weren't interested in finding out. They didn't see the need to seek to have a relationship of any kind with me. They weren't curious about me. They obviously didn't pick up on my "hood pass" or my "street credibility". The fact that I was brown too was lost on them. My identity to my constituency had been reduced to the black lady in the back room. My skin didn't matter. My lens didn't matter. My advocacy didn't matter. From these brown students' point of view, I didn't even matter.

It was an irritating itch I needed to scratch. However, at this time, I couldn't do anything about it; and, it hurt.

Chapter 32

Planning Black History Month – The Sequel

It was a particularly cold new year. A school district that rarely closes for inclement weather already had three snow days under its belt. The bite of the frigid air felt oddly similar to the gusts sent forth my colleagues, especially Luke. Last year, Luke had bequeathed Black History Month programming to me instead of brown students and I happily accepted the challenge. So excited I was about Black History Month programming that I had begun crafting an idea by mid-fall of year two. I wanted to create an experience for the Pleasantville students – both white and otherwise – to learn about the origin and significance of historically black colleges and universities.

As we neared the edge of and then slipped into the winter months, the sting of implicit bias (unconscious prejudice for or against a person or group) frostbit my original programming plans. It seemed apparent to me that we needed something more meaningful and direct which addressed the issues that were passing through the school hallways undetected so far. I believed we needed something stronger than a "push"; otherwise, I predicted we would never have a *real* conversation about race. The white folks were too comfortable and the brown folks were too vulnerable (whether they realized it or not) to freely share their true, lived experiences. We needed a "nudge" or perhaps a firm shove into some form of an honest conversation.

Months before in September, one of my Pleasantville counselor colleagues sent me a curious and peculiar forward. It was a question – I'm Not Racist, Am I? …Except the inquiry was actually a film. A small company in California had recently released a new documentary about a diverse group of New York teenagers who took a year to explore what racism meant to them. From the looks of the press release, a wealthy suburban private school was hosting a film screening and community conversation. So bold! I had to be there. I made it my business to get in that room.

On the night of the event, as is always the case, every conceivable obstacle in tarnation tried to prevent me from getting to the event on time. I even thought about not attending. Something told me that I needed to be in the room, though. Tons of cars were in the lot and I nearly missed the entrance because I was so mesmerized by the gorgeous school grounds. The school complex was located in Creamington, a suburb I never frequented; one that was known for not being welcoming to people of color. Creamington was created during the redlining era and this town unlike Pleasantville, Creamington found a way to stay almost exclusively white and wealthy.

I walked into the film screening and the high-ceiling room was filled wall to wall. Avoiding the drama of crawling over the folks who better managed their time and arrived punctually, I opted to sit in an unoccupied seat available in the front row. From the first few minutes of the film, I was fully engaged. While not quite 'in your face', I was immediately aware of how honest the next two hours were going to be for me. By the ten-minute mark, the honesty hit an entirely different level.

During a workshop scene in the film, students in the documentary were confronted with the concept of institutional racism. I watched their struggle trying to wrap their minds around the idea of racism as a form of systemic power. For the rest of the film, not just the students, but the audience fought through the discomfort we felt inside of our hearts and minds. Even as a biracial woman of color, I sat – at the end of the event – feeling tense, angry, hurt, emotionally exhausted and at the same time, validated. By the conclusion of the event, we didn't come up with any answers, but we had a ton more questions to ask ourselves and each other. That was the moment when I knew I needed to bring the film to Pleasantville.

Pleasantville needed to go through that internal battle. A fight with our hearts and minds. The hope was that we'd come out on the other side of the struggle closer. That evening, I grabbed every piece of material I could find and within weeks, I sent an email to the film production organization to find out how I could create this moment for Pleasantville. We needed its push.

In what was one of the most opulent educational facilities I'd seen in a while, I sat in the front row and took notes feverishly during the documentary. You must believe my intent was to view the film from an objective, educator's perspective. The challenge as a brown administrator working in a predominantly white environment, however, is that I can't forget that I am brown. Being brown is *always* personal. I soon realized it would not be possible for me to get through the documentary without being moved emotionally based on my personal racial identity, my current work experience through the lens of race and my human being experiences as a biracial woman informed by both white and brown communities.

The deeper I dove into the film, the harder it was for me to watch. I ordered myself to stay engaged and not shut down, though. The movie and I needed to experience each other, I felt. So, I watched and essentially journaled myself through 90 minutes of intense emotion. I filled seven or eight pages of a pad of paper with the notes, chronicling my reaction. My jots read like a hybrid of summarized annotation and a personal journal entry:

- *Catering to white people*
- *What do you gain from deconstructing racism if you are white?*
- *_____, what I need you to know is…*
- *Being numb*

- *Take responsibility every time you don't check someone on something they've done every time it offends you*
- *Go there and talk about the things people don't want to discuss*
- *Folks grow from bad experiences*
- *Guilt is a feeling, not an action*
- *White people will never know what it's <u>really</u> like to be a person of color*
- *N-word: Why white people can't say it*
- *Silence doesn't work*
- *What is black?*
- *What is nigger?*
- *Is black and the N-word the same?*
- *If I get too angry, I'll become ashamed of who I am*
- *Do white people put in real diversity and inclusion work without people of color present?*
- *Ouch moments*
- *Dealing with unaware people*
- *Say something!*
- *Brown people learn to not mess with the white people*
- *The need for empathy*
- *Black hair as a major issue in blackness*
- *Easier to see myself as pretty when there's nothing to compare myself to*
- *What is home?*
- *The feeling that people are staring at me because of my color*
- *It's cool for white culture to say N-word*
- *Does the n-word have meaning anymore?*
- *How many times per day do you hear the N-word?*
- *Visualization experience re: N-word*
- *The weight and heaviness of realizing you're being oppressed for the very first time*
- *You can tell how people feel about you*
- *To get so disturbed you can't talk*
- *Pessimism – can't change a system*
- *Parents who don't want their children to think about race*
- *Some think racism is a figment of brown people's imagination*
- *Do brown people have real role models?*
- *Jennifer Yim's game: The American Dream*
- *If you treat racism like meanness, you treat it by telling folks to be nice; doesn't address the real problem*
- *What if you treat racism like a power problem?*
- *Racism*
  - *Hurts and controls brown people*
  - *Helps white people*

- o *Designed as a construct*
- *Bigotry vs. racism*
- *Whiteness: history has never clearly defined whiteness; it just told people when they weren't white*
- *Who has power to collectively oppress others*
- *What does "at risk" mean?*
- *Do we prevent brown movements in systems?*
- *Who does hip hop belong to?*
- *Is racism not a pressing issue for everyone?*
- *Does everyone have the ability to talk about race?*
- *Statements that ignore the system of racism:*
  - o *If you really apply yourself...*
  - o *Everyone has an opportunity...*
- *Transracial adoptee and biracial people whose reality is if they never had a mirror, they'd think they were white*
- *Courage to face race*
- *White folks whose entire pool of friends just so happen to be white; possible that it was happenstance and not on purpose.*
- *Understanding racism intellectually vs. emotionally*
- *Safety within racism – possible?*
- *White skin = better life and better treatment*
- *Wanting people to SEE the real me as a brown person*
- *Telling people "everything's fine", but it's not*
- *The challenge of fitting in*
- *"Halfies" as a derogatory name for biracial people*
- *Why are people poor?*
- *Why do schools share less or no history of brown people?*
- *How do we approach diversity in the classroom?*

Immediately following the screening, two individuals who were involved in the making of the film led a very large, predominantly white and moderately liberal audience in conversation for reflection. As a professionally trained facilitator, I recall feeling unsatisfied and incomplete with the conversation. My brain was trying to process and grow from what I saw and heard in the documentary. I could not sum up my discomfort simply with a word or a sentence (which we were prompted to do by dialogue facilitators). I felt as if I just witnessed some of my Pleasantville students on the screen, grappling with racism in an authentic way. It was painful and leveling for me, but what I also sensed was dynamic tension that could lead to real progress and transformative change. We needed that change and I was hell—bent on at least trying to find a way to make it happen.

Chapter 33

The Invisible Knapsack and the Privilege of Numbness

After *lots* of conversation with some of my colleagues on the leadership team as well as Dr. Springsteen, I somehow successfully convinced them that should screen the documentary, *I'm Not Racist... Am I?* in mid-February. Per plans made and agreed upon in collaboration with my colleagues, there would be two screenings – a double-screening during the school day for the entire middle school and high school student bodies. Then, there would be an evening screening for the greater community. As a bonus for our screening event, we also decided to fly in the director of the film to lead us in dialogue after the viewing.

It is imperative to note that because of the high sensitivity of the *I'm Not Racist... Am I?* documentary, the film company which owns rights to the film does not allow it to be screened in advance, nor does it allow the film to be screened without a representative from their organization present to debrief the film after a viewing. Because of those extenuating conditions, it was decided that I would send a letter home to every middle and high school student residence to inform and prepare families regarding the film content. I was also advised to provide each parent with a waiver option if her or his preference was to *not* have their student view the documentary.

What is the right and quantifiable number of details that should be shared for someone to be properly warned of danger ahead? My letter had it all, I presumed. A general movie description. Explanations of film components including controversial language. A two-week schedule demonstrating how we were preparing students and teachers for the film content. Websites to check out additional details about the film. We even inserted a withdrawal letter if parents didn't want their children to watch the film. I wanted to ensure we could all have an awesome journey into self-discovery for implicit bias, but I wanted to make sure that it could be done in as safe of an environment for all human beings as possible. I communicated that our intention as a district was to show the film and have follow-up conversations about race by using the film as a source for critical thinking about perceptions of race. Similar to the film's description of itself, we sought to invite our school community into dialogue about race and privilege with educators, friends and family members.

Letters were mailed, which means that the events were set in motion. I was thrilled that Pleasantville was finally going to show courage and have a "root cause" conversation about race. To practice our courage and aid teachers in preparation for potential impromptu student dialogue on race, I facilitated a 60-minute professional development session with them.

Once all middle and high school staff had gathered in the designated auditorium for the professional development session, I led staff through an activity based on the legendary article and checklist, "Invisible Knapsack" by Peggy McIntosh, a white female scholar and activist. Educators sat in pairs and shared personal stories prompted by examples from McIntosh's list, which included the author's perceived realities of white privilege that white people experience every day but seldom notice. I walked the room and watched as educators read through McIntosh's list, listened and shared stories with each other in the dyads.

We transitioned out of the activity with a TedTalk featuring Mellody Hobson who, in the video, discussed the difference between being "Color Blind or Color Brave". I wrapped up the dense professional development hour with reflection on isolated conversations I'd had with some of the brown students and parents. I shared with the staff that I knew of real instances where racism was reading its ugly head in our schools and how important it was that we have the forthcoming conversation with an open mind. In the hopes that our staff might be and stay open to the topic of race, I ended the session with an article by diversity film maker Lee Mun Wah called "The Privilege of Numbness". Mun Wah's concept of a privilege of numbness examines the possibility that when a person with privilege interacts with another who does not share their privilege, instead of feeling empathetic, it is possible that the person with power or privilege may not *feel* anything. He asserts that a person is not being intentionally callous to the perceived negative experience of the person without privilege, but rather, they are <u>numb</u> to how that person feels. …And that not being able to feel the pain of marginalization *is* a privilege.

In summary, we discussed the fact that a presence of different identity lenses means a presence of different realities. This difference fuels instances when we benefit from a privilege of not having experienced others' pain. The main purpose of the professional development with educators was to get them prepared for all versions of reactions to the film (including their own) – both visible and invisible. We continued work to manage and improve our own implicit biases to better support students with empathy (where possible) and compassion. Key factors in our preparation for student support is having **curiosity** to know what students' stories and perspectives are, beginning the practice of ensuring we provide **safer spaces** for students to learn and <u>be</u>, and exhibiting an ability to **affirm** student stories once they're comfortable talking with us.

Chapter 34

Protecting the Good White Kids

How would you describe "protection"? Is protection an entirely different concept for white people as opposed to brown people's concept of protection? Can you itemize what would need to be in place for white people to feel "protected", particularly in a predominantly white environment?

Suburban life was a new thing for me. Only since my mid 20's had I been exposed to perfectly manicured grass, a posse of joggers and an overabundance of sources of fresh produce. Whenever I was rejecting the transplant into a suburban community, Jordan's advice for me to, "Act like I've been here before" echoed in my head. Right. The problem is that I *hadn't* been here before. I had never been the only brown person in a high level of leadership advocating for a body of students who mostly didn't look like me, all while the students who *did* look like me wanted nothing to do with me. There is no precedent for that. I had never been here. My brain was unable to construct some alternate social reality for what was happening. Therefore, I was reacting to my environment; and, per my recollection of the climate, the environment undoubtedly was reacting to me as well.

The saddest thing about people who have become invisible and expendable is that they begin to believe they don't need anyone. We think of them as prickly, angry people sometimes. The interesting thing about advocacy is that the people who need it most tend to be the most silent. Meanwhile, those who have the most power and protection seem to be the ones wanting *more* power and protection.

As Pleasantville administrators, we were "getting our ducks in a row" to host the big film and I knew that the material was going to be painful for some of those watching. Sincere advancement in social justice work always involves some degree of pain. It's simply unavoidable. The right kind of diversity and inclusion work should be transformative. It should stretch you. That kind of growth is impossible without some measure of pain and discomfort. In preparation for what lay ahead, my hope was that the letters which had recently been mailed home were preparing students and possibly the parents for the potential opportunity at transformation.

The first 48 hours after the letters were mailed home, I only received one hateful email about the film. I'm smart enough to know that where there is one, there are others. I was relieved, however, that the boat hadn't been rocked any more violently than it had. I shared the email I'd received from a man in the community who thought the school had no business hosting a conversation about race. It just so happens my colleagues knew the man who sent the email and informed me that he was a bit of a community Grinch. No harm; no foul. I could proceed as planned.

Then another email came in about a week later. This email was from a mom of a middle school student. Per her self-identification, she was the mother of a white middle school student. While she seemed generally supportive of the district's intentions to have conversations on diversity and inclusion, she felt very unsettled about our plans to include the topic of white privilege in these discussions. They'd never really discussed any concepts like that – or any other topics of diversity, frankly – in their home and there was clearly a discomfort with me mailing information about a diversity talk home in the form of a letter. This wasn't the first time I was scolded for "mailing" home diversity.

This mother and I emailed back and forth a couple times. While I responded to her inquiries about support, accountability and advocacy for students, the information I provided her left her insatiable; I didn't understand what else she needed. Either I was blind to her authentic concern or deeper her concern had not yet been authentically communicated. Finally, after several email exchanges, she clearly expressed her concern. As we were preparing to screen *I'm Not Racist ...Am I?* to our students, she was concerned about the support I was preparing to provide to Pleasantville's *white* students. All this time, my focus was on dismantling racism and exposing the symptoms of implicit bias. Yet, here, a white mother wanted to make sure I was doing all I could to protect white students. She wanted to know what I was prepared to do to make sure the white students weren't made to feel guilty or carry the burden of racism. Sure, there were those racist people "out there" somewhere, but this mother was advocating for the *good* white kid – hers and the other good white kids at Pleasantville, too. She didn't want them to be made to feel bad simply because they were white.

I thought I was prepared for potential backlash. I even believed I was prepared for an avalanche of waivers from parents who didn't want to subject their children to conversations about race. Apparently, though, I was not prepared to protect the potential fragility of whiteness and white guilt.

Chapter 35

I'm Not Racist ...Am I?

"It's a great day for the deconstruction of racism," I thought while stretching as I rose to start the day on a frigid February morning. Salutations, Black History Month! Today was the day I'd been waiting for since the beginning of the academic year.

I had big plans for this day. It had been an incredibly difficult fall and winter for me. I'd invested in this day's efforts as justification for the pain I'd endured. Today, hopefully, was going to make the endeavoring all worth it. I figured, we had an awesome opportunity to transform together and today was the day the paradigm shift would begin. I was all smiles and full of energy. All bad interactions I'd had with students and colleagues were forgiven. I was all about positive intentions today. I walked out the door of my home claiming victory for the day. Today was why I had taken this Pleasantville job.

I arrived at Pleasantville High School in the wee hours of the morning and met Catherine, the director of *I'm Not Racist ...Am I?* in the school parking lot. The morning sky was still dark, illuminated perhaps only by her flushed nose as she entered the building. I got her situated in my office and we jumped right into the day. I took Catherine on a tour of the school property so she could familiarize herself with the spaces. She whipped out her film CD as if she was unsheathing her diversity sword. The high school auditorium was warm and ready. The middle school theater was not ideal, but we were going to make it happen, anyway. The events were scheduled to be staggered, so there was going be a lot of running back and forth, but the payoff was worth the inconvenience. Today was a day of atonement, amnesty and transformation.

Screenings began with our middle school audience and we could feel the angst and energy in the room. Due to privacies created by the production company, no one had seen the film but me. Websites were given and additional resources were made available, but I was the only one who had seen the film in its entirety. James, the middle school principal, gave a rowdy but obedient middle school audience directives as we adjusted for technology errors that had been discovered. Once all these issues were seemingly resolved, the lights went down and the journey began.

As an international baccalaureate middle school with high state rankings, my expectations were high regarding our students' intellectual capacity to process the film's content – even on a middle school level. Five minutes into the movie, though, I could hear them reacting to a student in the film who cursed. "If that ruffled their feathers, I thought, "they're not going to know what to do with themselves once we get ten minutes deeper into the film. Knowing that one of the most powerful moments in the movie was just moments ahead, the director and I sat in the theatre, waiting with baited breath to hear students' reactions to the film's take on defining racism and racists.

As predicted, when the line dropped, the entire room gasped, as if being signaled to do so by a cue card. Excitedly, my heart skipped a beat at what conversations might come from the film. Catherine and I popped out of the middle school theatre and paced down the main hallway drag to the high school theatre where students were being prepped to begin their assembly.

I looked out into the high school audience as the director and I took a seat near the front of the auditorium. A sea of white faces with little brown polka dots showing up here and there. For just a moment, a wave of uncertainty rushed over me. Had I made a mistake in trusting their ability to handle this moment? The next ninety minutes were about to contain a paradigm shift or the start of a mutiny. We did some stage setting for the high schoolers, lowered the lights and the roller coaster cars left the dock. Just as we'd done with the middle school audience, we waited until the section capturing the new definition of racism was given. Again, the collective disturbance in consciousness moved the room. I could feel the line hit the students all at once. It was uncomfortable and just what the doctor ordered.

Just as I was settling in to acutely tune in to the breaths, sighs, and body repositionings in the high school auditorium, I received a text on my cell phone that something was going wrong in the middle school theatre. Technical difficulties. Apparently, the film kept starting and stopping. The volume was irregular. At the moment, James tried to gain back control of a room full of pubescent teenagers after twenty or more minutes of solid non-play of the film. We had no technology and audio-visual support in the middle school theatre. Murphy's Law had entered the building.

Catherine and I continued running back and forth between the auditoriums, but by the time the middle school's technical difficulties were resolved, time was up. Students roughly completed much of the film, but the bell had rung for lunch, leaving no time for even a *brief* decompression session with the film director. We scurried back down to the high school students to see if we could do a cleaner wrap up of the film.

Upon the close of the film, the high school students offered a resounding applause and immediately jumped into a rich question and answer session with the director. Though my jaws were tightly clenched in apprehension when the dialogue session began, I quickly relaxed and was impressed with the amount of maturity and push students demonstrated in their questions. It was obvious that not everyone was able to catch every lesson to be learned, but there was no doubt that the documentary had made the students think about race in a deeper and broader way. While there were several students who angrily prickled over the notion that they could be racists

176

(by the film's definition), others had experienced ninety minutes of affirmation. One student even stood up in the auditorium and apologized for ever offending other students. Another challenged her white peers to stop thinking about themselves and their complaints about whose fault racism is. In fact, when the bell rang for the high school lunch, at least 10 to 15 students stayed after to have conversational moments with the director.

Predominantly young ladies and queer or transgender students. Wouldn't you know it? The human beings stereotypically known to be wired for having a higher empathy skill set were the ones most moved to continue the conversation. That moment... At that moment when 15 or more of Pleasantville's bright minds chose a conversation about race over eating lunch in the cafeteria, I knew that bringing the film to the district was the right thing to do. It had already changed some lives.

As the conversation came to a close, a student who I was beginning to get to know named Heidi came into the auditorium. Most of the other students had departed to grab a quick bite to eat before the start of their next period class. As Heidi, a board member, the director and I talked, Heidi looked troubled. When we inquired, she shared her frustration with her friends through a teary-eyed and vibrato-accompanied complaint. Though she was liberally wired, her friends had become angered by the film. Her cheeks were flushed and her heart was broken. Heidi felt, at that moment, like she didn't even know who her friends were. Their words laid on her so cold and crassly, that she left them in the lunch room. As the bell rang for the next period of classes, I gave Heidi a hug and wrote her a pass. She smiled with hope after the wise women gave her a pep talk and her long blonde hair swished through the auditorium doors to class.

Yes, the rewards were already coming in. I had done the right thing.

Chapter 36

The Scandal of Talking About Race

After the school screenings of *I'm not Racist ...Am I?*, I was under the impression that the day had gone well. No major issues came my way. I *was* visited by a white male student who didn't understand why I selected the film and told me his friends stopped watching the film and started listening to music on their phones within the first 10 minutes. Other than that criticism, there seemed to be no fires to put out.

By the evening film screening, though, tides had shifted. After school, many white students complained to their parents that they were told they were racist. Students were furious over the accusation and so were their parents. In response, a handful of angry white parents came to the evening screening; however, most parents and community members responded by *not* attending the evening screening. In an auditorium with the capacity to seat well over 400 people, Catherine and I hosted less than 70 people at the evening film screening. Among those 70 were a few who came and defensively engaged the director to express their disapproval and disgust. Their perception was that the school district endorsed a film which labeled all white people as racist. Additionally, some criticized the content Catherine's film as well as her approach on the topic of racism. It was an excruciating two hours.

Eventually, after the high school building emptied, I escorted Catherine to her car. Between the two of us, we struggled to formulate an intelligent thought about what had just transpired. She wished me luck in my continued work with the district and I wished her safe travels. That night, for the first time, I felt unsafe driving home from Pleasantville.

I had a sneaking suspicion that the ripple forming in reaction to the film was going to turn into a tidal wave – and I was right. I tried to shut off any connections to Pleasantville, but in the last year and a half, I had become hypervigilant about checking and responding to email messages. There had been too many times this academic year when I was required to battle via my inbox or rally the troops in a carbon copy message. Regardless of day or time, I had grown to believe I had to wear my armor at all times. I kept watch with email. Used it as my signal to let me know when I could rest and when I needed to fight.

That movie. That cursed movie followed me home. That movie friended me on Facebook. That movie followed me on Twitter. That movie invaded my privacy and broke my rule of never taking work home. It worsened my addiction to my smart phone. Instead of waiting for the bomb to drop back at school on Monday morning, modern technology allowed me to see my character being assassinated in real time. My phone signaled me at least twice in one evening. I received private

179

messages from parents in Pleasantville. One message was from a wealthy single brown mother of two children who wanted to feel me out and chat with me. It was as if she wanted to "told you so" me, but in an awkwardly supportive way. She requested a meeting with me as soon as school was back in session. Having the ability to navigate a little of both worlds, she wanted me to know what the conversation was in the white community about the movie and what narrative was being created in the school community as well.

I'd seen the high school dynamics play out, but in the mad dash to navigate two film screenings at once, I'd missed the middle school fall out – and apparently, it was bad. White students were hurt or furious at the news that they, too, were racist. They were horrified at discovering via a Black History Month documentary that they were being raised by white parents who were also racist. All this time, they'd believed themselves to be the "good" white people, some of whom had voted for Obama. Yet, here we all were. While I hid in the bedroom of my home, some thirty minutes away, Pleasantville residents were in their tree-lined suburbs, violently purging the notion of being called racist out of their bellies.

It was an extended holiday weekend and Pleasantville's residents had nothing but time and fury to process the film. They watched ninety minutes of material to critically think about race and the common theme that resurfaced repeatedly to them was, "All white people are racist." Another brown mother of a Pleasantville student reached out to me and made me aware that the white community was not pleased – with the film nor with me. What I'd launched as a platform for a community conversation on racism had been received as the highest form of confrontation from a brown girl, no less, who didn't seem to "know her place". I had taken the exploration of diversity a little too far.

My email inbox began filling up with emotions. I was copied on a single white mother's angry and tearful message to district leadership. I was copied on a message inquiry from one of our education foundation board members asking who was responsible for the film screening. He also inquired about why we used so much time and resources to talk about racism in comparison to how little is taught on the Jewish Holocaust. I was copied on a message from James to a powerful community leader where he stated that the school district "missed the mark with the film", that we did not properly prepare students or staff and that we did not offer the most effective ways for students to debrief. James further said in writing – in a message on which I was copied – that the film is not something he would approve again and that it was an error in judgment on his part to approve showing the film. I imagined him as Pontius Pilate, washing my blood and the film reel from his hands.

Dr. Springsteen replied to some of the email inbox chatter by sending out a message, supporting my bold move and suggesting that the film served its purpose to get people to talk. I also received an email from a friend who thanked me for showing the movie. Interestingly, though, there was silence from Pleasantville's brown families.

It had been a long week and I sat, mid weekend, on my bed and felt my mind beginning the process of dissociation. I was overwhelmed and alone. I'd always thought of myself as a pretty strong and resilient person, but my body was about to fail me physically, mentally and emotionally because of widespread freely verbalized negative opinions and words attacking me and my choice of educational tool. I could feel it. I felt myself shutting down and needed to go away to get through this. Halfway across town, I could feel how angry Pleasantville was with me. In some cases, anger was too soft of a word. Venomous hatred. Some loathed me. Some used this moment to write me off and prove me to be effectively irrelevant. And I heard that young white man in my head again, clearer than before, "They think you're a joke." I knew it was true.

"Stop reading them," Jordan implored. Put down your phone, turn off your laptop and stop reading them." Though the message receipts had slowed, I couldn't stop reading them. I didn't know what to do. As a leader, I believed I owed people replies; perhaps not apologies, but explanations. My character and credibility was on the line. More than that, though, I began feeling something I hadn't felt in nearly twenty years – hopelessness. The opposition was daunting.

My weary eyes scanned a message on which I had been copied and insulted in the electronic public company of six or more of my peers. My flesh burned as if I'd space traveled and floated too close to the sun. Cheeks hot and red, I was humiliated. I felt uncomfortable in my skin. I stirred inside, trying to get out of it but I couldn't. I wanted to be strong, but I felt so close to giving up the fight. My eyes blurred, covered with a storm of emotion and my hands slowly floated, palms up, to my face. I was so embarrassed and hurt, I felt compelled to hide my face.

Twice, maybe three times, I started email replies. I'd been working on an email to my colleagues and couldn't finish it. The shame was too heavy in my hands to finish typing. As I sat there, face in hands, my unfinished and unsent message glowed on the screen:

All,

Thanks for keeping me in the loop regarding responses to the film, I'm Not Racist... Am I?. I value being in-the-know about the internal and external conversation. As a matter of transparency, I thought I'd share this attempt at a fact-based response with our principals and educators so that we are all in the loop.

Regarding the film, I'm Not Racist... Am I?, I have received ongoing critical feedback from principals, teachers, parents, community members and students. Feedback has been both direct as well as indirect and about a myriad of points including but not limited to:

- *Lack of teacher prep to navigate conversations about race and racism,*
- *Developmental inappropriateness of film for MS and HS audiences,*
- *Lack of teacher and parent ability to see the film before student screenings,*
- *Lack of proper prep for students to digest film content,*
- *Lack of preparedness for technical/AV set up at the MS screening,*
- *Deficit in film director's ability to facilitate student dialogue after the film,*
- *Lack of solutions offered by me or the director,*
- *Void of format for students to immediately and meaningfully process the film after the screenings,*
- *Deficit in properly informing audiences of film controversy*
- *Lack of film presentation from an educational lens,*
- *Film's alienation of white allies re: race dialogue, etc.*

What is concrete and undisputed is that the buck stops with me regarding this initiative - and I take responsibility for its failure. Though I have also heard about some dynamic pro-social conversations that took place after the film screening, the loudest voice I hear is that the film was viewed, contrary to my assessment or point of view, mostly as being offensive, divisive and not seen as an appropriate tool for critical thinking about race, especially for middle school and high school students.

I clearly overestimated our readiness for the film's content on all levels. I also hear that my efforts in preparing both students and parents, concerning the meaning and intent were comprehensively a lost opportunity. Further, I believe my "privilege" as a diversity practitioner prevented me from processing prickly parts of the film accurately for a Pleasantville audience. I have a high tolerance for "prickly" and as a person who lives inside of several marginalized identities, I am a passionate advocate for the underdog. In my fierce urgency of "now" with regard to supporting the invisible yet existing minorities in Pleasantville, the lens I failed to empathize enough with our white community members. These community members were offended and hurt by the raw nerve hit within the first 10 minutes of the film. In this situation, I am proof that diversity and inclusion is a *practice* and that we never perfect its application as human beings. As I have said many times before, the only way to minimize implicit bias is to have increased interactions so we can seek to better understand a perspective we don't have. In an effort to practice what I preach, I am seeking to better understand the Pleasantville community so that I can help repair wounds from the film.

*My personal feelings aside (and I have LOTS of them), let's move forward.
Below is how I am proposing we do that and I need your help for the
execution of these plans.*

1. *A facilitated community conversation with middle school students
   comprised of many small group dialogues around 3 meaningful
   questions.*
2. *Teacher-facilitated dialogue with high school students in their
   homerooms. I am proposing that students complete a
   questionnaire on race in homeroom and then return the
   questionnaires to the high school office.*
3. *Brief scenarios for teachers to reflect on and discuss in staff
   meetings. I have developed a list of 15 concrete strategies for
   processing discomfort (attached). My suggestion is that existing
   or emergent teacher leaders talk other teachers through these
   scenarios – a little bit at a time – at staff meetings.*

*I would like a more public medium to address the many points of concern
- not in a defensive way, but in an accountable and "next steps" kind of
way. You know your school community best. So, what format would be
most appropriate for the Pleasantville audience - a letter home? a written
post on the website? a short video? ...Of course, this would be in addition
to plans we have to talk with students and community in smaller group
formats.*

*For what it's worth, I hope this answers some of your own lingering
questions. I tried to the best of my ability to think this response through
rationally. My apologies if you feel my tone is defensive. I don't mean to
be.*

Yours in wellness and diversity,

Kim

In second grade, I somehow contracted Scarlet Fever. For days, I held a
high temperature. So high, in fact, that a rash formed on my skin. I missed a short
but significant amount of school, so my mother was in a hurry to get me back to
school. Though I was well, the effects of the Scarlet Fever were quite visible upon
my return to school and my peers. The fever and rash were very real, but now that
I was healing, my body communicated that I needed a new layer of skin. Over the
course of the next week or two, my skin gradually peeled off especially on my hands
and feet.

At my elementary school, we started each morning – weather permitting – by lining up by grade, saying the Pledge of Allegiance to the flag and singing a patriotic song. Once complete, the younger students would hold the hand of their line partner and walk into the school building. My first day back after recovering from Scarlet Fever was a rude awakening. I had created a fantasy in my head that someone would have noticed I hadn't been in school and would have missed me. In reality, what they noticed was my peeling hands. My line partner's face scrunched up. I was a leper to her. If I thought the school nuns wouldn't have had a fit, I would have run off of the playground to somewhere far away where I could have never been found. But I stood there. I stood there and was shamed for my body healing itself.

Thirty years later, I sat on my bed with my face in my hands. I suppressed what tears I could, but the others made salt water trails to my lips. I couldn't move. In an instant, I was that same little girl again, standing on the blacktop, raw skin exposed, and not a soul to be found who was willing to stand up for me. No words came to me on what I should say. The more alone I felt, the easier it became to feel afraid, threatened and harmed. I knew, as my hands held my face and my head up, that I was entering another period of transition and it was going to be painful to my lambasted and lacerated psyche.

Chapter 37

When Internal Fighting Spills Out

There is a network of folks who were nerds in primary and secondary school. We were pedigreed into adulthood differently. We have different skill sets than those who were the recipients of crushes, fanfare, automatic acceptance, Valentine's Day carnations, sleepover invitations and first picks on dodge ball teams. We learned to pocket our enthusiasm about the joys of learning and knowing the answers to problems. We attracted attention for all the wrong reasons and we developed an entirely different arsenal of conflict management skills.

Though least prepared for confrontation, school nerds like myself often found ourselves at the center of tension on a regular basis. Though trying our best to be invisible, every fiber of our being cried out to lords of the top of the food chain, "Notice me! Exploit my weaknesses! Make me smaller!" Our wishes were often granted and as such, our skin transformed in a different kind of way as we got older. It didn't really get thicker. That would imply that we are tougher and suffer less when pain is inflicted on us. That's a lie. It still hurts as much now as it did then. In some ways, the pain hurts worse now because we're emotionally exhausted from the experiences which, in and of themselves, made pain a constant companion. Instead, the best way to explain our skin metamorphosis is to say that we develop a higher threshold for pain. There is a gift in expecting something to hurt and enduring the pain anyway. That's what old nerds are able to do.

You can't always tell who of us did time as a school nerd. We look different now. Application of our brainpower as a form of work equity served us well. Now we can hide among the normal. We purchased contact lenses. We sought braces or other dental and orthodontic treatment (or had them removed). With brains came degrees and decent jobs and a little money. We traded in the bus passes for cars. Then nicer cars. The tattered threads turned into woven billboards and with some important person's name written on an inside label. But this just counts for those nerds whose identity badges were one-dimensional and could be rendered invisible by choice.

What about disabled nerds? What about multilingual nerds with discernible accents from a native land? What about brown nerds? Even with enhanced vision, perfect teeth and stylish clothes, not all outcast identifiers can be helped. Success doesn't straighten bent limbs and give sight where it didn't exist before. Success doesn't take native tongues and flatten "R" and "L"s to sound like they're from the Midwest instead of South American or the middle east. And success surely doesn't make black or brown skin lighter and wide hips narrower. So, what of the nerds with hangtags? Nerds who translate conversations twice before answering? Nerds whose skin color would have made them "the help" fifty years ago? Remember, nerds do not necessarily develop thicker skin. We sometimes just get marginally better at absorbing pain. Where does that leave us?

It is still Black History Month and though the shortest month of the year, February is lasting an eternity. It is mid-February and my brown nerd body is still absorbing the pain from public reactions to a film I presented on racism. If possible, that resulting email thrashing made my skin feel thinner than ever before. ...Like it might tear if hit at just the right pressure point, but my nerd threshold for pain taught me to never let on how much things hurt. Never give folks the satisfaction of letting them know I was suffering. Never let them discover I was as weak as they may have anticipated or hoped to bow me down. Swallow pain.

My attempts at proposing different student and community forums to talk about the documentary together had failed. Students weren't ready. Logistics were unfavorable. My plans didn't often reach the main administration offices of my sincere effort to ease a strained situation. Our facilities couldn't house everyone at once. Teachers weren't trained. Teachers weren't ready to manage questions they had not anticipated having to answer. Emotions were still raw. Too many snow days had eaten up excess teaching time. There was simply no time to left talk about racism during the school day. Luckily, I had already carved out an evening forum for the school and community to come together. The conversation was carefully planned so we could collectively process what we heard, felt and learned from the movie. This was the next step in our healing and what we could do together and where we needed some help.

I selected my favorite elementary library in one of the Pleasantville elementary schools and set up the room with snacks, handouts and writing utensils. My body was still frozen with anxiety and I knew why. Emotions were still like electric in the air and I was still public enemy number one for showing a 90-minute film that, in one section approximately three minutes long, had upset Pleasantville by indicating under certain circumstances, all white people could be racist. I was a bad taste in the mouths of many community members who considered themselves to be good people. The aim was to be part of the solution instead of part of the problem. Folks who considered themselves to be against racism. Folks who I knew to be recipients of the benefits of a system of racism. Racism without racists. I was still an enemy. Here I was throwing a talk party and thinking people were going to come and give me a second chance to pitch a teachable moment. High threshold for pain was my skill set, though; not theirs.

Once the hands of the clock lined up perfectly from north to south and no one was in the library yet, I knew something was off. If this had been a parent booster meeting for theatre, band or gifted and talented, the room would have been packed. Folks would have arrived early. Chatter could have been heard from around the hallway before one arrived at the library doors. Instead, I could almost hear the spiders crawling inside the walls. Several minutes past start time, I began speaking. "We can't do the agenda I planned for you today because we don't have

186

enough people," I confessed to the seven bodies sitting in the library. A parent and student. A teacher. A school fundraiser. Luke, Dr. Springsteen and the public relations representative for the district. "Here is what I'd hoped we'd talk about," I began as I walked through the agenda. I showed them poster sheets taped to the bookshelves of questions written in perfect penmanship that we couldn't really answer together. I offered thoughts and background information. Then I braced myself for pain and counter-intuitively solicited them for feedback.

Dr. Springsteen backed me 100%. He talked about feeling uncomfortable while watching the film and how he believed that discomfort was a good thing; a measure of growth. The teacher mentioned how he'd led his homeroom students in engaging conversations about the film and about race. He credited the film for those conversations and mentioned that his completely white class spoke about the film differently than his class with even a few black students. For the first time, he shared, the black students spoke up. It was a big moment. The district public relations officer and the development officer also shared having productive conversations and appreciated honest introspection on race that the film asked and required. Positivity. Honesty. Support.

Then the parent and student spoke up and shared a disturbing experience about how the middle school student had experienced overtly racist comments about her appearance in our school – on our watch. With no protection, she hadn't trusted us to come forward. All of us in the room felt the mother's exasperation and frustration. How do you relieve this kind of pain? How do you ensure it won't happen again? How do you explain that a school full of white students has not had enough practice being around brown people like you and you just have to roll the rock up the mountain until they catch up to understanding your pain? The room fell silent with no answers and yet I understood personally how the mother felt. Was Pleasantville the right place for her beautifully brown girl? For her warmly brown family? Had moving here been a mistake? What was there to gain at Pleasantville? What were they at risk of losing if they stayed any longer? Did we even deserve their trust to do no harm to their family?

How could we answer that unspoken question? My personal experiences with Pleasantville alone had proven to me that the community wasn't ready to face its issues of race and racism. I knew she and her daughter were in pain because I was in pain, too. We were suffering together in many of the same ways. What hurt most though, is I knew that the white folks in the room – even those who were in touch with and sympathetic to our pain – still didn't understand how intensely we were suffering. How the very core of who we were had been violently shaken. Though the number of was small, we were getting somewhere with the conversation. I was grateful this moment wasn't turning out to be a waste of everyone's time. Still, I couldn't breathe yet. Luke was in the room and he hadn't spoken, which was bad no matter what. Either he wasn't speaking because he wasn't "there" or he wasn't speaking because he was loading his weapon.

As principal of the high school, Luke heard the mother and daughter's story with completely different ears as I could have predicted. He heard stories of white students using the n-word with his administrator training and his administrator hat on. He thought punitively, but I cautioned him that there was more to the scenario than punishment. From thin air emerged our conflicting schools of thought for the whole group to see. In a scenario where a white student used the n-word, Luke wanted to find the student and discipline him. My argument was that discipline for racist or bigoted behavior would not truly fix the problem. Sure, in the immediate future, the student might be slow to use the n-word in a public space where he could be caught, but the bigger challenge and the greater work is to stop the student from seeing an analogy between black or brown skin and the n-word. That kind of work takes longer, I argued, but was at the core of true social justice work.

Luke vehemently prickled at my words. From his lens, our work in K-12 school systems was not to teach principals (or students) about social justice. Our focus, in his opinion, should be on core curricular academics. Our focus should be on prepping students for strong academic success and mastery of competencies on standardized testing. His belief was that we should be focused on closing achievement gaps, not on social justice movements inside the school system. We went back and forth and the conversation escalated. I regretted losing my temper and coolness in public. I have more at stake than he does when I lose my cool. Angry white men are viewed as passionate debaters. Angry brown women are viewed as defensive, emotional and hood or "ratchet". Passion in public seldom serves us well.

The meeting reached a close with the other five attendees sitting in silence and Luke and I scarcely agreeing to disagree. He left quickly as did a few other attendees. Lingering after the meeting to walk out of the room with me was Paula, the foundation director. Having no prior knowledge of my recent history with Luke, she pulled me to the side in the hallway. I read worry on her face as her brows knit while looking up at me. "What's going on with you and Luke?" I felt my face heat as the remaining anger I was holding in released itself under my skin. I needed to confess. "Could you tell?" I asked her with slight embarrassment. "Yes; we all could," she confirmed. I felt both relieved and vulnerable.

As we walked to our cars in the parking lot, I shared a fraction of what I'd been going through with her. It was heavy. It was too much and I knew she didn't know what to say or do. I needed to hear I wasn't crazy. I needed to hear the pain I was feeling was worthy of tears and I was being a brave soldier for not crying. But I know she didn't know what I needed to hear. Instead, she offered a sincere, "I'm so sorry." Her eyes met mine and I swore for that moment she was hurting, too. She wanted to support me; I knew that I felt that. And yet for some inexplicable reason, just the fact that she could never feel or understand exactly what I was feeling made me feel even more alone.

I still had my nerd skill set. I sucked all the air into my lungs and braced myself, as usual, for the bully to punch me as hard as he could in the gut. When it inevitably came, I took that punch. I had tried to defend myself to the best of my abilities and thwarted off any hits to the face. I may have even got a few licks in, but when I slipped into the car, I finally let out a deep and labored exhale. My stomach hurt. My arms were sore. I wasn't sure how much more fight I had in me after living in too much tension of February's battles.

Chapter 38

The Shuck and Jive of Social Justice

The high school was scheduled to have an assembly to discuss the documentary in mid-March, but plans had been altered. The principals and I were in agreement that students needed something a little lighter after the heaviness of the last couple weeks. Already, we'd reached mid-March and the Pleasantville community was still recovering from the semantic misunderstanding the ugly little word, "racism" taken completely out of context in the school hallways just a month ago. Two community artists, Carl and DJ Mario, had been working with me all season for the big reveal of our Pleasantville Renaissance grant (formerly the Bronze Renaissance grant) for months. In collaboration with the principal, we decided the March morning assembly was the best available time and place to make it happen. Prior to the high school assembly that was about to take place, we debuted our grant showcase just before spring break at a middle school talent show with phenomenal success.

Carl, one of my Pleasantville Renaissance partners, couldn't be with us for the high school showcase this morning, but my other partner, DJ Mario, joined me and was prepared to hold down the show solo. As we began set up for the showcase, my excitement began building. I was nervous and understood the weight of the moment. This would be the first time I stood in front of the high school students since we screened the documentary on race. I reflected on the middle school showcase and hoped today's program, just moments away now, would be – at least – almost as fantastic.

Only a month ago, students roared with cheer and applause as Carl and DJ Mario dazzled them. A popular middle school teacher brought me on stage and I introduced the student audience to Carl and Mario as they took the show away. DJ Mario started their performance introduction with a rumble of bass and melody that filled the room. Students danced at their seats and recited the lyrics to the music. He then revealed to students that he'd be sharing the stage with some of his new friends. He first introduced Carl, a community actor, who began with a theatrical performance of "Still I Rise" by Maya Angelou. Carl's voice spilled into the air and students drank him in. He shared how his voice was silenced when he was younger due to shyness and a stammer, but he explained as he grew older and more confident, he came out of his shell and found the arts to be a way for him to own and use his voice.

Next, DJ Mario announced he'd be welcoming some student friends to the stage. The music track faded and a new song boomed while two girls ran through the aisles from the back of the auditorium onto the stage. I remember giggling at how ecstatic students were at seeing other students, barely their elder, under the

191

spotlight performing with such high efficiency. Their brown skin glowing, full-toothed smiles, braids swishing on cue and total rhythmic command of their bodies. The dancers beamed; they were so proud. They choreographed a dance especially for this occasion. Following the girls was a white middle school boy in love with hip hop. DJ Mario introduced him and played an instrumental beat while the young student began rapping. He was barely audible but his fellow students went wild cheering his fears away and commending his courage to perform. Rounding up the student performances was a white male high school student who beat-boxed. As he made incredible vocal percussion sounds, the students, Carl and DJ Mario were stunned by his talent. The energy in the theatre vibrated the walls. At that moment, Pleasantville belonged to those students and I was immensely proud of them.

To wrap up our invitation to the arts program which was scheduled to begin in April, DJ Mario shared how he found his voice through music as well. To the amazement of students, he scratched on his records and turntables to old school hip hop and testified that music saved him from a darker future, too. I wrapped up the final invitation and we turned the talent show back to the host teachers and student audience. Over the moon with the success of the showcase to our middle schoolers, Carl, Mario and I acknowledged each other with blends of hugs, fist bumps, handshakes, chuckles and grins behind the stage while packing up. We agreed to follow up for the high school showcase and began developing our arts program calendar for the remainder of the year.

Though not in the high school's talent show, our showcase became the placeholder of a high school morning assembly. This show was slightly different than the energy for a school talent show. There's a big difference between 8:00 am as opposed to the end of the day before spring break. There's a big difference between forgiving middle school minds who had long since forgotten about a little ol' conversation on "racism" just weeks ago and high school students who hold grudges sometimes for inordinate amounts of time. I hoped this high school – full of some of the most intelligent and well-read students regionally – would be open and willingly (if not pleasantly) "involved". I wished for them to be curious yet hospitable with some small smiles playing at corners of mouths. I wished for them to be anything but high school students.

We cut the passive music and Luke approached the stage to introduce me. There was no fanfare or ticker tape; he simply instructed students to welcome me. Applause was minimal, as if students weren't awake enough to order their hands to smack together with vigor at 8:00 am. I felt the energy level my spine and take a nose dive down into the pit of my stomach. The prevailing mood was bad; however, I proceeded with hope and didn't mince words. I used the word "empowerment" as sincerely as I could. "Every important movement in modern times has been led by students," I told them. "You don't realize how powerful you are. You will shape the future. Find and use your voices to change the world."

Invitations and permission are critically important to me in diversity and inclusion work. I asked students for permission to share a poem I'd written about using my voice. The poem I was preparing to share, I divulged, was about my brown mother losing her voice while integrating a school in the 1950s. I had written the poem after sitting on the curb by Kelly Ingram Park across from the 16th Street Baptist Church in Birmingham, Alabama. In a pin drop silent auditorium, I told a garden of lilies about a phone call to my mother from that curb. "She wept on the other end of the line," I recalled, "as if my biracial voice was some miracle to her muted existence." I read:

I didn't understand
My own voice
Inherited from her
Still gift wrapped
Just like new
She integrated school
Dark on playground
Nigger in class
Nuns said nothing
Neither did she
Half century silence
50 years later
Daughter takes trip
Civil rights tour
Freedom bus ride
Sits inside history
Edmond Pettis Bridge
King's funeral wagon
Trees with secrets
Four little girls
Dogs and hoses
Kelly Ingram Park
Then it clicks
This was real
This really happened
Someone died here
For my voice
These same places
So quiet now
Silence is deafening
Called my mother
From a curb
how are you
I'm in Birmingham
Her childhood
Flashed before eyes

A growing movement
On the news
every night, asking
Who died today
But this day
Her biracial daughter
Calls from Birmingham
Intact, empowered, free
Nothing but silence
Her usual voice
She starts crying
And I understand
My voice came
From my mom
From her mom
From Virginia plantations
Passed down generations
Parched vocal chords
From colored only
Water fountain drinks
Muted by history
Until right now
Full time voice
First time used
I'm her words
I'm her evidence
The world changed
And she lived
To see it
So I talk
When she couldn't
Made a promise
My voice would
Make bold mistakes
Tell this truth
Show today's lies
Play on playgrounds
Raise my hand
Talk in class
Because I can
With their blessing
and this voice
What will you
Do with yours?

The last line of my poem reverberated through the microphone. I felt stripped but daydreamed of the presence of my brown ancestral spirits with me as I told one of our truths about brownness to a predominantly white audience. Student claps were even weaker than before. Reality revealed I was naked, after all. Pleasantville was through with me. No, they were over me; past me. I felt their anger, their boredom, and their disgust scan me like I meant nothing to them. They wanted me to know the depth of their contempt for me.

I was only a 30-minute interruption to the day of Pleasantville High School's students. I stood there at the podium with my mother's PTSD in my mouth. I stood there like a new girl at a new school, praying to be accepted. I stood there feeling brown "as all get-out" with all those white faces staring back at me in indisputable disapproval.

My eyes quickly scanned the audience for the handful of brown students with whom I, supposedly should have had a relationship. They, too, sat slumped in their seats as if to say, "I want to help you, but I just can't. You're on your own!" Peaking sparsely in the sea of whiteness, the brown faces seemed to hide themselves from me. They denied and disowned me and my nappy locks. They melted in their seats like I mortified them with each utterance. A piece of my heart broke off and ended up in my throat. I swallowed it inconspicuously. Thanks to my experience in performing behind a mask, I didn't even asphyxiate while introducing DJ Mario. As their lukewarm applause seemed to reluctantly welcome him to the stage, I found my way to front row seating with the audience. Student whispers tickled my ears and my little girl esteem. Their bluest eyes sizzled my back like cigarette butt burns into abused skin.

Young hands like royalty "golf-clapped" Mario onto the stage and he began as he had in the middle school talent show; nevertheless, it was vastly different this time. There was no roar, cheering or applause. There was no dazzle and no rumble. There was no chair dancing or a group lyric recitation.

Mario revealed to students that he would be sharing the stage with some of his new friends. As before, the background music track faded and a new song boomed while our two girls ran through the aisles as they had done previously from the back of the auditorium onto the high school stage.

Deja and her friend's brown skin glowed and they flashed full-toothed smiles. Their braids swished on cue as they flaunted total rhythmic command of their bodies. Merely moderate claps from peers concluded the girls' veritable star-studded performance. Inside our abbreviated window of time, Mario invited only one additional student guest to the stage – our white male high school student beat-boxer. The crowd came alive with applause for him before and after his performance. He was a crowd favorite and the audience was used to loving him; he was easy. So still, I found myself grappling with my heightened sensitivity about race. Was this cultural appropriation? Did the students only find brown culture acceptable or praise-worthy as performed by white people? Did they really want just the return of another minstrel show?

"Calm down, Kim," I whispered. I steadied my temper and attempted to second guess my own mind. Perhaps students didn't realize the only person they warmly clapped for was the polite, soft-spoken Midwest suburban white male student performing one of the essential four pillars of hip hop, a culture created within brown east coast communities. There was already too much going on, so I dissociated those feelings and brought myself back into the room.

Mario revisited the topics of student voice and student empowerment. He was a charismatic jack-of-all-trades as a performing DJ and normally a mover of crowds. I'll bet it's me, I guessed. Front and center, Mario engaged students and gauged their interest in empowerment. They sat like dead fish. He asked if students had ever felt a desire to express themselves. Two to three hands poked up out of hundreds of students in the auditorium like prairie dogs emerging from grassland burrows. Among hundreds of students, three hands braved the quiet of the large, echoing room. I knew Mario well and could sense that he, too, was in disbelief at the stillness of so many students and coldness of the crowd. Perhaps the prompt was wrong – at least here in Pleasantville. He switched gears and asked students if they'd ever wanted to change something about the school. They did not budge. By this point, I was embarrassed by the students as if they were my own children and were misbehaving in public.

All else had failed, but music never does. Music is a universal language. Maybe Mario and I were speaking a language different from the high school students in Pleasantville and music could be our translator. Mario signaled that he was near done with the showcase. Students slouched in their chairs, not even remotely entertained. Mario asked if he could share his story of how he found his voice. They could not have cared less about Mario's voice or his story. I cringed for him as he continued dying a slow death on the stage. The feeling of guilt rushed to my fingers and toes; I feared he was being punished for being affiliated with me. Mario asked the student audience if they were familiar with hip hop legends, Run-DMC. Maybe they were; maybe they weren't. The point was that they didn't care. We all – including Mario and me – just wanted the assembly to be over.

Mario, who had, in his past, been signed to a record label, scratched on his records and turntables to old school hip hop. He demonstrated his testimonial after, again, testifying how music saved him from a dark path. I momentarily smiled at the familiar sounds until realizing, I was the *only person* in the room enjoying one of hip hop's greatest elements – true DJing. Mario finished and for a brief moment, I was uncertain the students were going to offer him any courtesy applause or recognition. I began clapping and thankfully, students followed my lead with what could only be considered another polite clap. He recognized the strangeness of the room and concluded by referring students to contact me if they were interested in participating in the Renaissance program. There it was; the kiss of death.

Time was up for them and for me, both figuratively and literally. Mario and I glanced over at Luke to return the stage and mic to him. To our surprise, he didn't come up to the stage. He failed to thank Mario for joining us. He didn't ask students, perhaps out of discomfort with their tepid response, to give another round of applause to Mario or to me. In fact, he did nothing to acknowledge our guest, Mario, at all. Luke stood from his seat in the auditorium and dismissed Pleasantville's high school students to their first period classes; then, he simply exited the room along with the students without a single word to Mario or me.

That was that. The pit of my stomach imploded as I watched bodies file out of the room. My eyes trailed each body as it exited the auditorium. I waited for the mics to be turned off so they weren't "hot" anymore. My face was scalding. My embarrassment had been replaced with disgust. This was a classically hostile environment and I had dangerously put a virtual family member in harm's way. "This," I thought, "will never happen again." I told Mario as we stood on the stage and looked out into the now empty auditorium, "I think this is it. I think that was my confirmation that it's time to go. I can tell when I'm not wanted." Mario chuckled in solidarity with me and echoed, "I think you might be right."

Later that evening, I learned the auditorium wasn't the only room in the school where I lost favor with mankind. That same day, a high school staff meeting took place and the emotions were fever-pitch. A high school teacher with whom I had a "good" relationship contacted me later that evening via social media private messaging. He confidentially disclosed that I was the subject of chatter at the staff meeting earlier that afternoon. While I was disheartened to hear that I had been "hated on" by a room full of adults, supposedly my colleagues, the chatter was not what hurt me most. I felt vulnerable and abandoned yet again. Though I had thought a *handful* of allies in the room during that staff meeting, **no one** stood up for me. **No one** spoke on my behalf. **No one** risked being excluded or exiled to protect me. No one dared extend the staff meeting to stand in allegiance with me. There were too many opposing me to take on. This time, my work was too prickly and too polarizing. I was too non-traditional and my methods too unpleasant. My work just felt too <u>intentionally</u> uncomfortable. And frankly, I may just have been too rebelliously brown.

The truth is that inside, I was feeling unguarded. I was, again, alone in my misery. I was, *again*, misunderstood. Apparently, in the meeting, Luke and his staff labeled me as a deficit model thinker: too much doom and gloom; too much negativity. My confidante whispered to me, too, how disconnected my showcase was for teachers. "How did they miss the message of empowerment?" I fussed. How did they miss our "ask", more like begging, for student voice? "What did the teachers see?" I begrudgingly inquired. He replied in quotes, "Two girls dancing for a minute, a beat box boy, and kids standing up who don't like our school."

197

Deficit approach is what they saw and Luke agreed with them. My colleague and the leader of the high school teachers said out loud and in front of his staff that I had a deficit model approach. Gravity pulled me down from inside my gut. I had officially lost connection with the entire high school.

Soon after this series of events, my grant program was killed. Once I witnessed the tepid reaction of high school students whenever my energy was in the room, I knew there was danger. The situation was serious. I met with an outside grant vendor to seek an explanation for the tension in order to manage her distance or position outside of the contention. She, in turn, graciously pulled out of the grant as a vendor because of the climate and extenuating circumstances. Her concern was that I did not have the support or buy—in to attract student participants. I understood her concern; she was probably right. Why have innocent people wounded by shrapnel from Luke's and my battle?

I followed up with Paula, the grantor. We'd already had so many conversations about the Pleasantville Renaissance grant. It had been rewritten to ingratiate white students and still, they turned their noses up at its invitation. When I updated Paula that a vendor connected to the grant had pulled out, due to tension between myself and Luke, she informed me I had no real choice but to cancel the program. The foundation was not comfortable allocating funding for my grant project as it no longer had the key components outlined in the grant application. In a move that was unprecedented to my knowledge, I had to return grant funding. I gave back money that was earmarked to benefit brown students because white teachers and administrators didn't understand me, or more accurately the work I was trying to do and the awareness I wanted to bring about.

Timed perfectly, just as we were cancelling the grant, an article was published in Pleasantville's town paper highlighting the fantastic middle school talent show with special guests, Carl and DJ Mario. A colleague of mine shared the article with me, assuming I'd be encouraged to see the manifestation of my hard work. I chuckled out loud. The photo accompanying the article was of the young, white middle school boy on stage performing hip hop. No image of Carl or DJ Mario was included. Perhaps it was a microaggression. Perhaps it was nothing. Perhaps choking on waves of microaggressions without help from bystanders watching yet not moving to perform makes you a little more paranoid about that last gasp.

I was in the deep waters and no one threw me a life preserver. I am hydrophobic. I cannot swim. I was bleeding in the water and the Pleasantville sharks were beginning to circle.

Chapter 39

Brown Safety is White Threat

The aftermath of the documentary screening *I'm Not Racist ...Am I?* seemed to have waned a bit and my primary objective by this time was to complete the final year of my Pleasantville contract with some semblance of dignity and whatever remaining sanity I could muster. Multiple opportunities to debrief the concept of racism, especially as it related to Pleasantville, had fallen short of my expectations. As the weeks went on, the Calvary of brown Pleasantville parent help I had hoped might rush in to stand in agreement with me never arrived. I withstood the Pleasantville battle alone. Out of respect and, in truth, a bit of curiosity, I hosted a final parent meeting – this time, for parents of *brown* students at Pleasantville – to gauge their pulse on the temperature of race relations in the town since the screening of the film.

I decided to hold my final meeting with Pleasantville's brown parents at one of the elementary schools. This particular location also happened to be the building which employed our highest number of teachers of color in a singular school, which totaled <u>three</u>. My hope was that the school and its more diverse surrounding neighborhood might attract a few extra brown parents to attend – and in this instance, I was correct. To my satisfaction, the elementary school library filled with a smaller contingency of brown parents and a few white advocate educators. Finally, I thought, we can have a *real* conversation.

Though the weeks following the film screening had been accompanied by deafening silence from Pleasantville's brown folks, this meeting was bursting with commentary. I never used my prepared agenda, but instead, fielded questions about racism and implicit bias in the district. While one might assume my misery in Pleasantville loved the company, this meeting also frustrated me. I had served as a leader and a fierce advocate for marginalized students in Pleasantville Schools for nearly two years and I never perceived the brown parents "had my back". I knew I couldn't go to another meeting with my white peers and report what would sound like gossip about "what the brown parents told me". I needed something substantive – and concretely helpful – to share.

I put a demand on the spirited folks in the room to tell me <u>exactly</u> what their wants and expectations were regarding diversity and inclusion in the district. I asked them, "What would a safe, welcoming and inclusive Pleasantville look like for brown students?" With assistance from a couple social justice scholars who came to the meeting to support friends living in the district, here is the list of needs brown parents shared with me:

A safe, welcoming and inclusive Pleasantville for <u>brown</u> students would look like:

- Policy of advocacy: co-creating (with students and teachers) a script for students to use when they feel/experience discriminatory situations. There will be a series of "professional development" workshops with students, a series of workshops with teachers, on the challenges students brought up and their preliminary script. Teachers ass their input about the script. In conclusion, students and teachers practice the script. Students practice being empowered and teachers are aware of what student advocacy will look like.
- <u>Diversity</u> in educators, administrators and head coaching
- What happened to <u>Black History Month</u>?!
- <u>Choosing</u> the big "3" [focusing on race, income and disability] over the already high performers
- Power shift …for once
- My student feels as <u>valued</u> as anyone else
- Clear, consistent response <u>strategies</u> to create safe space
- School board: 50% of time at yearly retreat (diversity, empathy/compassion, student advocacy)
- Administration: mandatory professional development hours for diversity and inclusion
- Staff: mandatory hours for evaluation of evidence of diversity and inclusion classroom practice
- Provide support and opportunity for brown students to excel in honors / AP courses
- Self-advocating brown students would be supported (not disciplined) by staff, faculty and administrators
- If the district embraced a diversity construct, there would be more teachers that were brown throughout all the Pleasantville Schools
- There would be no tolerance for ignorant racial comments made and dismissed
- There would be a minority parent council
- There would be no failure to rescue struggling minority students
- Principal would not support a brown student and parent achievement program as a self-help support group for brown students because "the scores" show only brown students have low scores. Own and lead in the truth of the district's opportunities to grow in this space.
- Teachers have high expectations of brown students and <u>believe</u> they are as capable and intelligent as any other.
- Higher sensitivity to racial issues would be present. Flawed value system that has developed over years and ingrained by unchangeable staff has been counteracted by increasing the presence of African American staff and intentionally employing

those who embrace diversity… Resulting in a paradigm shift that traveled from staff to inevitable change in students
- System of change would come from focus that looks similar to a building's best practice. Our entire staff, meetings, professional development would be dedicated to that focus. If we want to have a paradigm shift, it needs to be embedded in every day. Then, we will establish a cultural norm. Right now, diversity and inclusion is an event.

On my way home from the meeting that evening, I was at a loss for words at how powerfully the brown parents – and *white advocates* for brown students – showed up and shared clear, concise and well-articulated appeals for our school leadership. It hadn't happened as soon as I had hoped, but, I wondered, were we finally about to work together and gain some traction in the diversity work for the Pleasantville School District? Could true social justice and true race equity be on the horizon? As the day sunset on me and my aspirations, I recalled the quote by Will Smith, which was posted on my office door:

"I think there's a certain delusional quality that all successful people have to have. You have to believe that something different than what has happened for the last 50 million years of history... You have to believe that something different can happen, and that you can be the one to do it."

Maybe I was delusional; but, I still hoped there was time for good work to be done in Pleasantville. I couldn't "move the needle" by myself and I couldn't rewrite the past, but perhaps with the help of the town's brown parents, we could change Pleasantville's future.

About a week later, I met with Abby, the public relations officer. She was still waiting to publish dates for my winter programming, including follow-up conversation we'd promised – in writing – to have with students and staff about our critical thinking on racism. However, no significant conversations had taken place, with the exception of my meeting with the brown parents. Though attempts were planned and scheduled, on several occasions, Luke and James felt that either the teachers and/or the students weren't ready. Believing it was in our best interest to demonstrate there was at least minimal follow-through on behalf of the district, she decided to write a short piece about the meeting and included vague hints that there was more diversity programming to come.

The pen is, in fact, mightier than the sword. Before even reading Abby's article, its controversy found me – again – in an email. I received feedback from two teachers that staff were troubled and disturbed by the article Abby wrote about my recent meeting with brown Pleasantville parents. One line in the article had, apparently, greatly offended the high school teaching staff. This one line was so egregious; it was specifically referenced in a departmental chair meeting hosted by Luke. Luke, a passionate advocate for his teachers, immediately followed up by aggressively confronting Abby, questioning her submission. She was accused of writing a puff piece that was "embellished, divisive, paints staff and administration in a negative way for public consumption, [and] negligent". When courageously she stood by her article, Luke approached Dr. Springsteen and asked that the article be rescinded from print and pulled down from our district website. Dr. Springsteen refused Luke's request, which enraged Luke even more. What could Abby have written to incense so many otherwise astute and reserved Pleasantville educators? Embedded in a paragraph summarizing my meeting with some of Pleasantville's brown parents, Abby wrote, "Students and parents expressed that teachers and administrators do not adequately address racial tensions at school".

Literally, that was all she wrote.

Luke's explosive reaction didn't really surprise me. Pleasantville teachers taking offense to the singular line about "not adequately addressing racial tensions at school" didn't totally catch me off guard. If you can believe it, the most troubling response to Abby's article, in my opinion, came from the high school librarian. …The same gentle soul who let me in the library on the night I discovered Pleasantville High School used to host minstrel shows. Having had much time to think and carefully craft his words, Dale shared what seemed to be a representative sentiment from other white educators at Pleasantville. As I read his words, I better understood why the high school hallways felt so cold to me. After a staff meeting and follow-up conversation with some teachers in the meeting *after* the meeting, Dale emailed me and stated:

- Staff felt that article (and I) suggested teaching staff is incompetent, uncaring, ignorant and at fault
- Belief that article was a complaint and that complaint was made publicly
- Staff was not informed of complaint or given a chance to address complaints before they were aired
- Staff is in the dark about what issues are
- Staff is embarrassed and humiliated
- Article was perceived as divisive and not playing on the same team
- Desire for plans to ease racial tension
- Request for research-based, prove, best-practice approach to follow
- Desire for advance toward common goals in a more collaborative fashion

In a comedy of errors, my final community dialogue meeting was scheduled just days after the article fiasco. The topic: A critical analysis of the *Black Lives Matter* movement. Right around the time of Abby's article being published, I had just extended an invitation for all teachers and staff to attend the conversation. Because of the sensitivity and scarce knowledge, the general public had at the time about what the Black Lives Matter movement was really about, I thought it might be insightful for us to learn together as a community. What I didn't realize is that Luke had taken it upon himself to become educated on what Black Lives Matter was really about. He "Google'd" the movement and then contacted me via email – with several people (including Dale, the librarian) carbon-copied on the message – and began his line of questioning.

Luke asked how the Black Lives Matter organization's mission about ending state and police violence and brutality toward black citizens related to the district's educational mission. Knowing Luke and his peers, who were also my colleagues, didn't identify me as an educator, I attempted endearment as a diversity practitioner. I re-invited all who were carbon-copied on Luke's email message to attend the event so we could *critically review* the movement together. I was careful to respond, in very few words, that the intent of the conversation was not confrontational, but for critical thinking. Luke curtly replied that he was not convinced by my explanation and stated that *all* lives matter. He questioned if "his" students were the intended audience. I breathed through all those baiting statements without "losing my cool". He then channeled Pleasantville's chief of police and wrote, again, with the same larger group carbon copied, that he had fear that the community conversation would be a bashing of the police departments and that casting blame is not a viable solution [for pro-social race relations]. He feared the event would be divisive.

No Pleasantville High School teachers attended the Black Lives Matter community dialogue session. In fact, as the end of the academic year drew near, very few of the high school teachers engaged me in *any* dialogue, for that matter. I heard rumors that teachers were afraid I had invited black political vigilantes to come to the event. Some white teachers feared for their safety. Yes, that sounds like something I would do, I sarcastically joked with myself. Start a race war at work on Thursday and then, return to the office on Friday; business as usual. Pleasantville had become a political cartoon. Luke and I were now drawn as opposing forces. And I needed Dr. Springsteen to step in before somebody, namely me, got hurt.

Chapter 40

Death by 36 Lashings

The first Monday in April, I scratched and crawled my way into a birthday. I turned thirty-nine years old. Honestly, my mind was so distracted by surviving my job and my children and my marriage that I wasn't certain reaching another birthday was a good thing. Lately, I'd felt more punished than rewarded and I really needed things to turn around.

The email chatter regarding the Black Lives Matter community dialogue exceeded the lows Luke and I usually spiraled down to in our regular visceral interactions. Our fighting had now become commonly public and in my opinion, incredibly disempowering. Luke had tremendous social capital; therefore, my concern was that his dismantling of my credibility had contagiously spread to others. I needed to maintain what dignity and credibility I had left. Tension had grown so high between Luke and me that I requested a meeting between us and two other principals in the district to be mediated by Dr. Springsteen. Dr. Springsteen granted my request and the meeting was set for later that week.

Leading up to the meeting, several pep talks found their way to me. Friends, family members and one or two colleagues talked me up and filled my spirit and I bet I told myself that I appreciated the support and encouragement but I thought I didn't need it. I'd been so angry for so long about Luke's treatment of me and I could not wait to sit down with him amongst our peers and see what he'd say in front of them, our boss, God and country. Over the past year and a half, he'd said some incredibly bold things to me, but I was pretty sure he had more professionalism than to bully me among mixed company. I also felt confident that more bodies in the room would mean that the playing field would be even. If a confrontation did break out, I wouldn't have to contend with him alone.

I waited until the very last minute to walk upstairs to Dr. Springsteen's office. Caution had me thinking something wasn't right. My head was clear and my notebook was in hand, but inside, my body was already starting to go into a panic. My arms felt like wet hand towels that were being wrung tightly, expending all my energy out in droplets on the high school hallway floor. I walked in the central office and down the hallway like I was John Coffey and the corridor was The Green Mile. The planets weren't in alignment in my favor. Something was off. Suddenly, this seemed like a bad idea.

Entering the room, everyone was sitting around the round table. And again, as was the case most of the time in Pleasantville, I was the only brown face in the room. Time was moving slower and my notebook felt like a cinder block in my hands. They watched me walk in like I was a gazelle in some sub-Saharan grassland, prancing into a circle of lions starved for protein that looked just like me. I searched Dr. Springsteen's eyes for fight and he looked as helpless as I felt. He was the most powerful man in the district and (supposedly) my ally.

One chair was left unoccupied. I knew it was mine. Beautiful blue printed cloth. As I sat down and mouths opened to begin the meeting, the chair hardened. Leather arm and leg bands came out of the chair and buckled and tightened around my limbs. I tried writing notes, but I was nearly lightheaded with anxiety. My smile had melted off my face minutes ago and was replaced with heaviness. Dr. Springsteen, who had seen the entire movie that started the hub bub, opened the meeting with a little stage-setting, but it only seemed to be landing comfortably on me. I know he wanted to help me, but at that exact moment, I knew he couldn't. as soon as he paused to bring others into the conversation, Luke reclined further in his chair. He was a large, comfortable man and there I sat across the table from him, laboring to breathe. He was engaged, but in all the wrong ways. Everyone else straightened up a bit in their seats, not knowing what to expect once the conversation officially begun – and it had. I felt a wet sponge drip water on my head as the black cloth covered my eyes and the metal helmet was firmly pushed over the crown and buckled securely under my chin. This was not the meeting I had originally requested. I had walked into the place of my own execution.

Luke's mouth opened and delivered words that sounded, to me, like the executioner now pulling down on the lever, sending those deadly volts through my body. Each point he made must have unburdened his chest from expressing his true feelings about me; little by little, they picked away at my battered soul. At times, the intentional words were so vile and hurtful, they felt as if they were potent enough to lift me out of the chair, my nails scratching into the arm rests, trying to remain seated. Here are some of the most notable energy surges that lit me up in the meeting.

1. They don't believe the gap in achievement for students of color is related to social justice issues.
2. Dr. Springsteen stated that the issue between Luke and me was bad and needed to be resolved. He said he's known Luke for fourteen years and had never seen him react to someone the way he reacts toward me.
3. Administrators stated that their teachers are unclear on my expectation of them, my plan, how they fit into it and the process to access me as a resource or to access my networks
4. Dr. Springsteen said I behave one way everywhere else and when I'm around Luke, my whole demeanor changes.
5. Belief that I have failed to develop trust, leadership and relationships with the black students
6. Was responsible for teachers being ill-prepared and that I inadequately provided teachers with improper training in preparation for the film
7. Belief that diversity and inclusion work should first be intellectual and then be practical. I debated against their feedback and tried to explain that minority community is looking for practical skills first and then intellect.

8. Statement that I've made several mistakes during my time at Pleasantville.
9. I didn't provide faculty with diversity and inclusion training and professional development and then I insulted their abilities publicly.
10. My commentary, programs and initiatives are militant, reactive, inflammatory and radical.
11. I was told by all at the meeting that I am not an educator.
12. Black student programs died on my watch and Luke is going to restart them on his own next year.
13. The district's purpose is not to engage in social justice conversations.
14. Black students were starting to do better before I arrived.
15. The black students who are doing better are not tied to any of my work.
16. Macro issues happening at a national level are not relevant in Pleasantville and have no place in education. They don't fit in with the concrete "right now" needs of students.
17. The Black Lives Matter World community conversation was perceived to be militant because they read the content on the Black Lives Matter website.
18. When presented with argument that other differing perspectives exist in the district that counter predominantly white lenses, I was asked to flex to Luke's [white] cultural lens.
19. I failed to develop relationships and become a resource for black students.
20. I was called defensive, passive, passive aggressive, divisive, negative and unapproachable.
21. Kelly said she knew the work would be messy but she didn't expect it to be "slop all over the floor mess".
22. I was told I need to gain back the trust of the high school teachers.
23. Regarding the article that mentioned parents and students stating that teachers "don't do an adequate job of responding to racial tension", I was told that the article was not factual, that the fault was thought to have been the district's PR representative but then discovered to be mine, Dr. Springsteen "refused" to stop the article from being published externally, I "betrayed" middle school and high school teachers
24. They are "frustrated" by my work.
25. They are "disappointed" by my work.
26. Luke will not attend my community dialogue sessions until he sees progress with this work and *his* students.
27. Teachers hated/prickled to the film and didn't find it to be valuable.
28. Luke (and James) found the film to be developmentally inappropriate for students.
29. Teachers disliked in-service, especially a session with two alumni telling their addiction and recovery stories.
30. I failed to be collaborative and was not inclusive.
31. Luke mentioned that an African American male colleague of his did a great job of intellectualizing diversity and inclusion for him (instead of my practical application of diversity and inclusion) and helped him make exponential progress in just one year.

32. Faculty say there's lots of tension and discomfort now that wasn't there before.
33. It was frequently stated that I didn't have a background in education and didn't know how to put my initiatives in an educational setting.
34. I need to compromise and see things from *their* point of view.
35. It was stated that families of students of color had no complaints or issues before I arrived. I challenged that there were issues. Luke disagreed. I told him I know there were because they told me there were. My statement was rejected particularly based on the point that families of color had not complained to other (white) administrators.
36. Finally, they brought a list of desired expectations for me for future work, which included:
    - Better engagement with families of color
    - Better understanding of what makes people of color feel valued
    - Training for staff
    - Train school climate committee on how to be liaisons
    - Set one to two diversity and inclusion goals and stick with them
    - Show link with social justice and curriculum and tie the two together
    - Set a calendar far ahead of time and advertise it
    - Be a resource for students of color
    - Be a resource for staff

I labored to breathe. After this meeting, I was stunned. Acid churned from the bottom of my belly to the back of my throat. I wasn't sure if I was going to vomit or breathe fire. I could feel all of the muscles in my arms, shoulders and neck tightening, as if a snake was constricting on the top half of my body. My hands were so tingly and numb, I was unable to write notes. My heart raced and pounded out of my chest and my face was raw. My soul was being sanded with a pumice stone after two or three layers had already been shaved off and the underpart was already so raw; now it will undoubtedly bleed.

Luke mentioned that he had another meeting to attend; so, he stood up and walked out of the room. The four remaining souls sat in the room in awkward silence. Clearly, Luke was the main talker with the most feedback. It was almost as if Luke was the oxygen in the room and once he left, the fire went out. We attempted to not look each other in the eyes. ...Or perhaps they were all trying not to look me in the eyes. Dr. Springsteen looked as if he'd just sent his child to be sacrificed. Like had just dismissed himself without seeking permission from or officially making Dr. Springsteen aware he needed to leave. He just took it upon himself – and left.

Stunned and not quite sure what to say, Dr. Springsteen looked at me and asked if I had anything to add to the conversation. But my words were gone. My blood was water. My face was emotionally botoxed. I was a taxidermy sitting duck. I recalled I hadn't answered Dr. Springsteen yet; all I could do was shake my head,

"No". "No, I have nothing to say." My response barely came out as loud as a whisper. Struggling to maintain any form of eye contact, I said to Dr. Springsteen, "Thank you for this meeting. I'll be in touch."

Chapter 41

From Wise Woman to Little Girl

Once, while listening to the testimonial of a woman in recovery, I heard an explanation of what proverbially "hitting the bottom" is like and it stuck with me. She described the experience of being deep in addiction and at her "bottom" as being in a pitch-black room, isolated from all human contact. Your own hands around your neck, choking you. Cold, scared, alone and in pain. She reflected, "You think you're dead. You feel dead. But when your hands slide up to your neck, you can still feel your heart beating, reminding you that you're still alive." I could definitively relate.

I walked out of Dr. Springsteen's office having to consciously remind myself how to walk. Right foot, left foot. Right foot, left foot. I clung to my pen and notebook like a child clutches a favorite woobie. All I wanted was to get into my "safe place" – my cave of an office space; and, hide from the atmosphere in the Pleasantville building and the feeling of being out on a limb – naked. I believed, apprehensively, that I was approaching absolute desperation. Once my key unlocked the door to my office, I meandered toward my desk and flopped into my chair. I looked around as if I was lost and then leaned over onto my desk. My arms and limbs felt foreign to me and I didn't know what to do with my hands. My breathing was still labored and my stomach unsettled.

My hands found their way to the phone receiver and I intuitively called Jordan. We weren't phone talkers, but, in that instance, I needed to hear his voice. "This is Jordan...", his voice greeted from the other end of the phone. Strong but low pitched so as to not bring attention to himself in a cubicle farm of important people. All I could mumble out was, "I need you to take me on a date tonight." "What's going on?" he inquired. My eyes welled over and my heart was about to burst. "I can't talk right now; because, I'm about to cry. I just need you to take me out on a date tonight," I told him. He heard something peculiar in my voice but knew that any additional conversation would further provoke more tears from me. I had never before cried at work. I had never felt the need Jordan, in a protective tone simply replied, "Understood."

Before I was able to place the receiver back on the phone base, tears base-jumped down my face. Unstoppable trickles like a hole in a levee. I had shed more tears during the last couple months over Pleasantville than I'd shed for grandparents' deaths and marital issues Jordan and I were struggling with to survive. **Being Black in Pleasantville had become more painful for me than death.**

I had to get out of there *immediately*. These tears weren't stopping anytime soon, and the last thing I needed was for one of my adversaries to see that they'd gotten to me. Anything on my desk was shoved into my book bag, and I wiped away endless tears while shutting down my computer. Just as I stood up to walk out, Craig walked into my office to bring me budgetary paperwork. In my emotional stupor, I had forgotten to close my door. He walked in talking, but as soon as he saw my face, he knew I was crying. I saw the look on his face. He froze in his tracks. He was as alarmed as I was that I had been caught crying. All he wanted to do was get out of the room as quickly as possible, and I wanted the same thing – for both of us. He stammered, puzzled with what to do. Should he attempt to comfort me or just run out of the door like he'd seen a ghost? He asked if everything was alright, but in a way that suggested he hoped I would say I was fine. I did and it was a lie. We both knew it but the lie was so much faster than explaining the issue. The issue was that I was battered and bleeding where he couldn't see it. Craig scurried out the room and I made a b-line for the back door as if a getaway car was waiting for me.

Walking down the back hallway, the crying pulled on me more. This hallway always seemed to signal bad times for me, such as coming in to work on the chill of a silent treatment the night before with Jordan. Zombie walking through after a battle of wits with the girls. Coming from or going to a meeting where I was sure no one wanted to see or hear from me. I had essentially grown weary of Pleasantville School's hallways.

Luke's words echoed in my head repeatedly. It sounded shrill and piercing, like the class bells over intercom. All I could see was James and Kelly sitting in that room, watching me being attacked. They said and did nothing to protect or defend me. No one came to my rescue. It was as if my body had been tied to the railroad tracks, and the Luke locomotive speeding by had carelessly cut me in half. And passersby simply stepped over my body and kept going. No, the body was fine but they'd left my soul in tatters.

I kept picturing Dr. Springsteen's face when I glanced at him after Luke left the room in a whitewashed face. We were **both** shocked and embarrassed. This man had been on the right side of social justice all his life. On the right side of history for the major changes as our nation grew. And here we had this singular person receiving ongoing attacks from another individual and even Dr. Springsteen didn't know how to bring a halt to it. Watching my mistreatment was truly disturbing for Dr. Springsteen; but, the reasons for his total lack of bystander intervention was in conflict with what I knew of his value system. He looked stunned and helpless as though confused by what had just happened. And as usual, I was abandoned and left to fend for myself, I, too, was confused at the course of events that had just transpired.

As if scripted like a Greek tragedy, once I reached my car, I was blocked in my parking space by a service delivery man's truck. Pleasantville just couldn't stop being unpleasant for me, even on one of the worst days of my life. There I sat in my car on a spring afternoon while a momentary sprinkle dampened the empty truck bed from which an ice cream machine had a while ago unloaded. I *desperately* searched through my emails, address book and text messages to reach a means of contacting the custodial supervisor. I could barely text a message, due to the trembling of my hands and tension in my arms. They were, as a matter of fact, beginning to feel numb. I was trapped in Pleasantville's staff parking lot unable to leave the site of the shocking, most humiliating and vilest experience of my career as an educator and trainer. Truck in front of me and a cinder block behind me. I was literally stuck between a rock and a hard place.

My body began suffering an emotionally-charged allergic reaction to Pleasantville, and I could see no route from escaping this place, the trigger. "Right now! Right now!" I thought. "I need to talk to someone who loves me right now!" So, I called my mother, bawling on the other end of the phone while sitting in my car behind Pleasantville High School. "Hi Dollbaby." Her voice was warm and soothing. I nursed on the comfort of her tone. Where I had intended to speak words, indecipherable moans and wails fell out of my throat. I whimpered my location to her. Emotionally, I was still unable to speak what had just taken place in the meeting. As I downward spiraled on the Bluetooth speaker, her cool comfort heated into deep yet calm concern. "Call somebody," she kept urging. "Call or text somebody to move the truck and get you out of there!" Something in my voice frightened her; I realized it, but I was so far gone, I had no strength to reassure her it would be alright. She needed to know that I was okay, but I wasn't.

As my sinuses began to congest from the crying, the service delivery driver returned to his truck and extended an apologetic wave as he drove away. I'd, by then, been sitting in the parking lot for 10 minutes on the phone crying with my mother. Be that as it may, instead of me feeling reassured and soothed since I was now able to get away, my escalating emotions were pushing me, giving me the feeling I was falling apart. Driving out of Pleasantville that afternoon, each block of wealth and perfection reminded me that this was the community in which I did not fit. Their trees **hurt**. Their stay at home moms jogging while pushing thousand-dollar baby strollers **hurt** me. Their perfectly coiffed lawns **hurt** me. My heart was punctured at each red light leaving Pleasantville.

By the time I reached the highway to merge, I was in a full throttle tantrum. "I just need to be around people who I know love me!" I screamed and sniffled inside my car. If it were possible to die a hysterical death, this was probably it for me. While my mother listened to me and tried to calm me down, Jordan called on my other line. He must have been worried by the monotone in my voice and had stepped away from his desk to check back in with me. I swapped calls and was unable to steady my voice. "Jordan...!" My rambling, mumbled words were inaudible.

Still screaming and crying, I was trying to respond to Jordan's inquiries with no success. "Did they see you cry?" he asked. "Where are you right now?" Jordan feared I would wreck my car due to the high state of my emotions. Honestly, he had cause for concern. I was crying so franticly, I could barely breathe and the road was only vaguely visible through my tears. My eyes burned and I was nearly slobbering on myself. My comforting, compassionate spouse ordered me, "Don't come home like that; I don't want the girls to see you crying. Find a coffee shop, get yourself a coffee or tea and calm down before you get home." He heard something edgy and irrational in my tone. His request, though, was unrealistic. The *only* place I wanted to be was home.

By the time I pulled into the garage, Luke, James and Kelly's words were etching themselves into the gray wrinkles of my brain like hieroglyphics. The impassioned verbal attack felt so vicious to me, I ended up in physical pain. My muscles were so constricted, my arms and legs ached. I'd been crying so long and so hard my eyes were beginning to swell shut. The whites of my eyes were blood moons and my face was flushed red. Gathering my breath a bit, I stepped through the door and Charlotte, my oldest daughter met me in the kitchen. More than anything, I wanted her to know me as a strong brown woman, but she knew all too well that Pleasantville was winning its fight against me. I lied to her. More lies to hide the pain. I told her I wasn't feeling well so I could hide myself away in my bedroom until I could portray the grown woman and strong leader she deserved to have as a mother.

Two steps. I two-stepped the stairs and pulled the bedroom door closed behind me. Kim, the little girl, had taken over my body. I had been reduced to that same eight-year-old girl with a Jheri curl who ran home crying afterschool when she'd been so badly bullied. The bullies got the best of me back then and today, they seemed to have triumphed again. Words could hurt so much more than blunt force injuries; they certainly felt like they did. My wise woman had regressed; she had shrunken out of existence. I had been disempowered and minimized into a little girl. I drug all parts of myself into the bed. Curling into a fetal position, I gripped my blanket with bird bath showers dripping from my eyes until my face sunk into the quicksand of the pillow.

I was defeated. Broken. This, I assumed, is what they had wanted.

I had survived poverty. I had survived a house where mental illness lived. I had survived divorced parents with a joint custody agreement. I'd survived school changes across two different states. So, why was this curious school district and community such an unbearable weight on my chest?

My bedroom was bright, sunny and airy. My pet dog crawled under the bed to keep me company. My older child guarded the first floor of the house. I wrapped my hands around my neck and imagined choking myself from the outside while my muffled wails were choked out from the inside. Still I was cold, scared, alone and in pain. I thought with rhetorical inquiry, "Am I dead? I feel dead, but I can still feel my heart beating." I couldn't tell, at that moment, if signs of life were a good or a bad reminder. "I don't know if or how I'm going to survive this, but I *am* still alive."

Later that evening, after Jordan invested hours in calming me down from the day's trauma, I submitted my letter of resignation to Dr. Springsteen.

Dear Dr. Springsteen,

After six months of careful exploration of my head and heart, I have decided not to sign a new contract with the Pleasantville City School District following the completion of my current contract. The past two years have required laborious tilling of the social-emotional wellness land – especially in the areas of diversity and inclusion. And while I would love nothing more than to see this beginning work to fruition, I believe the next phase requires different eyes, fresh hands and new leadership.

My initial commitment was to 1) tell the truth and 2) seek action-oriented ways to address unearthed non-academic barriers. Though this work was met with incredible dynamic tension, I believe I fulfilled my commitment. The conversation has been ignited and it's up to Pleasantville Schools to decide if the conversation is worth sustaining.

I am humbled by and have great appreciation for you and several other educators, parents and community members who have shown unwavering support since my arrival. It takes courageous leadership to push this effort and I find your moral imperative around this work to be highly respectable. Thank you for the opportunity to begin this journey with Pleasantville and I wish the district all the best in its eventual harvest of an entire school community that is empowered to be the very best versions of themselves.

Yours truly,

Kim

Chapter 42

Ridiculous Thoughts

I was in the midst of my out of body experience at Pleasantville. Still, there was no peace for me. My resignation had been submitted, but I hadn't heard a thing from the powers that be. As a matter of fact, they'd already sent me a new contract and I refused to sign it. The pink paper in the interoffice envelope sat on the corner of my desk, stinging like a lingering slap in the face. My decision did not phase them. My feelings were of no concern. The only message I could understand was that losing the second administrator of color ever – let alone the one responsible for diversity – would be *bad press*. They were asking me to stay for the students and to keep up appearances. I was not even sure that the Board of Education had <u>any</u> <u>clue</u> about what I'd gone through over the last year.

Prior to the debacle of a mediated meeting between Luke and myself, I had agreed to partner with a Pleasantville-affiliated nonprofit organization to host a mental health event. The event agenda included a movie screening followed by a facilitated dialogue session. The evening of the behavioral health community conversation, I still felt like a fraud. The irony of leading a conversation on the stigma of mental illness, all while I felt that I was, in fact, losing my mind was not lost on me. My mind, body and soul felt nowhere near functional, but I knew that the last thing Jordan and my family members needed to hear was that the white folks of Pleasantville won by finally and completely driving me crazy.

The rooms inside the school building were set up perfectly by the time the professional event planner arrived in preparation for the film and discussion event. Springtime in a school district is absolutely nuts and you have no clue who is and is not going to attend. Though there were lots of competing events, our event crowd began trickling in. "Fake it 'til you make it," my head said. At the go signal of the professional event planner, I picked up the microphone and put on my best extemporaneous speaking face. I pulled out of my back pocket what I hoped was a little charm and warmth and I gave a preview of the evening and introduced the film.

Pitch blackness befell the room as the film began playing. Opening scene was a young white woman being haunted by voices while studying alone in the library. The scene was already a bit creepy when I noticed that the audio from the movie was dragging. I texted the event planner to see if she knew what the problem was. Turns out that we had no technical support for the event. A high school theater set was being built and apparently took precedence over mental illness in the community. Two minutes. Then five minutes passed. More than seven minutes passed. The audience displayed incredible patience as I ran down the school corridors to find Sam, the professional adult who was slated to provide us with A/V services. He was in the high school theatre, painting a wooden set for the next school play. I'll never forget, it was a pink staircase. That's what was more important than my event.

After tracking him down and notifying him of the problem, the A/V technician signaled to a school boy, perhaps sophomore in grade. Sam spoke to the student in an indiscernible tone and assured me that everything would be under control soon. Satisfied, I briskly walked back to the middle school theater in hopes that remote operations controlling from afar had now magically repaired the movie audio.

When I walked back into the theatre, my eyes first found the event planner. I let her know everything was going to be fine. She reciprocated the vote of confidence and told me that a student had stopped by to repair the sound. A student. I was hosting a community wide film and discussion session and my technology had been entrusted to a fifteen-year-old student, who didn't even stick around for the duration of the film.

To ensure my ability to, at least, control the house lights, I ascended the staircase leading to the balcony and took a seat higher up to watch the film from there. I felt an odd sensation sitting on "the top". Looking below, I could see many of the audience members and yet still had a unique behind the scenes vantage point. Then it began happening.

Intrusive thoughts. Dangerous intrusive thoughts. "What if I fell?" I pondered. "...Or what if..." I hesitated to think. Rumination then began. "What if I lost control of my body and mind and leapt off the front of the balcony?" I looked below and tried to guess where my body might land. Would I fall on people or would I collide into one of the room's vintage seats? Would I die instantly or only mangle my body with injuries in the fall? Would I black out or keep consciousness? Would they call an ambulance for me? Would they be happy that I was hurt, or even better, had perished? The thoughts became more and more violent as they progressed. One came on the heels of another quickly. I had constant dark thoughts about plummeting and feared I wouldn't be able to resist the urge to cast myself like a fisherman's line. What was wrong with me?

My palms perspired and I tightly gripped the arms of the chair where I sat. What I reasoned was if I held onto the chair tightly enough, I wouldn't be able to throw myself off the balcony. I could feel my heart beating in my throat and I presumed my eyes looked wild and crazy. I didn't want to crash land, per se. I was just curious about the results of falling. What would it be like to let go of Pleasantville and just freefall? Would they feel any remorse for their part in contributing to my death? My tailbone ground itself into my balcony theatre seat in an attempt to re-engage with gravity. But, the temptation remained. I was tempted so much so that I removed myself and went back to sit in a seat on the ground level. I found out this had been a smart move for my current state of mind.

Finally, my heartbeat slowed. My sweating slowed. My wild eyes dimmed. My muscles, at last, began to relax. I reminded myself that today was a bad day to risk flirts with death. Ironically, when the film on mental illness ended, I put on my smiling façade again. Charm, inquiry and social justice for the rest of the evening and I think I may have convincingly fooled them and maybe myself that I wasn't losing my mind. Yet, on the drive home after the dialogue session, I could still feel that I wasn't completely okay. Something remained off.

My head felt like I was floating. I was spinning, falling, dropping with no parachute.

Startle! I jerked myself awake out of a restless sleep. It was 1:34am. I laid in the dark staring at the single small green light illuminating from the cable box. I was unfortunately wide awake figuratively pressing my forehead and hands against the glass box of insomnia, experiencing in some purgatory state of consciousness. I wanted to wake Jordan up and ask him to hold me. I couldn't stop falling and I was afraid. The room felt so dark and cold that night. My toes couldn't feel the bottom of the bed where my feet should have been pressed and tightened at the small of the fitted sheet. My gut seemed to be sinking like I was on a g-force amusement park ride. I needed to hold onto something or else I feared I might have just continued to sink into the floor or float away through the ceiling. This was it; night terrors. I was finally certifiably losing my mind!

Jordan calmly slept next to me, breathing slowly and deeply. His hands rested on his chest, stacked neatly, one on top of the other. He was fast asleep. There was no need to interrupt his REM stages. He didn't have to know how close to a mental breakdown I was coming. As the walls fell away from beside me and the floor fell away from beneath me, adrenaline rushed through my body. My heartbeat pulsed through my jugular vein. Yes, I could feel it again. The choking. The shortness of breath. I had to get some sleep. I extended my right hand behind my head and grasped at the headboard post just beyond my ear. My left hand slid up the front of the headboard until I reached the top. It felt like I was being pulled, ripped from my own sanity and the only way I could win the battle was to **not let go** of the headboard. So, I clutched onto it as tightly as a stirrup bed bar in childbirth. Gravity found me again. Brought my body back down to the bed. Brought my adrenaline back down to that of a resting body. Gravity brought my eyelids down, my energy down, and I finally rested for the first time in hours.

The next morning, looking and "acting" normal, I saw everyone off to school and work. As soon as the house was quiet, settled and I had a bit of privacy, I gave my primary doctor and my counselor each a call. Sometimes, you know when things aren't right, and this was one of those times. Fortunately, both were able to see me the same day and that was literally a life-saver. I felt like I was quickly unraveling, but I still needed to play my hand a little "close to the vest" and pretend like everything was cool.

Chapter 43

"I Think You Should Take Some Time"

I finally did it; I resigned from Pleasantville. No one knew of my resignation, though. Dr. Springsteen, in a "Hail Mary" attempt to retain me and right his district's wrongs, asked me to place myself in a *holding pattern* to reconsider. Then, I didn't feel relieved. On the contrary, I felt more anxious than before because my resignation felt like a dirty little secret. I was already carrying a boulder of the town's dirt up and down hills like the rock of Sisyphus. The tendons in my arms were tightly constricted and my breaths were shallow and labored. While I was done with Pleasantville, she was not yet done with me.

The very next day after resigning, poison arrived in an interoffice mail envelope. On canary-yellow paper was my brand-spanking-new contract for the next two-year term in Pleasantville. I panicked, my blood pressure drop drastically. No, this was not happening. I had submitted my official documentation notifying "the powers that be" of my intent to exit, but I couldn't escape? My fists pounded on the wooden drawbridge, still while inside Pleasantville, but my requests for it to be lowered for my official exit seemed to have fallen on deaf ears.

Fortunately, my irritation and panic were interrupted by a doctor's appointment. I had a session with my family practitioner to discuss my insomnia. My body and mind were exhausted, but I couldn't stop the intrusive thoughts or any thoughts anymore, for that matter. I spent days on the prison yard of Pleasantville and nights in the solitary confinement of my mind trying to problem-solve for all the suffering Pleasantville was covering up – including my own. Something was wrong with me and I knew it. The urge was getting stronger and stronger to scream, "No!" when asked, "Are you okay? Is there anything I can do?" A two-parter, the answer to which I could not fully disclose.

The nurse took my vitals and my body inaccurately believed it was alive and well. The paper lining crunched under me as I sat on the table, waiting for the doctor to join me. Like a visually-impaired person squinting to read a blurred line, I felt myself voluntarily trying to appear sane. As I spoke with him, I kept reminding myself not to appear "crazy".
Don't bounce your leg. Don't twiddle your thumbs.
Unclench your jaw. Decorate your eyes with
sarcasm instead of pain. Lilt your voice.
Straighten your back.
I deliver dismissive comments about how bad work is. It's fine. Everything's fine. I'm pretending! "My God," I thought to myself. "I'm really not okay."

"Hey there; how are you?" Dr. Wilson asked while knocking on and entering the door. "I'm good," I lied. I'm not sure I convinced myself or my doctor that time. Thankfully, my acting was sufficient enough to sneak past a depression screening. We discussed my overactive brain and how I simply could not stop thinking. A year before, I had been diagnosed with adult attention deficit disorder, so racing thoughts were nothing new. This "racing" was different, though. I was plagued with thoughts. I felt riddled with Pleasantville's problems and my credibility as the resident "black girl" and diversity subject matter expert was on the line. My brownness was being called into question by white people. Trouble was brewing and for seemingly the first time in my life, I couldn't think myself out of the imminent danger. My brain sure as hell was going to keep trying, though, and it wasn't going to let sleep get in the way.

Dr. Wilson's personality was quirky but warm. He reminded me of Jeff Goldblum, more like a detective than a medical professional at times. He asked me a series of questions. Once I passed the oral exam, he selected a prescription that, he explained, worked well with patients who also have A.D.D. When ingested, this medication simply slows the "idea" area of the brain. I was desperate and willing to try anything. Anxiety and sleep deprivation were an awful mix. Dr. Wilson wrote me the "scrip" and I whisked out of his office and across town to yet another appointment. It was time to check in with my counselor.

Unlike Dr. Wilson, Kevin, my therapist, would not allow me to get away with a lie about my mental state. He knew something was wrong because I called him and asked for an appointment after a bizarre evening of unrest. As Kevin began probing into my wellness (or lack thereof) in Pleasantville, my body went rigid and I began to cry. I struggled to walk him through my insomnia-filled night. The exact words escaped me for how to describe the zero gravity of falling that I felt last night. "Poor Jordan… I was squeezing his arm with one hand and the searching for the headboard with the other, just to keep myself grounded." Kevin never lost composure. He didn't stir and his eyes didn't bug out. Knowing me well, his therapeutic mind identified me as not feeling like "myself" and honestly, so did I. Kevin affirmed that the Pleasantville situation was out of control and that I was disturbed for good reason. He explained to me in a soothing tone that I was experiencing trauma. Because of our past session discussions, he went on that Pleasantville might even be triggering "old childhood trauma". I felt both comforted and somewhat more afraid than ever. He then asked me two odd requests.

Kevin: "Do you have any leave time?"

Me: "Yes, lots," [I answered while staring off into the corner of the room.] "Maybe almost a month's worth."

Kevin: "I want you to take some time off."

Me: "Okay, I'll take a couple days…"

Kevin: "How many days can you take?"

222

Me:	"I'm not sure."
Kevin:	"Were you planning on going back in to work?"
Me:	"No, I'm off for the rest of the day and I was going to take tomorrow off, too."
Kevin:	"Good. I think you need to take as much time as you can right now."

I startled at his request. Kevin strongly suggested that I not return to work for **several weeks**. Following this request was another odd request. "I want you to consider going on a mild prescription for depression and anxiety." My pride recoiled, but I couldn't prudently deny that I felt like I might be in danger of losing my mind. This was the "dark and twisty" feeling my sister and I had always discussed about some of our childhood experiences.

"Okay," I agreed. It was as if I had slipped into some kind of trance. Where was I? I had lost who I was. I was in no shape to lead others and I needed my circle to take care of *me*. Kevin asked me to call my doctor for a prescription. "I will...," I started to bargain, but Kevin interrupted me and our session. "Go ahead and call now." Oh, my God, I was just in the doctor's office, I thought. They're surely going to think I'm crazy. Kevin made his phone available and I awkwardly called to the physician's office which I had just left. Dr. Wilson called the order in immediately.

It was only after all of that was done that Kevin and I finished our session and I was somewhat relieved. I knew I had done a wise thing to call him the moment I was fairly sure I was not okay. however, a part of me began to realize that it was impossible I could be even more broken, fragile and alienated than I originally presumed. Nevertheless, my instability had been professionally confirmed. Did Pleasantville win? Did Luke win? Had they beaten me into submission? Had this experience used my worst nightmare against me and turned me into a crazy brown woman? My consciousness wasn't in my body. I'm not sure who this being was because it certainly wasn't Kim. Kim was strong. Kim was brave. Kim was a cultural translator. Kim was a lovable, golden child. I didn't know that lady named Kim anymore. I had forgotten who I was.

Chapter 44

Ding, Dong the Witch is Dead

I believe that my life continually forms and purposes me to do the work I am doing – and I am very good at what I do. I'm good at what I do because my career is more than just a job for me; this work is who I am. It's the fire in my belly. My calling. So, when I discovered this Pleasantville position, I was absolutely thrilled. The job was big and dreamy and lofty and ambitious ...and so am I. I spent the better part of my first academic year in Pleasantville proudly telling anyone who might ask that this job was designed for me and I was designed for it – an appropriate match.

My charge as Director of Student and Student Services is to lead efforts to support the social-emotional wellness of students at Pleasantville Schools. To address all non-academic barriers to success. We know that the students who Pleasantville struggles most to support are students of color, low income students and students with IEPs. Those are our achievement gaps. My efforts are geared toward building a capacity to understand these – and many other – challenging student conditions. Right now for Pleasantville Schools, this includes race, class, gender, ability and behavioral health as well as addiction issues. The reason why I am so passionate about this work is because years ago, I would have been one of those students.

Over 20 years ago, I was a biracial teenager living in a very low-income single parent home. I'd attended 6 high schools and moved 9 times before leaving for college. My custodial parent, my mother, suffered from severe major depression, social anxiety, suicide ideation and PTSD from integrating a predominantly white school as a child. In addition to my mom's diagnoses, I had undiagnosed ADHD and my brother, sister and I were all struggling to manage our own separate childhood traumas without help from a medical professional.

I would have been your achievement gap. *Can you say - without a doubt - that Pleasantville Schools would have been motivated to remove my barriers to success? Would you have known what to do with me? Would I have believed that you cared about my well-being? Could you have closed my achievement gap? As a low income, ADHD student of color with childhood trauma, could you have maximized my potential to be successful?*

Now fast forward 25 years to my work in this position. As a district, were you motivated to remove my barriers to success to do this work? Did you know what to do with me? How did you demonstrate you cared about my well-being? Did you close my achievement gap as a professional? Did Pleasantville Schools maximize my potential to be successful?

I have kept documentation of a list of incidents over the last two years that have made me feel unwelcome, unsupported or implicitly biased against while working at Pleasantville Schools. I ask that you listen to this list and these incidents in their entirety without interruption. After sharing, I welcome the opportunity to provide clarity to any of your questions and/or inquiries.

A Pleasantville Newspaper Article Announcing My Departure

"Search for new director to begin this summer"

Pleasantville Schools will begin searching for a new director of student services this summer.

Kimberly Brazwell, who held the relatively new position for two years, has declined the district's offer for a new contact, deciding instead to move on to other endeavors, according to a press release from the district.

"We are very disappointed to lose Kim," Pleasantville Superintendent Dr. Springsteen said in the statement. "This is hard work, but the work must continue."

Pleasantville's director of student services addresses students' non-academic barriers to success and works to improve their social and emotional health. Currently, Springsteen and the board of education are considering some of Brazwell's suggestions about possible changes to enhance the position's impact and effectiveness.

Brazwell declined a new two-year contract, stating she plans to pursue her consulting career as an equity and inclusion advocate and community builder.

She and Springsteen both emphasized the school district may continue to benefit in the future from her expertise in this area.

"These have been two important years in analyzing Pleasantville's data, figuring out the issues and setting up programs to address them," Brazwell said in the statement. "This work required one person to till through the

growing pains ... and will need a new person to harvest that growth in the next stage."

Springsteen said he will assemble a team of educators and community members to conduct a search similar to the multi-step, collaborative process implemented when the position was created in 2013.

During her tenure in the district, Brazwell secured grant funding to provide the district with a full-time a behavioral health professional, who has been on site in the district since January. She provided guidance for the educational component of the school district's new drug and alcohol use policy. She also initiated innovative programming and staff training in the areas of social and emotional health, cultural competency and community engagement. Brazwell also coordinated community conversations on diversity, inclusion and race.

Letter to Concerned Friends and Family

Greetings family,

Well, it's official. As of today, a statement has been publicly released that I am leaving Pleasantville Schools. My last day is June 30th. As you all likely know, this last year has been incredibly difficult for me (and continues to be, in many ways). If it has not already been said, I would not have been able to pull through this challenging time without your prayers, support, phone calls, well wishes, positive thoughts and words of encouragement.

Pleasantville was an unbelievable ordeal and yet I <u>know</u> my resilience will allow me to come out of this new and improved! Just wanted to update you and let you know how much your unapologetic love and support has meant to me as well as Jordan and the girls.

Love,

Kim

Chapter 45

The Dust Settles, the Pin Drops and the Tumbleweed Blows

The road to college was paved with good intentions upon every move. Each address change was intended to signify a new beginning. Hope. Renewal. All those cardboard boxes. All those U-Haul vans. All those memories. All those smells. And would you believe not a single soul ever threw my family or me a going away party? Wouldn't you think that somewhere, somehow, someone at some point would have missed us enough to want to make an auspicious occasion out of sadness that we would no longer be a phone call or a borrowed cup of sugar away? It never happened. And since it never happened, I understood goodbye parties to be meaningless. They were a satisfactory excuse to eat cake or go to a restaurant and order pasta for a party of eight. However, from my vantage point, nobody was important enough to really need a bon voyage party.

Upon reflection, perhaps I had never seen any real goodbye parties with the exception of retirement celebrations. I'll never forget the first one I was a part of. The only bon voyage party that seemed worth having.

During graduate school, I worked with a woman who was a legend in the field of minority admissions. Ms. Totty was the pied piper of black student recruitment for Opulent College. I don't know how she did it, but year after year, she was able to convince parents of brown kids to sign big checks, apply for financial aid, write scholarship essays and hand over their students to her care.

Ms. Totty was like an older brown Mary Poppins – practically perfect in every way. She knew everyone but never name dropped. She was still mysteriously about the same size and shape she'd always been and that was after four children, menopause and whatever deal she made with the devil for her Dorian Gray-like youthful appearance.

Before Ms. Totty, I'd never seen an older brown person so attentive to her own healthcare. She was the first brown person I met who was gluten free. She, for whatever reason, weaned herself from strong caffeinated tea and trained herself to drink lukewarm water with a mere drib of tea herbs for flavoring. She was classy and sassy. Warm eyes and a contagious laugh. Perfect long dark curls in her not really coarse at all hair. Meticulous D'Nealian penmanship. She was a great listener. And when she needed to teach you something inconspicuously, she knew how to touch you and speak in a way that alerted you to pay close attention. You wanted her on your side. You wanted her stories. You wanted her knowledge. You wondered what kept her spritely, knowing all the while that she'd been places and seen things that were too painful to fully process. But no anger. No animosity. Somehow, after whatever skill set her journey had given her, she only showed up in spaces ready to love and laugh. You wanted to know the secret. You wanted to drink the Kool-Aid.

When Ms. Totty announced her retirement to me, I sat in her office stunned and a bit lost. "Well, what will the college do if you leave?", I asked Ms. Totty with both alarm and sadness. She laughed and casually said, "They'll move on." I was nearly offended at her insistence that she could be replaced without some sort of institutional and emotional breakdown. Her eyes sparkled and her voice lowered. I knew I was about to receive a gift from her.

"It's like this," she explained. "Imagine a bucket filled with water and your fist fully immersed in the bucket. When you pull your fist out of the water, the bucket will have no memory that your fist was ever there. The water will fill the space where your fist was and everything will keep moving." She leaned back in her seat and smiled, as if her wisdom was meant to be comforting. I should have felt at peace, but I was almost angry with her for not demanding that the college rename the admission building after her. It took me years to realize she was giving me a sneak peek at humility. Ms. Totty had served Opulent College for decades. Her first students had since paid tuition for their children as students to attend Opulent College. And, the best we could do at saying, "Thank you" for putting brown kids in white schools to get ready to make some green was a card and some balloons. No; it seemed wrong.

I, on the other hand, was built to say goodbye. Not only am I able to efficiently pack a trunk, but I'm a great partner-in-crime when it comes to quick tear-downs and I am most efficient at throwing things away, though items have sentimental value and I can get lost in transition. And just like my unrequited friendship with Bethany, the high school drama teacher in my first months here at Pleasantville Schools, little communication was extended to me upon my departure process. Pithy goodbyes, mostly. Few visits. Few phone calls. Few emails, texts, Morse Codes, smoke signals or doves with tree branches. It felt like a bunch of nothing …and that was fine with me.

Chapter 46

The Blessing and Curse of
Well-Intentioned Liberal White Women

"My spot." So much privilege is built into those two words. In many industries and most especially in the field of education, committees are where politics ferment. In my role, I oversaw a committee charged with leading social-emotional and multicultural efforts for the district on behalf of students and it was time to re-up for the next academic year. After a volatile year in the space of race, I knew it would be advantageous to get more of what miniscule diversity the district possessed on this climate committee. The "old guard" had laid claim to these positions, which only seemed to become available through death, desertion or divorce of the members from the seats. In what I believed to be the best interest of students however, I made a gutsy call to replace several of the sitting leaders with racially diverse educators who would be new to the team.

What had I done? Who did I think I was to take someone's "spot" and give it away? I had appointed new people to take over the positions that had, for a few years, been other folks' "spots". Were these spots formerly a wilderness of supplemental student support? Were there natives on these spots who were always doing student support work and when colonization turned that work into contracts, were the spots reclaimed in the name of contracts? And if so, does a position automatically and eternally belong to someone simply because she was there first? Can a professional "call dibs" on a spot? Can a spot belong to someone purely through manifest destiny? Was a spot theirs for me to take from them or did the spots belong to the district?

I had built a ring of decisions out of a pocket full of posies but white opposition turned them into ashes and they were all falling down. When you have nothing or are assumed to be nothing, you get used to having nothing or having something taken away from you. In fact, when you have no privilege, have something and it is taken away, sometimes you don't even fight about it for a myriad of reasons. No point in making noise; they're not going to listen to you anyway, some think. Make noise and then they'll take more away from you, some think. Make noise, fight and keep it now but they'll punish me or my family for it later, some think. However you slice it, fighting looks different on brown folks than it does on white folks.

When one usually has privilege and 'things', I imagine it is a foreign concept to lose it. I had never thought about what that might be like before now. By taking positions away, particularly from white women, I interrupted white privilege – and they were not pleased, so they fought it. Principals contacted me on behalf of teachers. A union rep contacted me on behalf of a teacher to inquire as to how my process of selection was conducted. No teacher spoke with me directly.

One nominated teacher who had accepted his nomination, rescinded his right; gave up his, so far, unoccupied position due to politics already in play – that quickly. The hallways had been so silent for me and so noisy in my absence. There was conversation brewing but I did not have the privilege nor the honor of being part of the conversation until it was complete.

Former spot holders were hurt and angry. Thankfully, they had folks in high places to advocate for them. Administrators. Union reps. Whiteness and other things more powerful than me. My nomination process was halted. Dr. Springsteen declared that the nominations would be "frozen" until more administrative conversation took place about the design of the nomination process. Conversation that would, of course, continue *far* beyond the end of my contract at Pleasantville. Politics as usual.

My last bit of power had been usurped. Sorry brown babies of Pleasantville, I tried. But it wasn't over. Jerri, one of the administrators who'd advocated on behalf of her teacher wanted to meet with me. She and I had been confidantes for the entirety of my two-year tenure at Pleasantville and this pissing contest dumped a weighty strain on our relationship, at least from my end. My perception was that she wanted to see what I was thinking. She wanted to explain her advocacy. She wanted to be heard and she wanted to provide me with an opportunity to speak. I appreciated the effort, but I was tired of Pleasantville and tired of talking.

We set a meeting to talk and clear the air about administrative political nonsense. Prior to our meeting start time, I sat in my office for a moment, waiting until the very last minute to leave my safe space. With one final inhale, sucking all of the oxygen in the room as if I was diving underwater, I hoisted myself from my seat. I surveyed my office and grabbed my favorite pen of the day and my trusty notepad. Inside, though, I felt as if I was scanning my inventory to select weapons for the coming battle. My pen as my sword and my notepad as my shield.

My shoes made clean, rhythmically patterned clicking sounds on the perfectly buffed linoleum floors as I walked through the hallway. Yes, all of this was wearing on me. Everything was white. White in a way that seemed to remind me I didn't fit in. That I was fighting a losing battle. That my blackness could and would be consumed by this place. White floors. White walls. White students. White teachers. White hallway posters. Dead white forefathers in a social studies hallway that praised white colonization for "claiming" land that had belonged to brown people. My skin felt like midnight streaking the hallway. My face had grown hard. My mouth tight at the jaw line. My eyes dead. My cool pose found me in Pleasantville and had accompanied me to Jerri's office for a final meeting.

I reached my colleague's safe space, now a threatening environment to me and she was hospitable as always. Jerri was one of few white allies who I felt understood what I was going through. Jerri had been trying for over a decade to start a sustained diversity conversation at Pleasantville. That would be all but impossible. While her efforts were valiant, a diversity conversation isn't quite a diversity conversation if there are no people of color in the room. And when no one in the room is living it, diversity is merely a talking point on the agenda. And when they finish talking about it, their community service work is done. Talking about diversity is uncomfortable and white privilege allows folks to not have to be uncomfortable. That wasn't Jerri's fault, though. That was just a symptom of Pleasantville and of all kinds of Pleasantvilles across the globe.

The first thing I noticed was Jerri's body language. Her spirit seemed nearly as languished as mine. For all parties involved, it had been a long academic year. We'd finally reached spring quarter and the finish line was in plain sight. As I sat down into one of the hard, wooden chairs in her office, I wanted to extend a few words of sympathy and care to her. I wanted to let her know I noticed she was broken, too. The truth, however, was that I could barely muster up strength for self-care. I made the quick decision that she would have to comfort and heal herself as I had nothing left. The truth is that I could not even draw my eyes up to look at her. I was so angry and tired, I was afraid she would see it. She would know that my connection to her had been weathered and broken. I didn't want to talk about it. I didn't want to try to repair it. I just wanted Pleasantville, this Satan, to get behind me and our eye contact would get in the way of that.

In my mind, I had agreed to this meeting on two conditions. I was either looking for an apology on behalf of Jerri, my colleague for my leadership judgment being questioned or I was hoping for a 'touch and agree' conversation where we could realize that we were on the same side of the fight. Neither happened. The conversation began to escalate quickly as she defended her teacher against my nomination and my wishes. I spoke about race. She spoke about data. We were not speaking the same language, but for me, the deeper level of the conversation went beyond the students for whom I was advocating. Students who looked like me. students whose poverty experiences felt like mine. At this moment, I was again talking about me.

Unless accurate memory eludes me, Jerri was in near tears but not for me. She confessed to feeling and behaving like that of a momma bear for her teacher. Shared how hard her teacher worked, and, how her teacher had data to show her productivity. Also, she shared how her teacher supplemented her income with the spot I just tried to give away. I found it hard to swallow in Jerri's office, for fear I'd choke on the bile of my disappointment in Pleasantville. I felt my spirit quit. The war was over.

I could feel burn hovering just above her skin. My cheeks were hot, too. Still, my eyes couldn't take her in. Not in full glances, but sips and peeks. But taking all of her in was too much at that moment. Jerri had become "them". I fought it. Fought losing her as a support beam in my personal system of care. Still, even in the earlier battles, I had felt her start to slip away from me.

A knot of anger and hurt rested under my larynx. Struggled, I did, to keep my voice and my pain low. To breathe and swallow around the knot. "I have two weeks left," I mumbled to Jerri while looking straight forward, daring myself to hold fast to my avoidance of eye contact. "I have two weeks left and I can't believe I'm fighting my way out the door with parents and teachers." "Do you mean me, too?!" Jerri queried? "Yes," I confirmed. Her heat oozed. She was smart. She knew right then I had re-categorized her in my heart and mind. I'd had two years of painful experiences with white people. Unfortunately, I had too few successful, pleasant, agreeable ones. I believe she felt, at that moment, that I had stripped her title of 'good gal' in Pleasantville. "I always supported you!" she told me with fire cheeks and raised voice. "I have been on your side and advocated for you from day one!" What I heard was, "I'm one of the good white people. I have always been kind and treated you well." For reasons I still struggle to explain, it may have been the very worst thing she could have said to prove her point to me. As many people of color do when we upset white people about race, I felt myself consider backing off of the strength of my statement and softening it. But I was still angry. Too angry for no one's microaggressions to be at fault. "I have two weeks left," I repeated. "I'll be gone soon and you all can do what you want. I'm done."

Final, concluding dialogue followed, soft and closure-directed. Confirmation. Affirmation. "Are we okay's?" and "For what it's worth's". I was dead but maybe Jerri needed that to capture a pulse in that very heavy space. Insert hug here. This is where it usually works. This is where warm physical contact usually makes things better. My arms did what they routinely do. I held the hug as long and as tightly as I knew to do, but I was having an out of body experience. I couldn't feel it because I had already activated my superpowers of emotional numbness. Yet again, a friend... A liberal white female friend was trying to acknowledge my perception of race and simultaneously dismiss it. In my mind, she wanted to repair something that was irreparable and erase from my mind the perception that something I experienced as being racially profound was inexplicable on the basis of race. And because of that, and so many other things, I just couldn't with my whole heart hug it out.

My shoes made clean, rhythmically patterned clicking sounds on the perfectly buffed linoleum floors back through the hallway. Back through the cafeteria, now silent. Back through double-doors of a quiet lobby leading to my office. The knot under my larynx... it broke into a million pieces and turned to pixie dust in my eyes. My heart raced. The muscles in my arms constricted. My face got hot. I felt overwhelmed with adrenaline. No! Not now... I flooded with emotion and felt the urge to claw or run, to attack the space or myself, or explode or implode. My therapist's voice echoed in my head. "The next time you're in your office and those feelings come up again, try to stay in the space and see those feelings all the way through. Try to figure out what it is about that space that triggers those feelings." So, I stayed.

I paced in my office, and whispered to myself, "Feel this, Kim. Feel this... What is this?!" A crescendo of tears gathered at the peaks of my eyes and swan-dove down my cheeks. I broke. "What is this?!" I kept asking myself. Why was I in so much pain? Why did this place hurt so bad? Why did the meeting with Jerri rock my foundation? I paced in the corner of my office so as to not be seen, should someone walk in without invitation. I murmured replays of quotes from the meeting, searching my soul for the source of the bleeding.

"Two weeks left..."

"Why are they fighting me?"

"They couldn't even leave me alone on my way out the door..."

"You want me to tell you you're a good white person..."

"Momma bear..."

"I wish I had a 'momma bear'..."

Yes, all of this was wearing on me. Everything was white. White in a way that seemed to remind me I didn't fit in. That I was had fought a losing battle. That my brownness could and would be consumed by this place. White floors. White walls. White students. White teachers. White hallway posters. Dead white forefathers in a social studies hallway that praised white colonization for "claiming" land that had belonged to brown people. My skin felt like midnight streaking the hallway. My face had grown hard. My mouth tight at the jaw line. My eyes dead. My cool pose found me in Pleasantville and would stay with me until Pleasantville was over.

Chapter 47

"If I Can Help One Person..."

My heart had been broken by Pleasantville and no one cared. The email account was empty. The mailbox outside my office was dusty. The doorway was an open space leading to nothing. It was as if grenades were tossed into my office for two years and everyone took cover so as to avoid their own harm from shrapnel. No one came back to see if the mission to hurt me was effective. No one came back to retrieve my body. They left me for dead and dead is exactly how I felt.

Papers had been sorted through in efforts to leave the next "me" a track record of exactly what happened. Anger tried speaking with me. He tried to convince me that I owed neither Pleasantville nor my successor anything. I understood, though, that my experience and my slow-to-heal scars from Pleasantville were not their fault. Further, they would need all the tools possible at their disposal to continue my work. Maybe Pleasantville would view my successor's primary work as "righting my wrongs". In any case, much had happened over the last two years and because I trudged the path mostly alone, few people knew what I tried to do. Few knew I had the students' best interest in mind. In fact, one of the things that hurt most is I don't even think the students knew I had their best interest in mind.

The lights were dim in my office, as always. I'd long since decided to never use the fluorescent lights and further "institutionalize" the space. What was once a space filled with illustrated notes and quotes on a wall now looked like a barren cave. My eyes traced the perimeter and I saw bars where walls should be. I felt like a prisoner who was soon to be released after a two-year sentence.

My life had been changed while I was locked up, but I wasn't sure if anyone changed around me. Pleasantville took a toll on my body, my mind and my marriage and my family. It chipped away at my ability to be present at home. It stole my sleep and my security. It left me to serve only Pleasantville, but the service was in anger. Pleasantville was angry with me, and I, angry with her. I believed she was glad to see me go. I imagined Pleasantville could not wait for my release date so they could watch me walk out the door one last time and be rid of me for good.

By now, there was nothing much left to pack. The personalized items found their way in my car. Momentos were in three-ring binders, heavily-labeled and on remaining a bookshelf. I made copies of important items and tacked them on a bulletin board. To the best of my ability, I buried all of my secrets and hid the "keys to the kingdom" in my notes. My God, the office was quiet and the school building hummed. HVAC was the only sound communicating with me. Then, Satin and Sissy peeked their heads into my office. My spirit filled! My heart opened like a time-lapsed flower opens to sunlight in the spring.

When facilitating dialogue sessions or meetings, I know how to make the room go dead silent. All you have to do is ask for a volunteer to begin the conversation. As a facilitator, your prayer is simple. You don't need the entire room to explode in witty banter. You have no use for the slow clap voices building chord by chord as they settle in the comfort of group dialogue. No, all you pray for is one. All you need is one brave soul who is willing to go first. Willing to break the silence. Someone has to move forward into the unknown path and clear the brush for those to follow.

My human weed-wacker was Satin.

From the very beginning, we sensed something familiar about each other. I knew who she was and therefore, she inferred that I must be cut from a similar bolt of cloth. She and I both had survived a challenging year. And in many cases, I was only able to pull through because of students like her. Satin was only at the beginning of her journey at Pleasantville. She is still forging her path and finding her voice and it wasn't going to be easy.

Satin was not built to fit into a place like Pleasantville. She had a keen ability to see through the town and its residents. She didn't covet their belongings. She had a very clear idea of who she was. Not only that, but there was precedent in her being affirmed for who she was as opposed to how convincingly she was able to pretend to be something she was not. One year of high school down and she had three more years on her bid. She was doing hard time in the suburbs with the potential of release on time with good behavior.

Every prickle she received from educators or peers raised her temperature, but the fever broke every 24 hours. She was learning how to reflect on things, gaining the invaluable ability to bite her tongue instead of lashing out in an attempt to defend herself. In addition, she was quick. She was dangerous, too; because she could *sense* when the teachers were wrong – when they *should* have known something that they didn't. Satin had more than an inkling of what it felt like to be cared for; so, she was acutely aware of what it felt like when folks didn't care and the trait of discernment seemed to be hereditary.

Sissy, Satin's little sister was a fireball in the making. Much less aware of Pleasantville's nuances, her bubble was working a little better than Satin's. Isn't that what we want, in a way? The aim is for school buildings' student populations to be doing so well? Cultivating safe, comfortable environments and making students feel like they matter. The shine of Pleasantville had already worn off for Satin, but it wasn't too late for her little sister. Perhaps, if Pleasantville took the advice of the social justice experts, a whole new reality could be created for students as young as Sissy. In fact, perhaps the district could get so good at caring about the whole child – every whole child – that Sissy would hardly even notice race, class or gender anymore.

Chapter 48

And So, It Ends as It Began

The hallways were once again empty and smelled of dust, paint and wax. Desks were piled along the outer hallways of classrooms as the first-rate maintenance and custodial staff began preparing the summer marathon of making the school buildings spotless. They prepared perfect classrooms for practically perfect students. A small smile tickled at the corners of my mouth. I had survived, though I was somewhat broken. I was badly wounded and needed a spiritual healing, but I **was** still standing. Pleasantville had not been able to kill the spirit within me, though it did try. These same hallways that had nearly suffocated me for months in my travels were utterly vacant and were powerless over me! In the end, this proved to not be an unsolvable labyrinth where lurked the path to my supposedly assured death and destruction. Boogymen at my windows and monsters under my bed turned out to be light winds stirring in bare trees and dust bunnies dancing whirls in the breaths of air vent blasts. It was just a preposterous and inane ol' school building filled with other human beings, specks of dust in the universe, such as myself, I had nothing to fear anymore.

"One last thing," I promised to my girls. They'd always hated coming to meet me in Pleasantville's schools. Charlotte, Paris and I walked down the hallway together in pursuit of Central Office. I might as well have had broken limbs that were in the process of healing and my girls were my crutches. I don't know if I could have walked this final journey alone. It was fitting that my last building walk wasn't in isolation. In the beginning and in the end, my girls were by my side. Older now, taller, smarter and especially cognizant of the negative energy in the building, they at least seemed more at peace with the people missing.

Charlotte and Paris walked ahead of me by a few feet. Illuminated now by the emptiness of the building and the absence of loathing in the air, they giggled. Paris sang songs with toothy smiles. Charlotte watched over Paris and I watched over them both. They obviously felt more at ease now. They knew it was over. Fluorescent lights that once hissed at me on my way to meetings now bowed before my daughters. In the absence of Pleasantville's residents, my girls did not feel the need to guard my soul. Their laughs were authentic. Their joy was real. No fake smiles to extend. No poop-eating grins and mental courtseys at colleagues whom my daughters could not distinguish as friends from foes of mine. All of that pretense and senselessness was over. Now, I would take some time to heal.

That final walk down the hallway to central office was the longest walk ever. I had my final district belongings in a maize yellow envelope and could not wait to return them to the office. Anything that belonged to Pleasantville was still, for my purposes, more or less contaminated and toxic. I needed their energy out of my spaces.

Envelope contents: keys to my office, identification badge, parking hang tag and building swipe card for access. I felt like Dorothy, returning to the Wizard of Oz with the witch's broom. Similarly, the hallway out felt more like the yellow brick road. Or, perhaps I was a double agent spy retiring from the agency. I had completed my final "kill" and didn't have it in me to do the work anymore, suffering from battle fatigue. This was my secret meeting with the boss who called in the "missions". I was turning in my agent badge and moving on to greener pastures, one with less stunts and gun fights and villains and car chases. I just wanted to be myself at work again. I just wanted to remember and honor who I knew "myself" to be.

As the three of us reached the central office door, we couldn't help but notice that all the lights were out with the exception of hallway storm lights. **Curiously, everyone had already left without a word.** I tried sliding my envelope under the door, but it didn't budge. I tried my keys on the lock, but stopped shortly thereafter. The last thing I needed was school camera footage showing a former employee ambiguously fidgeting with the Central Office door lock. A small wave of panic bled into my body. My journey in Pleasantville HAD to end today. I could not manage another delay in ending this phase of my life. These items had to be turned in **today**. I needed to walk away with a clean slate **today**.

Just as we were preparing for a plan B, we heard a loud and moderately obnoxious sigh come from a nook with great acoustics. A sigh, a cough and a throat clearance. These were all signs indicating that the maker of said noises had no clue he was not alone. As if it were my responsibility, I found myself hoping the person would either quiet himself or at least not be mortified once he discovered his opera of noises had a small audience. My shoe clicking on my way got progressively louder as the mystery person walked out of one of the bathrooms. To my pleasant surprise, it was Dr. Springsteen.

Dr. Springsteen looked taken aback by the girls and I just standing there silently outside of the men's bathroom. We greeted each other in the hallway. Though looking shocked and slightly embarrassed for just a moment, Dr. Springsteen quickly smiled and engaged my girls in conversation. As a new grandfather, his eyes delighted at the sight of my daughters. Heading back in his direction toward the offices, we trailed behind him in rank and file. The lights were still dim and he stood in the near dark lobby of central office with the girls and me. I handed my envelope to him and explained its contents. He took what he needed and gave the rest back to me. I was witnessing his sadness and embarrassment. It felt like a "failed mission". He was hurt and disappointed just as I was. He possibly felt a different kind of pain and for different reasons, but we both looked like we'd been through something we wouldn't soon forget. Racism. That was our last conversation in the lobby of Central Office.

The spring and summer had brought a couple more deaths, keeping the Black Lives Matter movement active, alive and well. There was a distant gaze in Dr. Springsteen's eyes. He wiped his eyes a couple of times; but I couldn't tell if he was suffering from allergies or from the hurt of battle wounds from over the years. The soft resonance in his voice reflected remembrance of something still working to heal itself in his soul. I could see his mind playing back the memory as if he knew a moment, a room and could recall his face – younger then and his hair less frosted with wisdom. "This is as bad as it was in the sixties!" I could feel the gravity in his voice. This frosted hair communicated to me that he'd seen his fair share of news stories about black and brown people dying. It appeared to reach within him as deeply now as it did then. Maybe more.

And then there was an apology. I didn't need it from Dr. Springsteen, but it felt so good to hear it. It wasn't one of those polite, "This is what I'm supposed to say" apologies. It was sincere, heartfelt and searching. He apologized that I wasn't supported enough and that my journey in Pleasantville had been so accompanied by such strife. Again, there must have been more dust in the air, or maybe more allergies causing him to rub at one of his eyes. The world had changed now considerably from when Dr. Springsteen had begun his career decades ago leading school districts.

About the Author

Over 15 years of passionate service through social justice advocacy has made Kimberly Brazwell a highly-requested speaker and dialogue facilitator for engagements ranging from training workshops to keynotes around the globe. Kimberly is a diversity practitioner who designs trauma-informed experiential workshops. Her programs aid in reshaping organizational perspective on "fit", engagement, and cultural code-switching. Kimberly founded KiMISTRY, a consulting firm that coaches organizations on how to let their people be who they are where they are.

With a master's degree in educational policy and leadership from The Ohio State University, Kimberly's unique approach to diversity work applies the practice of mindfulness to implicit de-bias work. Her drive stems from her own biracial identity and rich diversity in race, religion, language, sexual orientation and class identity.

After attending six high schools, Kimberly went on to graduate from both college and graduate school at an early age. She has worked in education–both K-12 and higher education–for over 15 years. In addition to leading KiMISTRY, she serves as the executive director for a nonprofit community development corporation in Columbus, Ohio. Outside of social justice work, Brazwell is also a visual practitioner, writer, performing artist and blessed mother of two daughters.

For booking information, please contact KiMISTRY:
www.browningpleasantville.com
www.kimistry.net

KiMISTRY

KiMISTRY LLC

@kimistryllc

Made in the USA
Lexington, KY
10 September 2017